Gender and History

GENDER AND HISTORY

THE LIMITS OF SOCIAL THEORY IN THE AGE OF THE FAMILY

LINDA J. NICHOLSON

New York COLUMBIA UNIVERSITY PRESS *1986*

Library of Congress Cataloging-in-Publication Data

Nicholson, Linda J.
Gender and history.

Bibliography: p.
Includes index.
1. Feminism—Philosophy. 2. Feminism—United States
—History. 3. Liberalism. 4. Marxist historiography.
I. Title.
HQ1206.N7   1986   323.3′4′01   85-21281
ISBN 0-231-06220-6

Columbia University Press
New York   Guildford, Surrey
Copyright © 1986 Columbia University Press
All rights reserved

To
Gertrude Nicholson
and to the memory of
Samuel Nicholson

Contents

Acknowledgments

THIS BOOK owes much of what is valuable in it to many different people. First, there are those who donated large amounts of time, not only reading and commenting on the entire manuscript, but in many cases rereading the same chapters through several drafts. These include: Sandra Bartky, Mark Berger, Joan Cocks, Ann Ferguson, Kathy Ferguson, Russell Keat, Steve Seidman, Larry Simon, and Iris Young. I particularly appreciate the efforts of Alison Jaggar, who carefully read through the manuscript twice.

Many others gave various forms of help: Kathy Addelson, Asoka Bandarage, Seyla Benhabib, Larry Blum, Drucilla Cornell, Dion Farquar, Judith Fetterley, Nancy Fraser, Nanette Funk, Marlene Fried, Roger Gottlieb, Sandra Harding, Adrian Hayes, Nancy Holmstrom, Marcia Homiak, Susan Kaplow, Hy Kuritz, Joan Landes, Jane Martin, Dieter Misgeld, Jim McClellan, Bert Nepaulsingh, Philip Nicholson, Richard Olsen, Francine Rainone, Richard Schmitt, Joan Schulz, Janet Farrell Smith, Glenna Spitze, Karsten Struhl, and Larry Wittner.

Thanks must go to the members of those groups who listened and gave criticism to sections of the book as these were proceeding through various drafts, to the participants of: the Society for Women in Philosophy, Marxist Activist Philosophers, the Philosophy and Social Science Course of the Inter-University Center in Dubrovnik, 1984 and 1985, the Yankee Conference for the Study of Political Thought, and the Research on Women Colloquium of SUNY Albany.

I benefited from secretarial assistance during the course of this project, from the work of: Maribel Gray, Barbara Grubalski, Cecelia Ormsby, and Myrtie Roosevelt. I wish to thank Donna Wilkie for her work on the index and Maureen MacGrogan and Karen Mitchell for their wise editorial assistance.

The State University of New York Research Foundation awarded me a summer research grant which was particularly useful in the beginning period of research.

I wish to pay a special tribute to Alasdair MacIntyre, not only for the specific help he provided me with on several chapters, but for what he taught me many years before this project began on how to think about social theory. As his student, I alone bear the responsibility, of course, for how I interpreted and used his teachings.

Finally, I wish to thank all of my friends and family whose love encouraged me throughout this project and to the women's movement which has grounded this work, politically, cognitively, and emotionally.

Gender and History

INTRODUCTION

Thou shall not sit
With statisticians nor commit
A social science.
—W. H. Auden, "Under Which Lyre"

UNDERSTANDING Western society from the sixteenth century to the present requires comprehending the changing relation between the two spheres of private and public life. Until relatively recently, this comprehension was impeded by a belief which has been central to Western culture throughout these centuries: that the family as the sphere of the "private" is a universal institution, fundamentally different from other more variable forms of social institutions. As a consequence of recent changes in the family and in its relation to the rest of society, many are coming to realize the falsity of this assumption and are beginning to see the family as a contingent, primarily modern, social institution, in complicated interrelation with other modern social institutions. Feminist scholarship is an important though not the sole source in the development of this new perspective.

This altered view of the family poses serious challenges to modern Western political theory. Political theory, as it has developed in the West from the sixteenth century to the present, is primarily about what has been seen as distinct from the family. It has conceived of its subject matter, "politics," as being about forms of interactions or types of institutions whose nature and history exist independently of the family. This construction of political theory was shaped in part by the contribution of John Locke who, in his rebuttal to the writings of Sir Robert Filmer, decisively separated the "political" from the "familial." Even Marx-

ism, which several centuries later remedied liberalism's exclusion
of the economic from the political in its concept of "political
economy," never took up as a serious question the relation between
political economy and the family. Rather it tended to think of the
latter as merely epiphenomenal to the former. As a consequence,
liberalism and Marxism, two of the major political theories of
modern Western society, could not comprehend the important
dynamics occurring between family and society in their own times.
Such dynamics, I shall argue, shaped the content of both theories.
Since neither theory had the tools for making these dynamics self-
conscious, they surfaced within the theories in the form of un-
analyzed reflections, or reifications of the forms of social organization of their times.

For example, I shall argue that seventeenth-century liberalism
was a reflection of a new form of social organization wherein the
family and the state as we now comprehend them were being
created out of the older institution of kinship. Thus kinship systems,
which at one time had been the major mechanisms for regulating
food production and distribution, sexuality, crime and punishment,
etc. were replaced by the twin and separate institutions of the
family and the state. Seventeenth-century liberalism reflected this
emergence of family and state by separating in its theory the
familial and the political. Because it did not recognize the real
separation its theory was reflecting as historical, it tended to reify
the separation, that is to portray it as endemic to social organization
per se. By so doing, it lost sight of the origins of both the family
and the state in kinship and the consequences of such origins in
the structuring of both.

In the early modern period of the sixteenth and seventeenth
centuries, the family was not only, as we now know it, a place
for the bearing and raising of children; it was also a unit for the
production of food and objects necessary for survival. The sphere
of the family, in short, was not differentiated from the sphere of
the "economic" in the way that it is today. The differentiation
occurred as a result of industrialization, wherein the organization
of the production of food and objects ceased to be governed by
familial principles and instead became organized through the prin-

ciples of the market. This movement of production from the interior of the household to the exterior of public space was recognized in the political theory of Marxism, which decried liberalism's description of economic activity as "private enterprise." Marxism rather insisted on an awareness of the "public" nature of economic activity and its close interconnection with the activities of the state. However, as liberalism reified the early modern creation and separation of the family and the state, Marxism has also reified features of its own time: in particular the growing separation and dominance of the sphere of the economic. One consequence has been that it has tended to ignore the historically contingent nature of the separation of the family and the economy, tending to understand these as cross-culturally separated spheres.

Industrialization did not mean only a change in the place where productive activities took place; it involved a fundamental change in the nature of familial relations. The family, to a large extent, ceased being a unit of production. For poor and working class families this meant that the family became more like a "collection and dispersal" agency where the wages and services of all were pooled and distributed to maintain survival. It also meant that those individuals from these or more middle class families who could earn wages, or who had access to property that could ensure survival, could exist outside a family altogether. In short, a market economy based on wages and payment for factory-produced goods undermined the necessity of the family as a means of survival, at least for adults able to obtain incomes of a certain size. This feature of an industrial society has had different consequences for males and females and different classes at different points in time since the nineteenth century. At a very general level, it has brought about an increased individualization of social life, with individuals replacing families as the basic social unit.

The increasing individualization of social life has meant a new realignment of the private and the public. The private has increasingly come to be defined as that which concerns the individual alone. Many formerly familial activities, such as childrearing, nursing activities, care for the aged, etc. have become commoditized and/or become a concern of the state. Industrialization has also drastically changed the relations between men and women. In the early modern period in the West, where the household was the basic social unit and a male headed that household as a consequence of older patriarchal kinship principles, the male represented the household politically. Political participation was not based on the principle of "one man, one vote" but rather on the principle of "one household, one vote." Men without households and the property able to support them were as unable to vote as women, children, and servants. The individualization of social life meant the replacement of the household by the individual as the basic political unit. One consequence of this change was that denying women the vote in the nineteenth century became contradictory in a way in which it had not been earlier, analogous to the inconsistency of slave ownership in a wage-earning society. As women have also become more autonomous economically in the course of the twentieth century—and this has been particularly true for white, middle-class women—older norms defining women by their position within the family have also become less consistent with present reality. As a result of such contradictions, the modern women's movement has developed.

Just as I claim that both liberalism and Marxism are manifestations of the changing dynamic between private and public in the seventeenth and nineteenth centuries, respectively, so I also claim that feminism is a manifestation of the changing dynamic between these spheres in the nineteenth and twentieth centuries. As liberalism and Marxism often uncritically reflected these dynamics in the content of their positions and theories, so too does much of modern feminism. However, insofar as twentieth-century feminists have come to focus on the family, have come to think of it as a social and not natural institution, and have come to recognize its complex interconnections with the rest of society, they have begun to develop the means for becoming self-conscious about the very historical forces which have brought modern feminism into being as well as liberalism and Marxism.

In other words, I am arguing that contemporary feminism, while itself a manifestation of changes in the relation of private and public in the nineteenth and twentieth centuries, provides us with resources to construct a perspective from which to comprehend the centrality of these changes and of their historical precedents in shaping our present and past. Several important caveats must be made to this argument. For one, feminism is not the only contemporary resource for constructing such a perspective. In part the same social dynamics that have brought contemporary feminism into being have also brought into being other social movements and forms of scholarship that are similar in many respects to feminism and feminist scholarship. Other manifestations of the contemporary reorganization of private and public include such diverse phenomena as: Freudianism, and the growth of psychology as an academic discipline and cult-psychology as a cultural practice; the emergence of the beat and hippie movements of the 1950s and 1960s; the development of family and social history within the discipline of history; the attention the New Left gave to issues of "consciousness" and "subjectivity"; the emergence of twentieth-century welfare liberalism; claims within the philosophy of science on the theory-laden quality of data, and new views on the relation of the subjective and the objective within epistemology and theories of learning.

This list could easily be extended; the point can be drawn, however, that it is not only feminism which is a manifestation of changes in the relation of private and public or a source for becoming self-conscious about such changes. But while the same social changes that generated contemporary feminism have had parallel manifestations in social movements other than feminism and in innovations in disciplinary perspectives other than women's studies, contemporary feminism has often provided some of the most extensive, dramatic, and articulate expressions of these changes. For example, while in the mid-1960s many hippies believed that "The personal is political," it was not until later in that decade, with the emergence of "women's liberation," that the belief became articulated as a slogan.

A second important caveat must be made to my claim that contemporary feminism provides us with resources for constructing a perspective to rethink our past and its political theories. Contemporary feminism, as I will illustrate in the opening chapter, is a widely diverse political movement. While there are certain unifying threads, particularly a growing attention to the family, there are also substantive differences. Most fundamentally for the purpose of my argument, not all feminists have endorsed or have even thought about that position which I underline as central in contrasting feminism with traditional political theory: that we understand the relation between "private" and "public" as historically changing. Those who have most explicitly endorsed this position in their theoretical work have been socialist feminists, inspired by the deep attention to history which Marx transmitted from nineteenth-century philosophy and by the attention to the family that came out of radical feminism. Thus much of the theory and scholarship I shall draw on in this book will be from the writings of socialist feminists. However, even among socialist feminists, there has not been the kind of focus on this position that I believe is needed. One of my primary purposes in this book is to provide such an elaboration.

The argument thus necessitates two different kinds of messages to two different audiences. To those whose commitments lie largely with some version of classical liberalism or Marxism, I shall be pointing out that feminist theory requires a rethinking of such commitments. To feminists, I shall be claiming that feminist theory, to fulfill its potential for radical challenge, must adopt an explicitly historical approach.

To clarify what I mean by "an explicitly historical approach," I must turn to a debate on the proper mode of understanding social life which began in the nineteenth century and which continues today. By the latter part of the nineteenth century, many were inspired by the progress that natural science had made in explicating the natural world and wished to borrow its methods for analyzing social life. This group took on the label of "positivists," following Auguste Comte's demand that social inquiry become a positive science. Opposing them have been those such as Wilhelm Dilthey in the nineteenth century, and theorists such as Hans-Georg Gadamer in the twentieth century, who have questioned the wisdom of transferring the methods of the natural sciences to social inquiry. Such theorists, following Hegel's insistence on the diversity of social life, argued that this diversity could best be captured not through the creation of universal laws but rather through procedures of interpretation, or "hermeneutics," as illustrated in the analysis of texts. They noted the similarities between textual analysis and what goes on in dialogue between human beings in normal conversational interaction, where scenarios of meaningful and thus possible action are changed in the pursuit of mutual understanding. This model placed the concept of "narrative" rather than "law" at the center of social inquiry and challenged the stance of objectivity often found in the self-conception of the natural sciences. If social inquiry essentially replicates ordinary communicative interaction, where meaning and values are connected, then social inquiry must be recognized as containing normative components.

Contemporary feminist epistemology has adopted aspects of this approach. In particular, most feminists now accept the claim that social inquiry is a value-laden activity. In part, this is because the claim has become more frequently articulated and more widely accepted in all contemporary discussions of methodology, regarding natural as well as social inquiry. Moreover, feminist theory, as an outcome of a political movement, sees very clearly how the theoretical claims of the academy, while pretending to be without bias, often reflect decided normative and political stances. Feminist theory, therefore, does not deny the normative motivation of its own activity; rather it proclaims that such motivation is endemic to all scholarly activity.

On the other hand, feminist theory, to a significant extent, still adheres to the goal of achieving cross-cultural laws. Such adherence is most obvious in its search for *the* cause of women's oppression. This search grew out of the early recognition that the oppression was more pervasive than the dominant culture was willing to admit and not explainable by the kinds of appeals to nature or to God that the culture supplied. The radical feminists of the nineteen sixties and seventies began generating alternative explanations, many of which brought forth responses from contemporary Marxists. Marx, as a student of Hegel, passed on to his followers the recognition that human society was decidedly variable. Ac-

cording to many followers of Marx, this variability was a consequence of historical changes in the economy, or in "the mode and
relations of production." Thus the standard Marxist response to
radical feminism was that all its explanations ignored the historical
diversity of the forms in which women's oppression became manifest. Marxists also aptly pointed out that radical feminists, in their
search for cross-cultural causes, ended up with the same kinds of
appeals to biology and thus to "nature" that they had initially
rejected from the dominant culture.

Thus Marxists have tended to push contemporary feminist theory
toward recognizing historical diversity in the content and causes
of women's oppression. However, several factors intervened to
make this push limited. For one, Marx, although a student of
Hegel, was also highly influenced by the growing positivism of
the latter nineteenth century. Because Marx often paid scant attention to methodological issues, his work conjoins in an uneasy
fashion both Hegelian, antipositivist components and elements
central to the emerging positivism of his time. One way in which
the positivist elements became most apparent was in his belief
that for any given social form, all elements within it are determined
ultimately by the shape of its economy or by reference to major
economic transformations, such as the privatization of property,
which crossed many specific social forms. Thus when radical
feminists pointed to the pervasiveness of women's oppression
across many different societies, Marxists responded by arguing
that it was the cross-societal fact of private property which accounted for such oppression. By doing so, Marxists became partners
with radical feminists in the search for a cross-societal explanation.

Thus Marxism failed to remain consistently attentive to historical
diversity in explaining women's oppression. Even the emphasis it
gave to such diversity became unfortunately conjoined in the
debate with what appeared as an insensitivity to the issue of
pervasiveness. Radical feminists argued that Marxism's linkage of
private property with women's oppression demonstrated Marxism's
belief in the secondary character of that oppression. They noted,
quite wisely, the convenience of this kind of explanation for making
feminism as a political struggle secondary to the more traditional

items on the Marxist agenda. And they raised questions about its validity, noting weaknesses in its classic formulation by Engels and pointing to manifestations of sexism in nonclass societies. In consequence, radical feminism resumed its quest for a cross-cultural cause.

What neither position contemplated was the following possibility: that radical feminism may be right on the issue of pervasiveness, i.e., that women's oppression may extend far back into human history or at least transcend the boundaries imposed on it by Marxism, but that radical feminism (and Marxism) goes wrong in searching for a singular cause. That search is mandated only by a positivist methodology. If one appeals to the historical-hermeneutic tradition, a different explanatory model becomes possible. We might view our own devaluation and oppression of women not only as importantly different from earlier versions but also as generated for different reasons. For example, one different reason for a form of such oppression in a later period would be its prior manifestation in an earlier period. Another would be differences in all those historical circumstances which touch on women's lives in the different periods. Thus, to explain women's oppression in nineteenth-century America would require an understanding of both women's oppression in eighteenth-century America and of all that was new about the family, economy, religion, etc., in the nineteenth century. The explanandum here, women's oppression in nineteenth-century America, might be viewed as a piece in a jigsaw puzzle requiring both vertical and horizontal integration with other pieces. One difference, as students of hermeneutics have long pointed out, is that each element in the explanation, or piece in the puzzle, cannot be viewed as discretely identifiable. Rather, the meaning we give to each depends in part on our understanding of the others and of the puzzle as a whole.

This type of explanatory model is antipositivistic in many respects. It rejects that model of scientific explanation which searches for similar causes to similar effects, and also it is not committed to any version of determinacy at all. To say that the oppression of women in nineteenth-century America might be accounted for by appealing to factors preceding and coexisting with it is not to claim it as the inevitable consequence of such factors. That a historical phenomenon coheres with factors of its past and present is compatible with the possibility that an alternative phenomenon might have cohered as well, and with the possibility that social life may be incoherent at times, both to those who are living it and to those trying to understand the lives of others. By comparing social explanation to the piecing together of a jigsaw puzzle I was drawing on coherence as an important criterion for determining the adequacy of any given account. However, while coherence is an important criterion, it is only one, superceded at times by overwhelming evidence pointing to the presence of incoherent phenomena. In either case, whether the pieces of our puzzle fit together neatly or not, the metaphor of a puzzle underlines the fact that in social explanations we are frequently dealing with unique combinations of phenomena, making difficult the construction of cross-cultural laws.

There is another, important sense in which the approach I am suggesting for analyzing women's oppression is antipositivistic. I am not claiming that any historical account of women's oppression is objective in the sense of exhausting what can be said of our past. The very telling of such a story requires locating and focusing on phenomena long absent from traditional history. After feminism, there will come other political movements with different explanatory demands which will ferret out aspects of our history irrelevant to present feminist concerns. A push toward such amplification can be seen even today when many black women rightly castigate much of contemporary feminist scholarship for its narrowness of vision. However, this rejection of "one right story" does not mean that in historical understanding, "anything goes." Not all historical accounts are as comprehensive, as coherent, or as respectful of the evidence as others. However, it does mean recognizing, without apology, the political motivation of the present feminist concern to create a story which accounts for present and past female devaluation.

There are a variety of reasons why feminist theorists ought to explicitly adopt such a method. One major reason is that a narrative, historical model enables feminist theory to make theoretically coherent some of the deep suspicions that have surfaced within it and within the political movement. One prominent suspicion within contemporary feminism is that there is something ideological and harmful to women about the ways modern Western culture views the relation of family, state, and economy—that the divisions between these spheres are not as rigid as we are led to believe and that conceiving them in such a manner obscures the realities of women's lives. This suspicion exists uneasily with the awareness that the divisions between these spheres are nevertheless a fact of our social world and its past which also needs to be taken into account in comprehending women's lives. The only way out of this theoretical dilemma is to adopt a narrative, historical methodology which would make possible the telling of a story similar to the one I began to sketch earlier. According to such a story, the divisions between family, state, and economy, which now form an important fact of life for modern Western society, only gradually evolved over time. Because what now appear as separated spheres share common origins and interrelated histories, there are connections which the new, if still partial, fact of separation has helped to obscure. For example, if we recognize that once upon a time, the political and the familial were interconnected in the institution of kinship—a beginning modern liberalism has obscured through its contract theory of the origins of the state— then we can make comprehensible contemporary feminism's awareness of the patriarchal, and thus political, component of the contemporary family, and its awareness of the patriarchal, and thus gendered, component of the contemporary state. Similarly, to the extent we can see the separation of the economy from the household as a historical phenomenon, we can also comprehend why the contemporary marketplace still bears traces of its origins in its present functioning.

Earlier I stated that I would be speaking two different messages to liberals and Marxists on the one hand and feminists on the other. Actually, of course, the message is fundamentally the same. It is that some of the most basic categories modern Western culture has constructed to understand its own and all possible societies, particularly the categories of the familial, the political, and the economic, do not describe aspects of human existence that are necessarily distinct, but aspects which have been made distinct at specific historical moments. Marxism made significant advances over liberalism in enabling us to see this point, but became limited by its submergence both in the growing positivism of the time and in the fact of the growing separation and dominance of the economic in the nineteenth century. Feminist theory can, therefore, modify and extend social theory as part of the process of incorporating women into history and women's struggles into politics.

To make this argument I will proceed in the following manner. In the first chapter I will illustrate the uniqueness of feminism as a political movement in its concern with the family and personal relations and begin to note some of the theoretical dilemmas generated by this concern. In the following chapter I will analyze why this concern developed by examining societal changes taking place in the United States over the past two centuries. Having thus described the concerns and context of contemporary feminist practice in the United States, in part 2 I will analyze some of the scholarship associated with that practice. The argument here, beginning in chapter 3, will be that it is only through adopting an explicitly historical methodology that contemporary feminism can resolve many of the theoretical dilemmas generated within it. This argument will be extended in chapter 4, where I claim that by employing such an approach for analyzing the modern period, it is possible to understand the historical emergence and separation of the spheres of family, state, and economy and also to better understand gender in this period. In chapters 5 and 6 I argue that this type of account would also enable feminist theory to avoid and go beyond certain central mistakes of liberalism and Marxism, particularly the tendency in liberalism to reify the spheres of family and state, and the tendency in Marxism to reify the sphere of the economy. In these chapters I also elaborate the relation between the content of liberalism and Marxism and the changing dynamics of private and public occurring, respectively, in the seventeenth and nineteenth centuries. Thus by the end of the book I will have sketched a historical pattern relating liberalism, Marxism, and contemporary feminism and developed a means for understanding many of their differences.

PART ONE
FEMINIST PRACTICE:
THE PERSONAL IS POLITICAL

CHAPTER ONE

THE CONTEMPORARY WOMEN'S MOVEMENT

IN THE LATE 1960s the women's movement in the United States formulated the slogan, "The personal is political." Many of the women who took up this slogan had been active in the various protest movements of the sixties. The slogan was directed in part to other activists and was created to justify attention to a new cause: the personal relations between men and women. Such justification was perceived necessary because of the widely held attitude that the practices which took place between women and men acting *qua* women and men stood outside the domain of politics. For the activists of the 1960s, if these practices were not political, they were not appropriate objects for the scrutiny and struggle for change that were demanded by the relations between, for example, different racial groups. The early feminists intended to challenge this attitude through this slogan.

At one level the slogan expressed what was clearly false. Modern Western society appears obviously split between the two spheres of family or personal life on the one hand and public life on the other. The term "political" has been traditionally limited to describing the interactions within the public sphere, supposedly different in content from the interactions of private life. The feminists responded that apparent differences in content were often illusory; they argued that power dynamics, for example, existed in both. They added that the relations between the sexes, like relations between other social groups, were regulated by societal rules. The difficulties individual women experienced in their "private" lives were shared by other women and consequently were not "personal." Moreover, they argued that the supposedly private nature of gender shaped and was shaped by the content of social relations outside as well as inside the home. Thus the early feminists proclaimed that the popular ideology which placed personal relations between the sexes outside politics created obstacles against an adequate understanding of such relations.

To use the terminology of contemporary philosophy, the slogan "The personal is political" expressed a stipulative definition; intended was a change in traditional understandings of the term "political." Something more than language use, however, was also at stake. Descriptions of social reality bear a curious relation to the reality they are about; in part such descriptions help constitute the reality. In this case, the popular belief in a distinctness of the realms of personal and public life has been an important ingredient in keeping the realms separate. To challenge this belief was thus in part to challenge the reality constituted by it. In short, the slogan "The personal is political" expressed a stipulative and constitutive definition. It was stipulative in that it sought to redefine the term "politics" and constitutive in that such a new definition must in turn affect the reality being defined. The slogan was thus itself a political statement; by its very utterance it sought to make a change in social reality.

The slogan provides, I believe, an important clue to understanding the significance of the contemporary women's movement and marks it as unique as a political movement. This uniqueness is reflected not only within the political practice. Rather I wish to argue, and this will be a central argument of this book, that the theory which is currently being developed by those active in the contemporary women's movement represents a comparably unique contribution to existing political theory. The attention contemporary feminist practice has given to gender relations and the family is reflected within feminist theory in the study of both as necessary components of political theory. The consequence, I intend to show, carries serious implications for existing political theory.

As a preliminary step toward making this argument, I shall describe in this chapter the role the slogan has played in the politics of the contemporary women's movement, particularly as this movement has existed in the United States. It should be noted that the slogan only arose within a certain section of the movement and so cannot be attributed to the movement per se without qualification. The different parts of the contemporary women's movement have had a changing and complex relationship among themselves. Indeed, at certain points in the 1960s it would have been misleading to talk about "the" women's movement. In the late 1960s there existed at least two very different movements. The mass media recognized this difference in their distinction between what they called the "women's rights" movement versus what they dubbed "women's lib," the latter a pejorative shortening of the term "women's liberation." The "women's rights" movement was composed primarily of those professional women who initiated activities in the mid 1960s and who were involved in such organizations as the National Organization for Women. "Women's liberation," on the other hand, was largely constituted by younger women who were active in the 1960s' protest movements of the New Left and whose concern with women's issues began to receive national attention only toward the latter part of the decade. It is from within "women's liberation" that the tendency "radical feminism" emerged, the label intended as a means of distinguishing it from the "liberal feminism" expressed in the "women's rights" movement. While radical feminism distinguished itself from a feminism more "on the right," there was also dialogue and confrontation with those "on the left" and in particular with women who identified more strongly with Marxism and labeled themselves "Marxist feminists."

One of the important sources of difference among "liberal," "radical," and "Marxist" feminists has concerned the nature of their respective endorsements of the slogan "The personal is political." Only within radical feminism was the endorsement unambiguous; some of the early exponents of radical feminism broke out of the New Left with precisely this banner. Liberal feminism and Marxist feminism have had a more complicated relationship to the slogan. In fact, an important source of tension within both has had to do with the question, "How political *is* the personal?" The differing assessments by liberal, radical, and Marxist feminists of the relation between personal and public life is related in turn to fundamental differences in the underlying theories of each on the nature of social life.

LIBERAL FEMINISM

To understand these differences it is helpful to go back to the early 1960s and the reemergence of "women's rights" as a topic of political discussion in the United States. Following the enactment of the Nineteenth Amendment to the Constitution granting women suffrage, the issue had remained relatively dormant for almost forty years.[1] Two events of the early 1960s are often credited as important in marking the end of the silence; the publication in 1963 of *The Feminine Mystique* by Betty Friedan and the establishment of a Presidential Commission on the Status of Women by John F. Kennedy in 1961.[2] That *The Feminine Mystique* became a bestseller soon after its publication seemed to indicate a widespread discontent with the prevalent national ideal of the "happy housewife." At least as articulated by Friedan, women's daily life in the suburbs deviated significantly from its popular image and possessed a multitude of negative features. Women consequently needed to begin questioning their exclusion from all those spheres of activity which had become predominantly viewed as the domain of men. A similar questioning of women's exclusion from non-domestic life was expressed in the document *American Women*, released in 1963, the official report of Kennedy's commission. While that document did not challenge traditional conceptions of women's place within the family, it did argue forcefully against women's exclusion from other domains. While endorsing "the fundamental responsibility of mothers and homemakers and society's stake in strong family life," the commission also put forth such recommendations as for the increased availability of day care services for everyone regardless of family income and for tax deductions for the child care expenses of working mothers.[3] Kennedy's original commission spawned a variety of governmental agencies, including a Citizens Advisory Council on the Status of Women, an Interdepartmental Committee on the Status of Women, and various state Commissions on the Status of Women. These groups began to provide a forum for discussion of women's status within the law as well as a means of contact for those interested in making changes in that status. Of special importance was a meeting of the National Conference of State Commissions, held in the summer of 1966 in Washington, D.C. Out of that conference emerged NOW, the National Organization for Women. It grew out of the need felt by some that an extragovernmental action group exist which would put pressure on existing governmental bodies, such as the Equal Employment Opportunity Commission. The existence of NOW was officially announced at a press conference on October 29, 1966, with Betty Friedan becoming its first president. The purpose of the organization was stated as the following: "To take action to bring women into full participation in the mainstream of American society *now*, exercising all the privileges and responsibilities thereof in truly equal partnership with men."[4] The political stance of NOW is further illustrated in the Women's Bill of Rights which it drew up at its second national conference in November 1967 in Washington, D.C. The Bill of Rights was to be presented to the platform committees of the Democratic and Republican parties as well as all major candidates running for national office in the 1968 election.[5] It was composed of the following eight demands:

1. Equal Rights Constitutional Amendment
2. Enforcement Laws Banning Sex Discrimination in Employment
3. Maternity Leave Rights in Employment and in Social Security Benefits
4. Tax Deduction for Home and Child Care Expenses for Working Parents
5. Child Care Centers
6. Equal and Unsegregated Education
7. Equal Job Training Opportunities and Allowances for Women in Poverty
8. The Right of Women to Control Their Reproductive Lives.[6]

Two of the above planks brought controversy. The first demand supporting a constitutional equal rights amendment was opposed by women from the United Auto Workers. That union with others was officially against such an amendment on the grounds that it would conflict with various state protective laws. Demand 7 was fought by other women who argued that abortion was not a women's rights issue; they subsequently left NOW when NOW endorsed this demand.[7]

The statement of purpose and statement of demands express a particular emphasis: a concern to eliminate those obstacles barring the full participation of women in nondomestic activities. Certainly some of the above demands, such as demands 5 and 8 concerning childcare and reproductive rights, also touch on issues relating to women's "personal" lives. However, even these in the context of the other demands and the statement of purpose appear as means to ensure a more primary end: the ability of women to participate equally with men in activities and occupations outside the home. What also can be concluded from the above is an emphasis within NOW on making changes within the law to bring about this end. All the above eight demands are ones that could be brought about by legal means. This, of course, is not surprising, in that the demands were developed for endorsement by political parties and candidates. The point, however, is that NOW viewed such activity as crucial on its agenda. That it did so followed from the motivation behind its genesis: that there exist an extragovernmental action organization which would work to put pressure on existing governmental bodies to bring about legal change.

However, while in the mid and late sixties it may have been correct to describe the politics of NOW or other liberal feminist organizations such as WEAL (Women's Equity Action League) or BPW (Business and Professional Women) in this way—as concerned primarily with women's ability to function equally with men outside the home—this characterization has become increasingly problematic. Liberal feminists, like many others, have steadily focused their attention on women's personal lives. Thus liberal feminists, with others, have discussed such topics as "the politics of housework," the demeaning portrayals of women in television and advertising, the oppressive nature of traditional understandings of women's sexuality, etc.[8] There are complex reasons for this growing attention by liberal feminists to personal issues as ends in themselves. Many follow from widespread societal changes which will be discussed at greater length in the following chapter. For now it simply can be noted that issues associated with personal life have, during the twentieth century, steadily become issues of public concern for American society at large, and this has been manifest in many aspects of American life, including but not limited to the women's movement. Thus a defining aspect of the New Left of the 1960s and that which distinguished it from the old left was a concern with matters of "consciousness" and "lifestyle." The New Left itself was affected by the "beat generation" which preceded it and the "hippie" movement which was a part of it, both of which placed a strong emphasis on matters personal and viewed them in political terms. Apart from the New Left there has existed a widespread national concern over social mores regarding marriage and sexuality. Thus that many liberal feminists have come to incorporate a focus on personal relations within their concern for "women's rights" is understandable within the context of an existing general societal concern with such issues. Moreover, many liberal feminists, as a consequence of their feminism, have taken note of the strong arguments made by more radical feminists, that the achievement of parity with men outside the home necessitates changes in traditional patterns within the home. They have thus increasingly come to recognize the interconnection of domestic and nondomestic life.

Of course, the degree to which domestic life is believed to be in need of change varies widely within the national culture, and part of this variance is also reflected in the women's movement, still creating important differences between liberal feminism and its more radical allies. It is one thing to argue that women should retain their surnames in marriage or that women and men should share housework responsibilities. It is something quite different to protest the privileged status given to heterosexuality as a mode of sexuality or more radically to argue against its desirability for women. Thus an increasing unanimity on the position that traditional mores governing personal relations need to be changed coexists with important divisions concerning the extent of the changes believed to be needed. Thus while liberal feminism may have increasingly accepted the dictum that "The personal is political," this has coexisted with a tendency toward caution in making such politics revolutionary.

Connected with the difference in conceptions of how radically domestic life needs to be changed are other differences concerning how radically nondomestic life needs to be changed. Liberal feminism has tended to accept the basic structures of existing political and economic institutions, pressing hardest on the need to make them accessible to women. This contrasts with the leftist perspective present in varying degrees in radical feminism and strongly in Marxist feminism which sees such institutions as hierarchical, competitive, and individualistic.

This latter difference between liberal feminism and its more radical allies has had important consequences concerning their respective positions on the relation of private and public life. While liberal feminism, like other versions of feminism, tends to be sympathetic toward redefining the relation of private and public, for liberal feminism this often means the subsumption of the private under the public. In this respect there is a close similarity between liberal feminism and twentieth-century welfare state liberalism, as both look to the extension of state functions as a means of alleviating social problems. Both positions reflect that movement within the twentieth century for the state to extend its domain, taking over in many contexts activities thought previously to be the province of the family and the household. Examples are the further development of public education and the emergence of social security, welfare, and public health agencies. Such phenomena, in conjunction with increased state regulation, both in regard to familial matters and also in regard to economic activities, have caused some to speak of the creation of a new domain altogether: the sphere of the "social," a sphere of state control arising on the collapse of old boundaries between the private and the public.[9] Liberal feminism, insofar as it advocates extending this domain to meet the needs of women, can thus be described as supporting that realignment of the private and the public which entails the subsumption of the former under the latter.[10]

This tendency within liberal feminism to view problems in private life as solvable by an extension of public regulation both ties it to classical and contemporary liberalism and differentiates it from many other forms of contemporary feminism. It ties it to classical liberalism insofar as liberalism has classically celebrated, though in different forms in different centuries, the public realm as articulated reason, or law, in ordering social life. Classical liberalism, of course, has also worried about infringements of liberty made possible by a too powerful state. Contemporary liberal feminism, like contemporary welfare state liberalism, tends (though not unequivocally) to view the good accomplished by the extension of such reason or law as outweighing the personal liberties diminished in consequence. Both stances, however, can be differentiated from a growing tendency in radical and left-wing feminism to argue that such a conception of reason or law emphasizes traits associated with masculinity, such as the inclination to abstract from particular differences in needs and circumstances and to deemphasize the importance of compassion and care.[11] Neomarxists and anarchists have argued that in its twentieth-century instrumentalized form, public "reason" has been employed as a means of domination, giving power to the "expert" and turning others into passive clients of state control.[12] Neomarxist and anarchist feminists have pointed out that in the institutionalized form of such "reason," in public bureaucracies, masculine control over women has taken new forms, going beyond traditional paternal modes. They have argued that while the state here may be undermining "patriarchy," at least in its traditional form, this has not necessarily entailed the promotion of gender equality but rather has often merely changed the nature of gender *in*equality. Women's personal dependence upon individual men has frequently been replaced by a more impersonal subordinate position within the workplace and by a mass dependence on the states' welfare institutions. Private patriarchy, in short, has itself become public.[13] What all these positions share, therefore, in opposition to liberal feminism, is the recognition that the breakdown of the separation of private and public is insufficient to satisfy feminist requirements but must be conjoined with a restructuring of the public.[14]

RADICAL FEMINISM

We can further understand such differences by looking more extensively at that political position known as radical feminism. In part, radical feminism was created by women who had been active in NOW and were dissatisfied with what they perceived of as NOW's conservatism. Thus in 1967 at the annual meeting of NOW subsequent to the one in which the above demands were formulated, a group of New York women allied with Ti-Grace Atkinson left NOW and subsequently formed an early radical feminist organization, "The October 17th Movement," later called "The Feminists."[15] Radical feminism was to a large extent also constituted by women whose previous political activity had been in the diverse organizations of the New Left. This was the case, for example, with such women as Shulamith Firestone and Jo Freeman, who founded an early radical feminist organization, Radical Women, in New York City in the fall of 1967. These two women, with others, had earlier presented a series of women's demands to a New Left conference, the National Conference for a New Politics, in the spring of that year. None of the demands were taken seriously, causing them to begin thinking about the necessity of separate women's organizations outside existing groups.

The early organizers of radical feminism shared with the rest of the New Left a belief in the systemic nature of much of political injustice. Thus when these women began to perceive the situation of women as representing a case of this injustice, they employed the adjective "radical" to describe their stance. It signified a commitment to look for root causes. Radical feminists viewed the activities of women who had been involved in NOW or other existing business and professional women's organizations as "reformist," helpful and necessary but fundamentally inconsequential. This view stemmed both from a belief that the criticisms liberal feminism made of relations between women and men in both domestic and nondomestic life did not go far enough, and also, from a belief that liberal feminism had no sense of the importance of gender, and the social relations of domestic life, in structuring all social life. For radical feminism, liberal feminism's belief in the power of the law to remedy inequalities between women and men testified to a lack of insight into the fundamentality of the "sex-role system," those practices and institutions which were important in creating and maintaining sex-role differences. Of particular importance was the family, for it was here that biological men and women learned the cultural constituents of masculinity and femininity, and learned about the fundamental differences of power which, according to radical feminism, were a necessary component of both. A quotation from a manifesto of New York Radical Feminists illustrates the political position:

> Radical feminism recognizes the oppression of women as a fundamental political oppression wherein women are categorized as an inferior class based upon their sex. It is the aim of radical feminism to organize politically to destroy this sex class system.
>
> As radical feminists we recognize that we are engaged in a power struggle with men, and that the agent of our suppression is man insofar as he identifies with and carries out the supremacy privileges of the male role. For while we realize that the liberation of women will ultimately mean the liberation of men from their destructive role as oppressor, we have no illusion that men will welcome this liberation without a struggle. . . .
>
> The oppression of women is manifested in particular institutions, constituted and maintained to keep women in their place. Among these are the institutions of marriage, motherhood, love and sexual intercourse (the family unit is incorporated by the above).[16]

In sum, for radical feminism, women's inferior political and economic status were mere symptoms of a more fundamental problem: an inferior status and lack of power built into the role of femininity. Radical feminism challenged prevailing beliefs that the constituents of this role, such as women's abilities and interests in childrearing or lack of assertiveness or even the content of women's sexual interests, were "natural." Rather the argument was made that all but certain limited biological differences between women and men were cultural. The constituents of the sex-role system were social constructions, and more important, such constructions were fundamentally antithetical to the interests of women. The norms embodied in femininity discouraged women from developing their intellectual, artistic, and physical capacities. It dissuaded women from thinking of themselves and from being thought of by others as autonomous agents. Whereas "masculinity" embodied certain traits associated with adulthood, such as physical strength, rationality, and emotional control, "femininity," in part embodied traits associated with childhood, such as weakness and irrationality. The norms of femininity created an emphasis in women's lives on achieving the roles of wife and mother whose outcome was a comparable imbalance between men and women in economic and emotional autonomy. Moreover, while the norms embodied in femininity often worked against women, the norms embodied in masculinity served to create many unattractive beings, those who too frequently were aggressive, selfish, instrumental in their dealings with others, and unskilled in the arts of nurturance and caring. The source of the problem, according to radical feminism, was to be found in the home and family, where girls and boys received their initial and most primary lessons on the differences between the sexes and where adult women and men played out the lessons that they learned. The lessons of gender differences learned and practiced in the home were in turn transferred to the outside world when women did leave the home. Thus when women took paid employment, they replicated and were expected to replicate the practices and inferior status of women which were a part of the home. In sum, according to radical feminism, the inferior status of women as political or economic beings was merely the symptom of a problem whose roots were to be located elsewhere.

Radical feminism also generated new forms of political organizing. Organizations such as NOW, WEAL, BPW had engaged in traditional political means to improve women's status. Such groups sent telegrams and lobbied in Congress. Members of NOW sometimes marched or demonstrated. The primary intent of such actions was to bring about changes within the law. While radical feminists also marched and demonstrated, the intent of the action was not always the same. The point was not necessarily to change people's thinking so that they might vote differently but sometimes to change people's thinking so that they might live differently. This conception of political organizing was embodied in the phrase "consciousness-raising." In the early years of radical feminism, this was occasionally attempted through street theater, itself a practice carried out within the New Left. This tactic was employed in Atlantic City in the fall of 1968 at an event which first brought "Women's Lib" to national attention. The New York Radical Women demonstrated outside the Miss America contest, crowning a sheep "Miss America" and throwing such feminine articles of clothing as bras, girdles, curlers, false eyelashes, and wigs into a "Freedom Trash Can."[17] It was from this event that the media's description of "Women's Lib" as "bra-burners" was generated. The more prevalent form that consciousness-raising took within the early years of "Women's Lib" was small-group discussion. Women came together to discuss the implications of gender in their own lives, which included its personal as well as its political and economic components. What is notable about such groups is that they expressed, and were consciously designed to express, a political statement in their very purpose. The attention that radical feminists gave to the dynamics of personal relations was accompanied by a belief that attention to feelings and personal experience was a necessary condition for eliminating the present sex-role system. Since the components of that system were embedded in deep and complex ways in daily life experience, it was only through careful examination of that experience that the multiple manifestations of gender could be understood and thus changed.

This attention to "personal experience" had immense significance for the direction contemporary American feminism has taken. On a practical level it entailed a rethinking of the nature of social change. On a theoretical level it entailed a new focus on the family as a central institution in structuring social life. To be sure, radical feminism was not the first social movement to devote attention to the family and personal life. Psychoanalytic theory has also been concerned with both the family and sexuality. For many radical feminists, however, much of psychoanalytic theory appeared to reflect uncritically prevalent assumptions concerning gender. For example, psychoanalytic theory did not question the dominant position that men played within the family or within society at large. It often assumed the universal existence of the family type which prevailed in the middle classes in late nineteenth- and early twentieth-century Western society. In short, psychoanalytic theory did not treat the family as a social institution whose dynamics might be susceptible to criticism and possible change; it did not address the family and gender relations in political terms.[18]

Thus the initial task which faced early radical feminist thinkers was that of creating a theory which both treated the family as a social institution and recognized its centrality in structuring social life as a whole. Thus if for liberalism the state, or public law, has been seen as possessing priority in structuring social life, and if in certain interpretations of Marxism the economy, or sphere of production, has been viewed as the base from which might be explained all other social phenomena, so for radical feminism the family, sometimes described as the sphere of "reproduction," occupies an analogous role. This point was made explicit by Shulamith Firestone, one of the early radical feminist theorists, in her rewriting of Engels:

> Historical materialism is that view of the course of history which seeks the ultimate course and the great moving power of all historic events in the dialectic of sex: the division of society into two distinct biological classes for procreative reproduction, and the struggles of these classes with one another; in the changes in the modes of marriage, reproduction and childcare created by these struggles; in the connected development of other physically differentiated classes

(castes); and in the first division of labor based on sex which developed into the (economic-cultural) class system.[19]

An important problem with Firestone's argument, which surfaces in much, and particularly early, radical feminist writing, is a tendency to resort to biology to ground the analysis. In Firestone's case this tendency manifests itself in her claim that the ultimate causes of women's oppression are biological differences between women and men. That women bear and nurse children makes necessary a basic family form in which women are fundamentally dependent on others in a way in which men are not. This power imbalance between women as a class and men as a class is replicated by a similar imbalance between children and adults. From such biologically based imbalances result the imbalances of power which have marked all human societies. However, for Firestone, biology need not be destiny. Technological developments in the reproduction of children conjoined with cultural changes in childrearing would end the so far universal "tyranny of the biological family."[20]

As many critics have pointed out, Firestone's account suffers from the obvious problem of ahistoricity. That we associate childbearing or childrearing with dependence and devalue those who perform such tasks need not imply that all other societies make or have made similar associations. Similarly, Firestone's account seems to project onto all societies a modern Western nuclear type of family with a certain gender division of labor. This projection seems allied with her association of childbearing and childrearing with dependence. If we abstract from our own nuclear family, where individual women are often dependent on individual men, to different family forms with different divisions of labor, then it is easy to see that a pregnant or lactating woman need be no more dependent on a larger social group than any other member of that group. To respond here that any other member possesses a greater possibility of leaving that group because of a greater ease in existing self-sufficiently is to belie both the social nature of human existence and the fact that women are as capable of forsaking children as men.

These problems in Firestone's account bear explicating only because they reflect methodological problems prevalent in radical feminist theory. Within the larger body of that theory there has been a tendency to create transhistorical descriptions and explanations and at times to resort to biology. As Heidi Hartmann notes, the radical feminist emphasis on psychology tends to blind it to history.[21] Also, the inclination to articulate a transcultural perspective follows from the need to create a theory which will explain the universal phenomenon of female oppression. The emphasis on biology is connected with this need and also with the radical feminist focus on the family, as the family tends to be viewed in modern Western culture in largely biological terms.[22] The contradiction here is that radical feminism's attention to the family and to gender has been motivated by the desire to denaturalize both, to enable us to see both as constructed and changeable. It has been one of the important contributions of radical feminist theory to make the point that women are made and not born.[23] The dilemma for radical feminism has been to retain this awareness of the social construction of gender and the family while also maintaining an awareness of the persistent and deep-seated phenomenon of female oppression and the importance of the family both in generating that oppression and in structuring nondomestic life.

Radical feminist practice and theory has also changed in many ways since its genesis in the late 1960s. One change is a growing attention to issues of race and class.[24] Another is an abandonment of the early reliance on the terminology of "roles" and the "sex-role system." As Alison Jaggar has noted, role terminology implies that women and men have a high degree of choice vis-à-vis gender; role terminology suggests that gender is a kind of mask or script which people may assume or relinquish at will.[25] Also, radical feminism in more recent years describes women's oppression less as a consequence of "the family" and more in terms of specific practices which have been associated with that institution, such as mothering and sexuality.[26]

Indeed, one of the most important changes in radical feminism since the late 1960s has been its increased, explicit focus on sexuality, a change associated with the extension of radical feminism into lesbian feminism. An article which greatly contributed to this development was "The Woman Identified Woman."[27] This paper claimed that women must eliminate the need for male approval and the practice of identifying with male beliefs and values, both central components of a misogynist culture. The authors argued that an important means for women to accomplish such tasks and to remove the self-hate women typically have toward themselves is to love other women, both emotionally and sexually. At the very least, women cannot let the label "dyke" stand in the way of developing such love and removing such self-hatred. More recently, Adrienne Rich has also tied together female self-identification and lesbian sexuality under the phrase, "a lesbian continuum." By using the term "lesbian" to denote not only female homosexuality but also instances "of primary intensity between and among women, including the sharing of a rich inner life, the bonding against male tyranny, the giving and receiving of practical and political support," Rich argues that "We begin to grasp breadths of female history and psychology which have lain out of reach as a consequence of limited, mostly clinical, definitions of 'lesbianism.' "[28]

However, radical feminism has gone even further than stating that there is a connection between lesbianism and women coming to define and love themselves. Made more explicit, both by Rich and others, is the assertion that women's oppression is constituted by heterosexuality. As Catherine MacKinnon puts it, "Sexuality is the lynchpin of gender inequality."[29] It is worthwhile examining the following passage from the article in which this point was made for its illustration of the similarities and differences between early radical feminism and more recent forms:

> Implicit in feminist theory is a parallel argument: the molding, direction, and expression of sexuality organizes society into two sexes—women and men—which division underlies the totality of social relations. Sexuality is that social process which creates, organizes, expresses, and directs desire, creating the social beings we know as women and men, as their

relations create society. As work is to marxism, sexuality to
feminism is socially constructed yet constructing, universal
as activity yet historically specific, jointly comprised of matter
and mind. As the organized expropriation of the work of
some for the benefit of others defines a class—workers—the
organized expropriation of the sexuality of some for the use
of others defines the sex, woman. Heterosexuality is its structure, gender and family its congealed forms, sex roles its
qualities generalized to social persona, reproduction a consequence, and control its issue.[30]

MacKinnon, like Firestone before her, defines feminism by contrast with Marxism. As Marxism has defined production, or human
labor recreating the conditions of its existence, as central to its
analysis of oppression, so feminism, according to MacKinnon,
makes sexuality the cornerstone of *its* analysis of oppression. Thus
MacKinnon is continuing that path well trodden by contemporary
feminists, of recognizing that Marxism, while providing a deeply
insightful tool for analyzing social oppression, has no means for
comprehending gender oppression. What is unique in MacKinnon's
argument is her explicit claim that the central lacuna in Marxism
and that which serves as the defining issue for feminism is sexuality.

MacKinnon's argument gives us clues for seeing both what has
been most insightful in radical feminism and its major problems.
Contemporary radical feminism has been relatively unique in the
concerted attention it has given to matters often thought of as
either natural or trivial, issues such as sexuality and the family,
and in arguing for the centrality of these phenomena in structuring
relations between women and men and social life as a whole.
The insightfulness of the first point, that in at least some cultures
sex may be instrumental in structuring gender is illustrated in the
English language where the word "sex" refers both to sexual
activity and to gender. Moreover, the illuminating power of the
second point, that both sexuality and gender are concerns not only
of "private life" but of all social life, must also be recognized as
a crucial contribution of radical feminism. For one, it enables us

to see the interconnection of gender oppression in domestic and nondomestic settings. Also, it helps us realize that the liberal feminist solution of extending the sphere of state control is not necessarily a solution for women: that to extend the realm of state control may entail merely a substitution in new forms of masculine power, or gender inequality, in women's lives.

However, if the strengths of radical feminism lay in its recognition of the interconnection of sexuality and gender and of their importance in affecting social life, its weaknesses result from its tendency to collapse gender into sexuality and to see all societies as fundamentally similar. Indeed the interconnection of these two problems can be seen in MacKinnon's analysis. MacKinnon argues that "sexuality is the lynchpin of gender oppression." A question one might put regarding this assertion is: does it hold true for all women? For example, one might say that the form of sexism experienced by contemporary, poor, black, American women at the hands of a white, male-dominated, state bureaucracy and corporate world seems at least as central, if not more central, a form of sexism in the lives of these women than the sexism experienced in the context of heterosexual relations. In other words, MacKinnon's analysis does not appear to leave room for the possibility that forms of gender oppression, such as those experienced in work, politics, or religion, might express or have come to express a central form of the oppression of some women. This is not to deny that sexuality might have played a central role historically in generating gender oppression, but that would constitute a historical and not an analytic truth, which would have to be integrated with historical analysis to explicate gender oppression in other periods. Indeed, as I will argue in later chapters, when one provides this kind of historical analysis, the insights of radical feminism appear at their strongest.

MARXIST AND SOCIALIST FEMINISM

The New Left, out of which radical feminism emerged, was composed of a diverse collection of political groups and contained a wide spectrum of political views. An important component of the New Left were individuals who described themselves as socialists or Marxists. The relation of Marxists to the contemporary women's movement has been complex. In the late 1960s and early 1970s there were many who believed that the women's movement could at best be described as reformist, demanding changes which were relatively superficial to the social order per se. Allied with this perspective was a tendency to see no important differences between liberal and radical feminism. According to many Marxists, the ultimate political demands of both could be summarized in the slogan, "Where there are men, there women shall be." This goal could be easily satisfied by working class women performing those working class jobs traditionally performed by men and ruling class women stepping into the positions of power of their husbands. Such a political transformation would not alter, however, the fundamental class structure of capitalist society, which would be relatively compatible with such changes. The notion that gender differences were relatively superficial societal differences stemmed from the position that the oppression women suffered as a consequence of their gender was insignificant in comparison with the oppression black people suffered as a consequence of their race and even less significant in comparison with the oppression black and white working class people suffered as a consequence of their class. Some Marxists pointed to women of relative privilege and status, such as Jacqueline Kennedy, to illustrate the absurdity of sympathizing with women merely as a consequence of their gender.

The above derogatory stance of many Marxists to the women's movement diminished somewhat by the early 1970s. Gender joined the ranks of race to become a worthy organizing issue. Persisting for a longer time was the question of how gender oppression was best to be explained. While many Marxists came to accede to radical feminism's claim that gender oppression was a significant type of oppression, the argument remained that radical feminism lacked an adequate explanation of its cause. Radical feminism employed the phrase "sex-role system" to explain female oppression and looked to the family as its carrier. For many Marxists such a framework was ahistorical; it tended to place the family and the practices associated with both masculinity and femininity outside history and class. Many believed that what was necessary was an analysis which could explain the initial genesis of female oppression, its evolution within history, and the specific forms it took within diverse class formations.

For many Marxists this analysis was available in Friedrich Engels' *The Origin of the Family, Private Property, and the State.*[31] Engels posited an initial state of social organization as primarily peaceful and egalitarian. The basic social unit in such societies was the collective kin group. All economic and political activities were communal and public. There was no difference in status between men and women; the political and economic egalitarianism that prevailed extended also to the relations between the sexes. Such societies operated mainly at the level of subsistence; the little social surplus that was created was passed on through the line of the mother. By a gradual evolutionary process the form of group marriage which existed in such societies was replaced by what Engels called the "pairing family," not identical with later monogamous marriage. The pairing family represented a loose association and did not undermine the communistic structure which still prevailed; that was destroyed only with the creation of a social surplus made possible by the introduction of cattle breeding, metal working, weaving, and agriculture. Within the existing division of labor, it was men who were in charge of food production. Men's role in creating the new wealth in turn became contradictory with the principle of matrilineality. Matrilineality needed to be overthrown; that it was, in turn, brought about the emergence of the patriarchal family:

> Thus on the one hand, in proportion as wealth increased it made the man's position in the family more important than the woman's, and on the other hand created an impulse to exploit this strengthened position in order to overthrow, in favor of his children, the traditional order of inheritance. This, however, was impossible so long as descent was reckoned according to mother right. Mother right, therefore, had to be overthrown, and overthrown it was. . . . The reck-

oning of descent in the female line and the matriarchal law of inheritance were thereby overthrown, and the male line of descent and the paternal law of inheritance were substituted for them. . . . The overthrow of mother right was the *world historical defeat of the female sex.* The man took command in the home also; the woman was degraded and reduced to servitude; she became the slave of his lust and a mere instrument for the production of his children. . . . The establishment of the exclusive supremacy of the man shows its effect first in the patriarchal family, which now emerges as an intermediate form.[32]

The attraction of Engels' explanation for contemporary Marxists was that it enabled a recognition of the radical feminists' claim that sex oppression was significant without necessitating an abandonment of the traditional Marxist framework. It was for Engels the same phenomenon, the existence of an initial social surplus, which was simultaneously linked with the oppression of women and the beginning privatization of property. Private property, responsible for class domination, was thus also connected with gender domination. The struggle for communism, as the struggle for that form of social order which replicated at a higher level of subsistence the communality and egalitarianism of primitive society, would bring about the simultaneous ending of both forms of domination.

This account by Engels has been subject to a wide variety of criticisms, many of which I will examine in a later chapter. For now, however, we might focus on some of the most widespread criticisms that were made of his analysis, particularly by radical feminists in the course of the 1970s. In counter to Engels' argument, radical feminists claimed that male domination, labeled "patriarchy," extends further back than even to the beginnings of class society. Thus they argued against Engels' claim of a single cause, private property, to explain all forms of social inequality. Engels' explanation, it was believed, by failing to give credence to the autonomy and persistence of patriarchy, also failed to give adequate recognition to its strength.

This specific criticism was conjoined with a more generalized suspicion of traditional Marxism's focus on the "economic." A persistent tendency within Marxism has been to interpret such terms as "economic" or "production" to refer to phenomena taking place outside the home. A consequence has been a tendency to dismiss both practically and theoretically the domestic sphere. Thus even when Marxists became sensitive to the radical feminist claim that women did indeed constitute an oppressed group, they tended to treat this oppression as a phenomenon most interesting in its nondomestic manifestations. For example, many appeared to equate their commitment to feminism with a concentration on the situation of women as paid workers.

I noted earlier that if liberalism could be characterized as giving theoretical and practical priority to the state as a means of social change, and radical feminism saw the roots of gender oppression and oppression in general as stemming from the family, Marxism could be characterized as giving priority to the sphere of the economy. Thus Marxists have believed that it will be from changes in the organization of the economy that changes in both the state and the family will follow. Marxists have tended to view the sphere of home and family, as presently constituted, as either nonproblematic or as vestigal survivals of an earlier form of social production, which would wither away as a consequence of the steady advancement of capitalism or the establishment of socialism. However, from the perspective of radical feminism, such a viewpoint suffers from a problem similar to that of liberalism: both liberalism and Marxism fail to see how gender dynamics are built into the operation of both the state and the economy. By failing to give credence to the dominating dynamics of familial patterns in all of social life, both liberals and Marxists tend to recreate such dynamics in all the social changes they instigate or envision.

For many Marxist women (and some men), many of these charges rang true. Many were drawn to radical feminism's claim that Marxism's emphasis on the "economic" entailed a dismissal of the importance and persistence of women's oppression and a lack of insight into its dynamics. Many were also sympathetic to radical feminist criticisms of Engels' account. On the other hand, many of those who were sympathetic to such charges were also critical of radical feminism's tendencies toward biologism and ahistoricity. If Marxism had ignored the persistence of women's oppression by concentrating on the economic sphere, it also seemed that radical feminism, by concentrating on the family, tended to ignore the diversity of such oppression. Moreover, many Marxist feminists believed it was important to retain not only Marxism's emphasis on history but other aspects of the theory, such as Marxism's concepts of "materialism" and "class." The task then became one of reinterpreting such concepts so that they were no longer susceptible to criticisms by radical feminism.

Those who took up this task identified their position by the label of "socialist feminism."[33] As a stance it represents less a particular theoretical position than a commitment to integrate the insights of radical feminism and Marxism. The results have varied widely. One of the most influential and representative examples was Heidi Hartmann's article, "The Unhappy Marriage of Marxism and Feminism: Towards a More Progressive Union." Hartmann, like other socialist feminists, criticized both a radical feminist approach for being blind to history and insufficiently materialist and Marxist categories for being sex-blind.[34] She argued that we need to understand the categories of patriarchy and capital as descriptive of independent sets of social relations which became, by the early twentieth century, mutually supportive. A form that this mutual accommodation took was the family wage, as well as a sexual division of labor which placed women in certain "feminine" low paying jobs.[35] This theoretical approach paralleled, for her, what was also required politically: "a practice which addresses both the struggle against patriarchy and the struggle against capitalism."[36]

Hartmann's position too has been subject to a variety of criticisms.[37] One, by Iris Young, notes a problem which follows from the very strength of Hartmann's argument. Young applauds the "materialist" component of Hartmann's analysis, that it does not limit gender oppression to the realm of culture or psychology but locates it in men's control of women's labor power. However, Young notes that if one describes "patriarchy" in this way, i.e., as basically a mode of production, it is difficult to differentiate it analytically from "capitalism," also conceptualized as a mode of production. Young claims that it does not help here to argue that "patriarchy" and "capitalism" are two distinct modes of production existing alongside each other, a position she attributes to Ann Ferguson as well as to other "dual system" theorists.[38] She argues that almost inevitably such an approach ends up situating patriarchy within the family and hypostatizing the division between family and economy specific to capitalism into a universal form.[39] Moreover, she argues that such an approach, by situating patriarchy within the family, fails to adequately account for women's oppression outside of the family.[40]

With Hartmann and Young I would argue that patriarchy is not limited to culture or psychology but must be understood as a distinct form of social organization, regulating work as well as sexuality. In this sense, it is in part, but only in part, "a mode of production," existing in the modern period alongside of, in conjunction with, and at times, in antagonism to capitalism as "a mode of production."[41] In other words, gender as well as the system of private property and wage labor organizes the production and distribution of resources in the modern period. However, I would claim against Young that if we identify patriarchy not with the family but rather as a certain type of kinship structure which in premodern times organized work, sexuality, religion, etc., we can understand how in the modern era aspects of patriarchy might be found both in the family and also in the spheres of politics, the economy, etc., as these progressively became separated spheres. The full telling of this tale, however, must await further chapters.

CONCLUSION

In the above I have attempted to point out the strengths and weaknesses of the different varieties of contemporary American feminism and to begin to suggest that approach which will best conjoin these strengths and eliminate the weaknesses. The fuller articulation of this approach will come in later chapters, where I also elaborate its advantages over traditional political theory as represented in liberalism and Marxism.

Needing to be stressed at this point, however, is that many of the strengths of all the variants of contemporary American feminism and some of the dilemmas came about as a consequence of something new in political theory: a focus on the family. While this focus has been strongest in radical feminism, it has influenced liberal feminism and brought about, through the work of Marxists, the construction of socialist feminism. As we shall see in the following chapter, this focus on the family has been more true of twentieth-century American feminism than it was of the nineteenth-century movement. To understand what has brought about this change and to provide a deeper understanding of the significance of the theory being created, I would now like to turn to an examination of the nineteenth-century movement and to changes taking place within this country over the past two centuries.

CHAPTER TWO

FROM SUFFRAGE TO SEXUALITY

The Doctrine of Sexual Spheres

MUCH WORK has been done in the past fifteen years on women's situation in nineteenth-century America.[1] A persistent theme in this literature is the doctrine of the separation of sexual spheres in structuring the social order. According to this doctrine, society was composed of two different and firmly separated spheres: the sphere of the home and family on the one hand and the sphere of business and politics on the other. The sphere of the home was the appropriate domain of women, whereas those activities outside the home relating to political or economic activity were the appropriate concern of men. At one level this separation possessed a certain spatial significance: women's lives were closely tied to the physical interior of the household. The spatial division separating the inner sphere of the home from the outside world had, however, a symbolic significance that did not correspond precisely with the spatial division. Certain out-of-the-home activities, such as visiting with or ministering to the needs of kin or community or taking part in the affairs of church or charitable organizations, were also permitted to women. Thus the separation is more adequately understood as a separation between two worlds governed by different norms and values. On the one hand, the world of politics and business was viewed as a sphere governed by the pursuit of power and profit; here individuals engaged in ruthless conflict. The personality traits necessary to function in this sphere were aggressiveness, cold-heartedness, intelligence, and a singular concern with one's own (which included one's family's) self-interest. The home, on the other hand, represented a refuge from this arena of incessant conflict; it was the domain where

morality, concern for others, sensibility, and feelings were allowed
to exist.

The above represents a very rough schema of the social order
of nineteenth-century America. It only begins to describe with any
accuracy, particularly for the first half of the century, the lives of
one sector of the society, those of the new "middle class" found
in urban centers of the northeast. As Ann Douglas points out, the
norm of female restriction to the home had little meaning for
countless American women of other classes and of other regions.
Speaking of the period from 1800–1865 and describing women's
restriction to the home as exemplifying what Douglas calls female
"disestablishment," she makes the following important point:

> One must start by stressing that feminine "disestablishment"
> hardly affected all women in all parts of the United States.
> For the majority of American women living between 1800
> and 1865, there was probably no economic dislocation and
> concomitant "disestablishment" process comparable to that
> affecting the northern middle-class woman. For the countless
> girls who moved from a life of labor on a farm to a life of
> labor in a factory, for the feminine immigrants who came in
> increasing numbers straight from a ship to a northern sweat-
> shop or a midwestern frontier, for the thousands of enslaved
> black women who served King Cotton, disestablishment clearly
> had little or no meaning.[2]

That the doctrine of sexual spheres only truly applied to a
certain class follows from the changing functions of the family
the doctrine expressed, which were most clearly exemplified within
only one class. The idea of the home as a refuge from the external
world of business only made sense of a home which itself was
not a business, i.e., did not engage in those productive activities
associated with, for example, the farm of rural America. This is
not to deny that there was an important division of labor between
men and women on the farm nor to deny that the division at
least sometimes had to do with a division between activities leading
to products for exchange versus activities leading to products for
home use. Rather the difference is that the home ceased being

the arena for the making of products at all. Unlike her rural counterpart, the new urban middle-class housewife was less concerned with the making of such items as candles, soaps, shoes, quilts, or rugs, let alone the tasks of growing food or minding the animals. Unlike her married working class counterpart, she did not take in laundry or sewing or even boarders, and certainly unlike her unmarried working class counterpart, she did not work in the mills. Thus allied with the idea of the home as a refuge from production developed also a new American ideal of women's idleness:

> The mid-nineteenth century middle-class lady I will be discussing was not necessarily as idle as her various critics and admirers on occasion painted her. . . . It is rather that the lady's leisure, whether hypothetical or actual, was increasingly treated as the most interesting and significant thing about her; her function was obscured and intended to be so. . . .[3]

What Douglas is pointing to here and further elaborates is a trend which was to spread beyond the Northeast and beyond this particular class of women, a norm of femininity which was equated with powerlessness and lack of industry. This equation is illustrated in many of the concepts by which femininity came to be defined, in concepts such as "silly," "dependent," "decorative," and "sentimental." The transformation that was involved in so defining women is illustrated in a story Douglas relates of a conversation between an Eastern "lady," Eliza Farnham, and a Western farmer. In response to Farnham referring to his wife as a "bird," the Westerner insisted that he was "not sheltering a delicate creature weaker and more sensitive than himself." The Westerner compared his wife's physical strength to that of several of his beasts of burden and concluded: "I don't know what you Yankees call a 'bird' but I call her a woman."[4]

The equation and even celebration of femininity with lack of industry certainly had its antecedents in prebourgeois aristocratic circles. New was its adoption by a culture which prided itself on being industrious and antiaristocratic. What it signified must be understood carefully. While the nineteenth-century urban middle-class American woman was being characterized as "frivolous," she was also being given more responsibility in certain areas such as childrearing. The cult of motherhood which flourished in the nineteenth century was tied to the idea that motherhood was itself an activity requiring study and thought. Mothers were now to be held responsible for shaping the characters of their children and were given many exhortations from both domestic educators and the church on the possible hazards of their task. Also treated with a high degree of seriousness was women's role as guardian of morality. Women were expected, both through their example and through their "influence," to bring moral considerations to a world otherwise lacking in virtue:

> The purpose of women's vocation was to stabilize society by generating and regenerating moral character. This goal reflected an awareness, also apparent in other social commentary and reform efforts of the time, that the impersonal world of money-making lacked institutions to effect moral restraint.[5]

In spite of the importance given to such womanly roles as child-rearer or moral guardian, women's activity within the sphere of the home was ultimately embedded within a certain context of triviality. Though the home and family were viewed as a necessary refuge and antidote to the external world, they were also denied an aspect of the seriousness granted to the latter domain. The consequence was that those activities which were allied with the home and family were also denied a certain seriousness. Thus an emphasis on women's activity in certain areas, such as childrearing, could coexist with a conception of women as idle. This type of conjunction of beliefs is illustrated even today by many assuming that it is appropriate for women to carry small children while also viewing women as incapable of carrying any other object of a comparable physical weight.

The Origins of the Nineteenth-Century Women's Movement

The women's movement which developed in the period immediately preceding the Civil War was composed primarily of
women from this new middle class of the Northeast. As many
late twentieth-century feminists began their political activity in the
civil rights movement of the 1960s, so many of the activists of
the nineteenth-century women's movement began their political
activity as fighters in the struggle for the abolition of slavery.
While on one level their activity in the abolitionist movement was
compatible with their female role as champions of morality, on
another level their involvement in a movement which was also
political generated contradictions with their female role. In part
because of such contradictions, many active as abolitionists began
to see the necessity of a movement geared to the needs of women.
This development is clearly exemplified in the story of the Grimké
sisters, Angelina and Sarah. These two sisters were invited to
speak on abolition by the American Anti-Slavery Society. The
setting was to be small parlor gatherings attended by women only.
However, the attendance at the first gathering was so large that
the meeting had to be moved to the parlor of a nearby church.
The subsequent meeting was also scheduled in a church, and the
popularity of the Grimké sisters soon led to them speaking frequently to large mixed audiences. Their speeches unleashed controversy over the propriety of women speaking "in public."[6] Similar
problems arose in other contexts. The American Anti-Slavery Society at its founding convention in 1833 ruled that women could
not join the society or sign the "Declaration of Sentiments and
Purposes," though it did allow a few women to attend and to
speak to the floor. Twenty women consequently met and formed
the Philadelphia Female Anti-Slavery Society.[7] A World Anti-
Slavery Convention held in London in 1840 ruled that only men
could be seated as delegates. Two women, Lucretia Mott and
Elizabeth Cady Stanton, forced to sit in the galleries as onlookers,
began to discuss the need for political activity concerned with the
cause of women. Their conversation eventually led to their or-

ganizing with others the first Woman's Rights Convention in Seneca Falls, New York, in 1848.[8]

To understand the nineteenth-century women's movement, we need to take into account more than the contradictions which stemmed from women's involvement in a moral cause which was also political. The initial organizers of the movement were not only angry about the prohibitions then existing against women speaking in public or being active in political organizations. The separation of the spheres of domestic and nondomestic life provided a deeper context for their anger. The extreme identification of women with the home and family meant that women, particularly when married, existed outside civil society. Eleanor Flexner describes what this meant:

> Married women in particular suffered "civil death," having no right to property and no legal entity or existence apart from their husbands. . . . Married women could not sign contracts; they had no title to their own earnings, to property even when it was their own by inheritance or dower, or to their children in case of legal separation. Divorce when granted at all by the courts or by legislative action, was given only for the most flagrant abuses: adultery, desertion and non-support, and extreme cruelty. With respect to women's ability to gain redress on an equal basis with their husbands, both law and practice varied widely, from the relative liberality in New England to the stringent limitations of the mid-Atlantic colonies. In the South divorce statutes were for a long time non-existent, and the legal dissolution of marriage was infrequent and difficult to achieve.[9]

From the perspective of many of those who became active in the nineteenth-century women's movement, such restrictions on women's rights were in blatant contradiction to the country's democratic ideals. Thus, the organizers of the Seneca Falls convention used the nation's Declaration of Independence as a vehicle to express their position. The following is taken from the Declaration of Sentiments which was read and adopted at that convention:

We hold these truths to be self-evident: that all men and women are created equal; that they are endowed by their Creator with certain inalienable rights; that among these are life, liberty, and the pursuit of happiness; that to secure these rights governments are instituted, deriving their just powers from the consent of the governed. . . . The history of mankind is a history of repeated injuries and usurpations on the part of man toward women, having in direct object the establishment of an absolute tyranny over her. To prove this, let facts be submitted to a candid world.

He has never permitted her to exercise her inalienable right to the elective franchise.

He has compelled her to submit to laws, in the formation of which she had no choice.

He has taken from her all right in property, even to the wages she earns.[10]

The outrage many felt over such contradictions was intensified with the Civil War and the passage of the Fourteenth Amendment which granted suffrage to black men but not black or white women. One consequence of this outrage was a strong and growing women's rights movement which, while focused on the right to vote during the latter part of the nineteenth century, also fought for and won other victories for women in the course of the century. Such victories included the extension of women's property rights and control over children, women's right to vote in various state elections, greater rights in the case of divorce, and increased educational opportunities.

The contradictions which were perceived between the country's democratic ideology and the manner in which it treated women should not be understood, however, as merely stemming from the fact that women were denied equal political rights with men. Women were denied such rights before the nineteenth century. We need explanations which will account for the fact that within the nineteenth century the discrepancies were seen as discrepancies when they had not been before.

One possible explanation can be derived from the work of Ellen Dubois. Dubois discusses the replacement of a political sphere constituted by families to one constituted by individuals:

> In seventeenth-century New England, all community functions—production, socialization, civil government, religious life—presumed the family as the basic unit of social organization. The whole range of social roles drew on familial roles. The adult male's position as a producer, as a citizen, as member of the church, all flowed from his position as head of the family. Similarly, women's exclusion from church and civil government and their secondary but necessary role in production coincided with their subordinate position within the family. . . . By the nineteenth century this relationship between family and society had undergone considerable change. Although the family continued to perform many important social functions it was no longer the sole unit around which the community was organized. The concept of the "individual" had emerged to rival it. In the nineteenth century, we can distinguish two forms of social organization—one based on this new creature, the individual, the other based on the family.[11]

Thus the change in perceptions had to do with differences in the manner in which political rights were becoming defined, from rights inherent in men as heads of families, to rights inherent in men as individuals. The nineteenth century's political sphere, rather than existing as a domain constituted by family heads in their role as family heads, had increasingly become a domain where family was irrelevant. The exclusion of women from this sphere became consequently contradictory in a way that had not been the case when political activity had been based on familial roles. Dubois describes this contradiction with respect to civil government:

> The contradiction between the alternative to familial roles that activity in the public sphere offered and the exclusion of women from such activity was particularly sharp with

respect to civil government. In seventeenth-century New England citizenship was justified on the basis of familial position; the freeholder was at once the head of the household and a citizen. By contrast, nineteenth-century citizenship was posed as a direct relationship between the individual and his government. In other words, patriarchy was no longer the *official* basis of civil government in modern industrial democracy. However, in reality only men were permitted to become citizens.[12]

One could make a similar claim in reference to the economic sphere. As men's relation to government was, by the nineteenth century, no longer seen as necessarily mediated by family role, so too industrialization and the beginning breakdown of the family farm as a productive unit meant that the accumulation of wealth or even mere subsistence was no longer necessarily mediated by familial relations. The family, of course, remained a unit of consumption and inheritance whose income was still controlled by the male head of household and whose property was still passed on through his name. The significance of industrialization, however, is that the family ceased being a major unit of production; in this sense the economic sphere, like the political, became a sphere of "individuals."

The above analysis also suggests that the individualization of the political and economic spheres was associated with the growth of both at the expense of the family. This is strikingly obvious in reference to production, where industrialization meant a real loss in family function. Thus the idea of the family as a "haven" from production, rather than suggesting a mutuality between the two spheres, might be better understood as a redefinition and consequent restriction of the family's role; what was now the haven had once been the whole. In this sense we can understand the social order of the nineteenth century as illustrating in part an extreme separation between the spheres of "public" or "social" life on the one hand, and family life on the other, and at the same time as evidencing grounds for the beginning of the collapse of the separation. To the extent that the nondomestic sphere was being constituted as a sphere of individuals, to that extent did the family become less important as an institution. This suggestion accords with much contemporary social theory which has discussed the decreasing importance of the family particularly during the twentieth century as many of even its nineteenth-century functions have been taken over by other institutions.[13]

Moreover, this growth of an individualized, nondomestic sphere must be related to another social change: the increasing individualization of social relationships *within* the family. In the course of the modern period, the family, again most strikingly in its white, middle class version, has increasingly come to be viewed as consisting of autonomous individuals whose relations with each other are of the nature of a contract. This conception of the family represents a departure from an older, more organic, more stratified version. As we shall see in chapter 5, early indications of this change can be found in the writings of the seventeenth-century theorist John Locke. Lawrence Stone, in his history of the family in England, traces what he describes as "the growth of affective individualism" within the family from the period 1640–1800. Part of what this meant was the growth of more egalitarianism between spouses, more freedom for children, and more affectionate ties among all members. Carl Degler, in writing on the American family, describes similar features for that family type which he claims emerged in the period from the American revolution to about 1830.[14]

The Politics of the Late Nineteenth-Century Women's Movement

Both the growth of an individualized social sphere outside the home and the increased individualization of social relations within it raised particular contradictions for middle class women. Increased autonomy within the family and new opportunities to function autonomously outside it remained tied to existing beliefs about women as necessarily dependent and private beings. The enlargement of a sphere of activities outside the household meant in part that women could engage in activities—such as teaching or working in benevolent societies—which took place outside the jurisdiction of the family. However, women, more than men, were still being viewed in familial terms, i.e., as most appropriately daughters, wives, and mothers, a viewpoint which often appeared to contradict such non-family-based activity. One task for late nineteenth-century feminism was to justify this new nonfamilial activity as appropriate activity for women. This was often accomplished by denying its nonfamilial nature.

An example is Catherine Beecher's argument for the extension of women's education on the grounds that it would make women better wives and mothers. Thus education, traditionally viewed as primarily for men in association with and preparation for non-domestic activity, was portrayed as a means by which women could become even more womanly than they were. A different form of the same strategy lay in the suffragist argument that women, if given the vote, would bring their moral sensitivities as wives and mothers to the immoral world of politics. Here again, suffrage, rather than being described as a means by which women would abandon their roles as wives and mothers, was depicted as a means by which they would enlarge such roles. As Degler notes, this kind of argument made suffrage more attractive than the earlier appeal to the "rights" of individuals, which placed women, as individuals, outside the family. As he and others have also claimed, the reason that women's suffrage was perceived for a very long time as a radical demand, and its supporters more extremists than those, for example, who fought in the Women's Christian Temperance Union, was because it did suggest a more nonfamilial, individualistic position for women than did the activities of the WCTU.[15]

Was it deceptive for late nineteenth- and early twentieth-century feminists to make such arguments, to describe their demands and activities as in harmony with traditional womanly roles? Moreover, if this kind of feminist argument was not deceptive, can it not at least be faulted as unduly conservative? This is the kind of argument that Jean Bethke Elshtain raises against the suffrage movement: that insofar as it justified the vote for women on the grounds of women's "special nature," it perpetuated, ideologically, the very division of spheres that was responsible for women's plight. She notes arguments made by Elizabeth Cady Stanton which espouse the moral superiority of women and similar arguments made by Stanton and others which envision a transformed social world once women were given the vote. Elshtain claims that such arguments, besides being fundamentally conservative in their assumptions, encouraged a misleading view of what women's suffrage could accomplish. This inevitably led to demoralization among suffragists when it became clear after the enactment of the Nineteenth Amendment that no such great change was occurring.[16]

Elshtain's arguments are in harmony with those of others who have criticized the late nineteenth- and early twentieth-century women's movement as unduly conservative.[17] Supposedly, one manifestation of this conservatism was its focus on the vote. Allied to this limited focus, as well as to its description of suffrage as an enlargement of women's traditional sphere, was its failure to challenge women's place within the family. It has been argued that the late nineteenth-century women's movement was insufficiently critical of the family, which, as we have seen, has been viewed by many twentieth-century feminists as the root cause of women's oppression.

Is such criticism justified? Can we fault the late nineteenth- and early twentieth-century women's movement for not being as radical as later feminism was to become? Answering this question can help us understand the nature of American feminism.

Most fundamentally, it is important to recognize that the very lines separating domestic from nondomestic activity were in the process of being transformed. If the jurisdictional labels late nineteenth-century feminists applied to their new activities appear to us as obviously misleading, this may be in part a benefit of hindsight. For example, we now can see that women's involvement in such types of activities as teaching or social work contributed to the growth of what we now describe as the welfare state. We thus see their activity as obviously public. They, however, saw such activities as suitable for women because of their resemblance to women's traditional tasks. That they therefore described this new activity as "bringing domesticity outward" must be understood in a context where the kind of fully articulated public sphere we are now familiar with had not yet been constituted.

A similar kind of caution is required in evaluating the failure of late nineteenth-century feminism to challenge the family. If women were beginning to operate as individuals, as beings not defined by family relations, this again was only in the way of a first step. While industrialization and urbanization may have begun to open up the possibilities for individual self-support outside of the family, few women in the nineteenth century were or could imagine the possibility of becoming self-supporting. Economically, there were few alternatives for women to marriage; culturally the unmarried woman was viewed as a social outcast. There existed comparable social pressures on women to bear children. The childless wife was an object of pity. In such a context it would have been unlikely for any large-scale movement to embody a criticism of marriage and motherhood; for most women there were no other options.

Of course, there were individual feminists, such as Elizabeth Cady Stanton and Victoria Woodhull, who were highly critical of marriage and the family. There were also feminists who proposed major alterations in traditional housekeeping arrangements, describing such possibilities as public kitchens and day care.[18] The point is rather that there was no large-scale social movement comparable to late twentieth-century radical feminism which proposed that women reject marriage or motherhood altogether. And again the difference has to be located in the fact that if late nineteenth-century American women were beginning to act and work outside of the family, this was only in the way of a first step.

The nature of the difference separating the late nineteenth-century movement from that which was to emerge later can be symbolized in the fact that the former movement lacked a concept which was central to the latter: the concept of a "role." This concept implies a solitary being who can move among different activities, taking on different norms appropriate to the activity in question. This new concept is a symptom of the increased individualization and flux of social life which has characterized the twentieth century. Elizabeth Cady Stanton hinted at such an idea in her statement that "womanhood is the great fact, wifehood and motherhood its incidents."[19] A late twentieth-century paraphrase of Stanton's remark would be that wifehood and motherhood are "roles" which women may or may not take on. The contemporary feminist would, however, even modify Stanton's remark to claim that as wifehood and motherhood are roles, so too is "woman-hood."

The point thus is neither that the first and second waves of American feminism are identical nor that there exists a great divide between the two. Rather I am indicating a historical continuum marked by an increasing view of women as persons able to exist as individuals outside the family. In this context, the late nineteenth-century movement's focus on suffrage might be viewed as the first step taken by women to achieve a self-identity not based on family relationships. While later steps might entail very different kinds of political demands, even the demand for a redefinition of the "political," the breaking away of women from a familial identity might be seen as the common thread.

THE TWENTIETH CENTURY

The Growth of the Nondomestic Sphere

I have claimed in the above that women in the nineteenth century, economically and culturally, were firmly tied to the home, whether that home was a productive unit, as it was for rural women, or unproductive, as it was for many urban women. This situation has drastically changed during the twentieth century. During this century women's participation in the paid labor force has steadily increased (see the table).

Labor Force Participation Rates

Year	Males	Females	Females as a percentage of all workers
1890	84.3	18.2	17.0
1900	85.7	20.0	18.1
1920	84.6	22.7	20.4
1930	82.1	23.6	21.9
1940	82.5	27.9	25.2
1945	87.6	35.8	29.2
1947	86.8	31.8	27.4
1950	86.8	33.9	28.8
1955	86.2	35.7	30.2
1960	84.0	37.8	32.3
1965	81.5	39.3	34.0
1970	80.6	43.4	36.7
1975	78.4	46.4	39.3
1980	77.8	51.6	42.0
1983	76.8	53.0	43.0

NOTE: Figures include both full- and part-time workers and those actively seeking employment. Pre-1947 figures cover persons 14 years of age and over; later years, 16 years of age and over.

SOURCES: U.S. Department of Commerce, Bureau of the Census, *Historical Statistics of the United States, Colonial Times to 1970*, Bicentennial edition (1975), part 1, pp. 131–32; U.S. Department of Labor, *Employment and Earnings* (August 1984), vol. 34.

These statistics indicate a growing contradiction between the reality of many women's lives and the dominant cultural ideology which still divided the society into familial and nonfamilial spheres and attached specific gender codes to each sphere. Not depicted by the statistics is also an increasing disparity between the prevailing ideology and a growing percentage of women working who were also married and mothers:

In 1940, married women constituted only 30 percent of all women workers, but that number had risen to 48 percent by 1950, to 54 percent by 1960, and to 60 percent by 1970. The increase of women workers did not come from single women; the percentage of single women at work rose only from 48 percent in 1940 to 51 percent in 1970. But the percentage of married women at work rose from 17 percent in 1940 to 40 percent in 1970.[20]

The increase of women working outside the home who were also married and mothers did not immediately bring into question women's traditional place within the family. For black and white working class women there existed a long tradition of practice deviating from prescribed norms. When these statistics came to incorporate middle class white women as well, changes in the ideology were demanded. One accommodation, emerging during the 1960s, was the idea of woman's "dual role." It is this concept which underlies the political position of the document *American Women*, the official report of President Kennedy's Commission on the Status of Women, released in 1963. The following comment by Judith Hole and Ellen Levine expresses certain of the assumptions of the report:

> Taken as a whole, the Commission's entire inquiry, Report, and its many broad-reaching recommendations appear to have been based on several implicitly (sometimes explicitly) stated assumptions. The most fundamental of them presupposed that the nuclear family unit was vital to the stability of American society and that women have a unique and immutable role in that family unit; accordingly, women who work, and who are also married and possibly mothers, play a dual role in society to a much greater degree than do men who work and are also married and fathers. Another fundamental assumption of the Report was that, notwithstanding women's dual role, every obstacle to their full participation in society must be removed. Today's feminists would argue that in fact these two assumptions are contradictory; the barriers against women's *full* participation in society cannot be removed until and unless men (and society at large) share equally with women the responsibilities of homemaking and child rearing.[21]

As Hole and Levine note, the concept of woman's "dual role" was highly problematic. It soon became clear to many middle class women that a woman's participation in the nondomestic sphere did carry implications for her activities within the home. There was something obviously unfair in the demand that a woman working outside the home also carry on the duties traditionally assigned to a housewife. Thus there developed throughout many sections of the early women's movement discussions on the "politics of housework."

Beyond the practical contradictions generated by old expectations being added to new responsibilities, the participation of women outside the home meant the development, particularly for professional women, of a new sense of self. Women who held responsible jobs, who gained through their work a measure of self-respect, and who earned a salary that could make them self-supporting developed a degree of independence incompatible with traditional conceptions of femininity. The domestic sphere as constructed in the nineteenth century contained as an important ingredient women not only performing certain tasks, such as housework, but also embodying certain traits. Such personality characteristics as being nurturant, self-sacrificing, and nonassertive were incompatible with at least a certain kind of nondomestic activity. Women's activity outside the home both generated conflicts with traditionally assigned tasks and traits within the family and provided alternatives to that family. As noted earlier, women of the nineteenth century had few alternatives to marriage and motherhood. For twentieth-century women, and again this has been particularly true for middle class women, both marriage and motherhood have become choices, with marriage increasingly a reversible choice.

It would be a mistake, however, to deduce from the above idea that it is the phenomenon of women working in the wage labor force that is the sole or even primary cause of what has been described by some as the "death of the family." Rather it seems more accurate to describe the increasing participation of women in the workforce in the twentieth century as itself merely one manifestation of the more fundamental realignment of the regions constituting the familial and the nonfamilial. Sara Evans' phrase the "socialization of social production" is useful to describe the economic aspect of this realignment.

Much of the work traditionally associated with the home has been brought into the public world of paid labor by the expansion of social services and white collar bureaucratic occupations since the second world war. . . . These changes constituted the socialization of social production, a process similar to the socialization of goods production in the nineteenth century. The earlier economic revolution had brought men into the labor force in order to produce goods. This time, however, many of the jobs created in fields such as health care, education, child care, clerical work, social work, and advertising constituted extensions of the traditional social role of housewife. . . .[22]

Not just service functions have moved outside the home during the twentieth century. In the nineteenth century, middle class women were assigned the role of guardians of the "inner life," and to the extent that "feelings" were allowed to exist it was primarily within women's sphere. During the twentieth century, the "inner" life itself has to some extent moved outward, gaining a degree of public attention. This is evidenced in the growth of psychoanalysis and other forms of therapy. Feelings have become worthy of professional attention and in the process have gained a certain stature. It has been argued that the greater regard given to the inner life during the twentieth century might be viewed as a component of the process of increasing individualization. According to this analysis, the old ties that bound individuals to family, to community, and to history have been steadily broken. As a consequence, there has grown a concern with the self, with its physical and psychological well-being.[23] This argument would support the ideas discussed throughout this chapter, particularly the description of the nondomestic sphere as a sphere of individuals growing at the expense of the family.

Moreover, in response to the idea that it has been women's increasing entrance into the labor force which has caused "the decline of the family," some recent scholarship by Barbara Ehrenreich must be noted.[24] Ehrenreich has claimed that since at least the 1950s, men have been steadily abandoning the family and forsaking their role as provider. An important cultural manifestation of this change was the emergence of *Playboy* magazine in the 1950s. As Ehrenreich claims, the underlying message of this magazine was that a male could spend money on himself, not be married, and still be considered "masculine." This broke with the then prevailing ideology which stigmatized the unmarried male of a certain age as "immature" and possibly homosexual. Ehrenreich also points to other movements of the latter part of the twentieth century, such as the beat and hippie movements, as continuing the argument for masculine singleness.

Ehrenreich's arguments supplement the thesis of the growth of the individualized, nondomestic sphere during the course of the twentieth century, only focusing on its implications for men. Men also have been more extensively participating in a nondomestic sphere throughout the twentieth century by leaving farmwork or home/craft activity. Thus it is to be expected that a new conception of masculinity would be developing, not defined by family ties, which would be comparable in some respects with those changes in femininity we associate with feminism.

Of course, there are important differences. Since men's participation in nondomestic activity historically followed *from* their position as head of household, such activity has been less problematic, more sustained, and better paid than women's. When initially men took on jobs outside the home, this was viewed as necessary to their role as head of household, and not in contradiction to it. Moreover, their wages were set to cover the needs of a family and were not perceived, as were those of women, as supplementary. As a result, when men today abandon family ties, they bring on themselves very different economic consequences than when women perform the same abandonment. As Ehrenreich argues, this important difference accounts for the increasing "feminization of poverty" which has marked the latter part of the twentieth century. As she also argues, this difference accounts for the fear many New Right women have about the instability of the contemporary family and the hostility they have to that which they perceive as threatening to it.

Of course, the above patterns cannot be said to be applicable to black people, particularly those low in social class. As Carol Stack's excellent book, *All Our Kin*, shows, social patterns among poor black people in the United States illustrate different dynamics from those of both working class and middle class white people and middle class black people.[25] Here, high degrees of unemployment for both women and men, incarceration and military service for men, and extreme poverty have contributed to the maintenance of extended kinship networks revolving around women. Such extended networks have been necessary to provide some cushion against the hazards of extreme poverty, though they have also tended to conflict with the demands of self-interest and self-enclosure experienced by those attempting to become middle class. Because of these differences in social dynamics, gender relations between poor black women and men cannot be described by the above patterns, a fact having important implications for the lack of appeal of feminism to such women.

Similarly, the preceding patterns, while perhaps more applicable to middle class black people than to those lower in social class, here also need a great deal of qualification. Because the ideal of female domesticity in the nineteenth century never had as much relevance for black people as for middle class white people (nor did it for many white immigrants), because certain middle class occupations such as teaching were more available to black women than to men (teaching, for example, being considered by the late nineteenth century a female profession), and finally because lower wages paid to black people have necessitated both female and male participation in the labor market, black women have always viewed themselves as potential workers in the paid labor force. This again has entailed different kinds of relations between black women and men from those characteristic of middle class white people. It has also meant that to the extent that middle class black women have become feminists, they have come out of a different heritage and have brought to their feminism differences in perspective.[26]

Twentieth-Century Feminism

The cultural and economic transformations discussed in the last section may help us account for the specific nature of much of late twentieth-century American feminism. Two phenomena are particularly important: difficulties experienced by many working, and particularly professional women, attempting to be successful in a work world still committed to the ideology of women as wives and mothers, and the growing public attention given to matters of private life and psychology.

It is the first phenomenon, the clash between work expectations and familial ideology, which must explain much about the goals of the women's rights movement of the early 1960s. For many women attracted to the issue of women's rights, the obstacles they encountered in the work world constituted a very real lack of rights. Moreover, related obstacles were recognized by many women at home, housewives, who on reading a book such as *The Feminine Mystique* came to comprehend much of what was being denied to them. However, as the phenomenon of the increasingly self-reflective housewife itself indicates, developing in accord with a recognition of obstacles existing for women in becoming public beings was a growing awareness of problems for women in private life.

The interrelation of these two developments can be seen clearly in the emergence of radical feminism and in the growth of radical feminism's concern with the familial and the personal. As earlier noted, many radical feminists had been involved in the New Left. They were women also who to a significant extent believed and had been encouraged by others to believe in the possibility of their own careers. Their presumption of their responsibilities and abilities to function outside the home and family was manifested in their political activity. However, and here the parallels with the nineteenth-century women's movement are obvious, the nature of their activity and self-perception became problematic in the context of still remaining expectations of women and femininity.

Interesting work has been written on the presence of traditional gender expectations within the New Left and how these expectations conflicted with the self-perception of New Left women.[27] Also needing to be stressed, however, is the clash between these expectations and developing political tendencies within the New Left. Like their old left predecessors, the 1960s activists proclaimed the goal of social equality. Of concern here as it had been for activists of the 1930s was the unequal distribution of wealth and power. Moreover, again like their predecessors, the New Left activists believed that this unequal distribution of wealth and power was not interestingly a question of differences among individuals but was more fundamentally a question of differences among social groups. Such differences could thus be best accounted for by social and not individual explanations. However, differentiating the new and the old left was a concern on the part of the former with the psychological, viewed not as a substitute for but as a component of the sociological. Developing within the New Left and marking it as "new" was an increased concern with "consciousness," the latter being interpreted as the manifestation of sociological phenomena in the perceptions and values of individuals. Thus, for example, 1960s activists had become sensitive to the fact that separating black and white people were not only different opportunities in employment and housing but also psychological differences in self-confidence and pride. They had become cognizant of the fact that the power imbalances between students as a social group and faculty or administrators also played itself out in the subtle arena of psychological attitudes and individual behavior. In short, within the New Left, the topic of inequality or of imbalances of power had grown to be defined as including relations between individuals in social roles, a concept which itself contained a psychological component. In the case of the New Left, the change can help us account for why, when the topic of women's rights did begin to be raised in the nation at large, women within the New Left could begin to relate their own personal conflicts to the political movement of which they were a part. In short, women within the New Left had grown accustomed to discussing the psychological implications of social group oppression. Once they began to perceive women as a social group, deprived of political and economic rights, the road was already open for examining the psychological implications of this oppression both in terms of their own lives and in terms of the lives of others.

Attention to the psychological implications of women's oppression necessitated, however, a focus on the sphere of family and personal life in a way in which no other political issue had. Whereas the psychological manifestations of power imbalances in other social roles could more easily be seen as effects of causes originating in the political or economic spheres, this was not as obviously so with gender norms. That white people felt more self-confident than black people could be seen as a consequence of the legal and economic inequality between white and black people. An understanding of the attitudes and behavior accompanying gender norms seemed to require, on the other hand, attention to the family and personal sphere, for it was most obviously here that gender norms were learned and played out.

While attention to the psychological components of social oppression followed from New Left politics, an examination of the family and personal life did not. A component of our modern domestic/nondomestic separation has been the prevailing belief that both family and personal life exist outside the domain of politics. Thus for New Left women to critically analyze the family and personal relationships associated with familial relationships required a self-conscious attack on this belief. This attack was carried out through the creation of the slogan "The personal is political."

CONCLUSION

The slogan and the self-conscious attention to the personal sphere that it called for represented a new turn in American feminism. This is not to deny the important continuity within American feminism over the past two centuries, which I hope the above analysis has indicated. As I have argued, the changing dynamics between the family and the world outside of it has meant a growing redefinition of women as beings not defined by family relations. In the nineteenth century, these dynamics made possible the demand of women for suffrage. During the twentieth century, the shifting alignment of spheres has had as one important manifestation an increasing participation of women in the paid labor force. This in turn has generated conflicts for women between their new abilities and expectations of functioning autonomously and the remaining norms that still defined women by familial relations. These conflicts coexisted with a growing national concern over matters of psychology and private life. The result was that many women, newly conscious of the issue of gender inequality, began to focus their attention on the domain of family and personal life. This marked an important shift in the nature of American feminism. It has made possible a discussion involving many, both activists of a wide variety of political orientations and scholars from a number of academic disciplines, on the nature of the family and its relation to other social institutions. It is time now to begin reviewing that discussion.

PART TWO
FEMINIST THEORY

CHAPTER THREE

TOWARD A METHOD
FOR UNDERSTANDING GENDER

IN PART ONE, I discussed the historical context and characteristic features of contemporary American feminism as a political movement. In particular I wished to stress the distinctive nature of this movement's concern with family and personal life. The degree to which feminism in the latter part of the 1960s focused on the family marked a turning point in the history of American feminism. As noted, this is not to deny the critical attention earlier given to marriage and the family by such feminists as Elizabeth Cady Stanton and Charlotte Perkins Gilman, nor more important, to miss the point that women breaking away from familial roles and definitions has served as the common thread tying together nineteenth- and twentieth-century American feminism. Rather the claim is that with the emergence of radical feminism and the slogan "The personal is political," the family and personal life became an object of explicit attention by a political movement which characterized its concerns as political. This entailed a rethinking, on a wide basis, of the lines traditionally separating the family from other social institutions and a questioning of the family as a biological institution. This new focus thus involved a recognition of the family as a social institution, as a product of history, and as capable of change.

These concerns in contemporary American feminism have had theoretical consequences. As many began to think about personal and familial issues in political terms, so also many came to perceive the need for theory which analyzed the family, which charted its origins, history, and interrelation with other social institutions. Some of the theory which has emerged from the contemporary movement, I believe, provides the basis for challenges to conceptual frameworks central in Western culture, particularly to important assumptions within political philosophy, as I intend to show in later chapters.

Before I can make the above argument I need first to examine contemporary feminist theory to illustrate what in fact makes it unique. I would like to begin by examining some of the contributions which have emerged from the discipline of anthropology. I focus on anthropology for several reasons. For one, anthropological issues have played a major role in contemporary feminist political debate. As noted in chapter 1, different sections of the contemporary movement have been divided over such issues as the origins of women's oppression or the cross-cultural nature of the family and its role in determining social life. Contemporary feminists have frequently looked to anthropology to resolve these issues. Thus the connection between feminist anthropological debate and feminist political debate has been very direct. Second, from an analysis of feminist anthropological discussion I intend to generate a methodological perspective which I believe can illuminate the uniqueness of the theoretical contributions of scholars working in other disciplines, such as history. In sum, I believe an examination of contemporary feminist anthropological theory provides us with a direct view to trends within the wider context of feminist theory.

THE UNIVERSALISTS

It will be recalled that two issues which divided radical feminists from Marxist feminists were disagreements over the universality of women's oppression and the role of the family in causing it. For many contemporary feminists there were attractions in both the radical feminist and Marxist arguments. Many agreed with the radical feminists that the Marxist account minimized the persistence of women's oppression. On the other hand, many also agreed with the Marxists that radical feminists ignored the diversity of such oppression. The task therefore became that of developing a theory which could reconcile both claims.

This theoretical need manifested itself within anthropological discussions, where the claims of both diversity and persistence appeared grounded. On the one hand what was obvious was the historical variation in gender roles; the traits and practices associated with women and men varied widely from culture to culture. To the extent that biological universals existed which differentiated men and women—and this was considered by some problematic— the cultural norms associated with gender went far beyond and could not be deduced from biology. Even sexuality could not be understood in merely biological terms. Thus Gayle Rubin introduced the phrase "the sex/gender system" to connote "the set of arrangements by which a society transforms biological sexuality into products of human activity, and in which these transformed sexual needs are satisfied."[1] In addition to sexuality, the psychological traits and sets of practices which were associated with gender seemed also a product of social construction. Michelle Zimbalist Rosaldo illustrated the variability involved:

> There are, in fact, groups like the New Guinea Arapesh, in which neither sex shows much aggression or assertiveness, and there are societies like our own, in which children of both sexes are more egoistic than boys in other parts of the world. . . . The same sort of variability attaches to almost every kind of behavior one can think of; there are societies in which women trade or garden and those in which men do; societies where women are queens and those in which they must always defer to a man; in parts of New Guinea, men are (like Victorian women) at once prudish and flirtatious, fearful of sex yet preoccupied with love magic and cosmetics that will lead the maidens—who take the initiative in courtship—to be interested in them.[2]

The problem, however, was that while anthropology seemed to reveal enormous diversity in gender roles, it also taught another lesson. The evidence of anthropology seemed also to attest to the apparent universality of the subordination of women. In cultures which on all other grounds looked widely remote, there appeared the common theme of female inferiority. Thus while women's assigned tasks and traits diverged widely from culture to culture, women were consistently judged inferior to men, whatever their tasks and traits. This anthropological lesson was also illustrated by Rosaldo:

> Among the Arapesh, studied by Mead . . . , the roles of men and women were seen as cooperative and complementary, but a wife was felt to be a "daughter" to her husband, and at the time of the dominant male ritual (when men played on secret flutes) she was required to act like an ignorant child. Among the nearby Tchambule . . . , the women were traders, controlling the family economics; yet there the men were artists and ritual specialists, and although the women had little respect for masculine secrets, they still found it necessary to adhere to, and engage in a ritual order that marked them as inferior—in morality and knowledge— to men. . . . For a final example, consider the Jewish ghetto communities of Eastern Europe. . . . In these communities, women had an extraordinary amount of influence. They were strong and self-confident mothers whose sons were their loyal supporters; as community gossips, they shaped most political events; in the household, a woman kept control of the pocketbook and effectively dictated family spending. . . . Yet, in spite of all this, wives would defer to their husbands and their greatest joy in life was to have a male child. A woman's work was rewarded by having the son become a scholar, a man whose actual activities might have little influence on the everyday life of the community but who stood, nonetheless, as its source of pride and moral value, its cultural ideal.[3]

Thus the problem encountered by early feminist political and anthropological theory was the need to reconcile the evidence of historical diversity in sex roles with the apparent universal subordination of women. What was needed was theory which accounted for the oppression of women in its "endless variety and monotonous similarity."[4] Appeals to biology might explain the similarity but not the variety. Existing social theories might explain the variety but not the similarity. What was needed was a theory which could do both.

Similar solutions to this dilemma were put forth by several theorists, among them Rosaldo. She noted that central to the universal inferior status of women is the fact that everywhere men have "authority" over women. This means that while it is certainly the case that in many societies women have a great deal of influence and power, such power is never culturally legitimated. The power women possess tends to be viewed as manipulative, disruptive, illegitimate, or unimportant.[5] Rosaldo argued that this universal delegitimation of women's power can be explained by a universal of societal organization: a differentiation between domestic and public spheres of activity. The fact that in most traditional societies a good part of a woman's adult life was spent giving birth to and raising children led to a general identification of women with domestic life and of men with such extradomestic activities as politics and military activities.[6] Thus "men are free to form those broader associations that we call 'society,' universalistic systems of order, meaning and commitment that link particular mother-child groups."[7] She noted that while this opposition between domestic and public does express a universal feature of human society, the degree to which any given society is differentiated between the two spheres varies. Moreover, those societies where the distinction is least present are also most egalitarian in the status accorded to women.[8]

A variant of Rosaldo's argument was articulated by Sherry Ortner.[9] Ortner also raised the need for an explanation which could account for the universal inferior status of women in the context of enormous diversity in gender roles. Her argument was that women, again because of their biological involvement with reproduction and lactation, have been universally associated with a domestic sphere which has also been identified with nature. Since nature for all human societies represents that which stands below culture or society, women as symbols of nature enjoy a comparable inferiority:

the family (and hence women) represents lower-level, socially fragmenting, particularistic sort of concerns, as opposed to interfamilial relations representing higher-level, integrative, universalistic sorts of concerns. Since men lack a "natural" basis (nursing, generalized to child care) for a familial orientation, their sphere of activity is defined at the level of interfamilial relations. And hence, so the cultural reasoning seems to go, men are the "natural" proprietors of religion, ritual, politics, and other realms of cultural thought and action in which universalistic statements of spiritual and social syntheses are made. Thus men are identified not only with culture, in the sense of all human creativity, as opposed to nature; they are identified in particular with culture in the old-fashioned sense of the finer and higher aspects of human thought—art, religion, law, etc.[10]

Ortner also qualified her thesis by noting that this identification of women with nature is never absolute. Women, as the primary agents of children's early socialization, are transmitters of culture and are viewed as such. It is also women who typically transform food from a raw natural state to a cooked state. Yet she noted that even these examples further illustrate her thesis. The socialization of young boys is always at some point transferred to male hands; the most elaborate and culturally respected forms of cooking are always performed by men. Thus, "women perform lower-level conversions from nature to culture, but when the culture distinguishes a higher level of the same functions, the higher level is restricted to men."[11]

One strength of the Rosaldo/Ortner thesis was that it appeared capable of supplementation from even a psychoanalytic perspective. Both theorists appealed to the work of Nancy Chodorow. Chodorow, in various writings, has argued that from the fact that it has been women who have been principally responsible for the care of infants and young children can be deduced certain traits of male and female personality structures.[12] Chodorow has argued that because the primary adult relationship of young girls, unlike young boys, is with a member of the same sex, feminine personality differs from masculine personality. A young boy must come to transfer his original identification from his mother to his father or other male figures who play a relatively remote role in his upbringing. One consequence is that his sense of gender identity is based on relatively abstract categories. Also, since in this process he must renounce his early identification, a young boy's sense of self is at least partially based on a "denial of attachment or relationship, particularly of what the boy takes to be dependence or need for another and differentiation of himself from another."[13] This denial of attachment is also related to a devaluation of women and femininity. A young girl, on the other hand, who grows up in the vicinity of her mother develops a gender identity which is more particularistic, based on daily association with a concrete person. Moreover, since she does not need to renounce her initial dependent and primary relationship with her mother, her sense of self becomes more highly defined in terms of her affective relationships.

As Rosaldo noted, Chodorow's analysis supplements a structural framework emphasizing the opposition of "domestic" and "public."[14] By Chodorow's account, young girls learn concretely how to be adult women in the context of their initial familial setting. Young boys have to "achieve" gender identity by breaking out of this setting. They are thus led to create extrafamilial "public" associations whose construction or entrance into represents an accomplishment. Such associations are defined in part oppositionally to the family and women. Whereas the relationships of young girls follow from the particularistic, affective relations of the family, boys "in contrast are apt to know manhood as an abstract set of rights and duties, to learn that status brings formal authority, and to act in terms of formal roles."[15] In sum, the opposition between "public" and "domestic" seemed to have a psychoanalytic analogue.

It should be pointed out that it was not only feminist theorists who stressed a domestic/public opposition as a key feature of human society. As Ortner noted, this opposition is also the basis of Lévi-Strauss' argument in *The Elementary Structures of Kinship:*

Lévi-Strauss argues not only that this opposition is present in every social system, but further that it has the significance of the opposition between nature and culture. The universal incest prohibition and its ally, the rule of exogamy (marriage outside the group), ensure that "the risk of seeing a biological family become established as a closed system is definitely eliminated; the biological group can no longer stand apart, and the bond of alliance with another family ensures the dominance of the social over the biological, and of the cultural over the natural." And although not every culture articulated a radical opposition between the domestic and the public as such, it is hardly contestable that the domestic is always subsumed by the public; domestic units are allied with one another through the enactment of rules that are logically at a higher level than the units themselves; this creates an emergent unit-society—that is logically at a higher level than the domestic units of which it is composed.[16]

DOMESTIC/PUBLIC: A FALSE UNIVERSALITY?

An explanation of women's inferiority which appealed to a universal domestic/public separation was attractive to many. The question arose, however, whether in the attempt to account for that which seemed universal, that which was diverse had become obscured. In other words, was the diversity in human social organization with specific reference to gender roles adequately accounted for or distorted by this type of explanation? Of significance here is an argument put forth in a later writing of Rosaldo.[17] Rosaldo claims that while the account earlier offered by herself and others did contain much that was compelling, it also had certain problems. For one, she maintains that it

assumes—where it should rather help illuminate and explain—too much about how gender really works. . . . By linking gender, and in particular female lives, to the existence of domestic spheres, we have inclined I fear, to think we know the "core" of what quite different gender systems share, to think of sexual hierarchies primarily in functional and psychological terms, and, thus, to minimize such sociological considerations as inequality and power. . . . What this means ultimately is that we fail to school ourselves in all the different ways that gender figures in the organization of social groups, to learn from the concrete things that men and women do and think and from their socially determined variations. It now appears to me that woman's place in human social life is not in any direct sense a product of the things she does (or even less a function of what biologically she is) but of the meaning her activities acquire through concrete social interactions.[18]

In other words, Rosaldo argues that an appeal to a universal domestic/public separation obscures the diverse causes and content of gender roles. One cannot look to any universal set of things which women do or still less to the ways women biologically are to explain the social organization of gender. The way women biologically are or the things that they do are always a part of a given social system which specifically interprets such biology and such activities. Moreover, the specificities in cultural interpretation themselves reflect particular relations of power which are lost in an appeal to a universal domestic/public explanation. There is nothing inherent in a domestic/public separation per se which can account for female oppression. To understand such oppression we need to comprehend the power dynamics of gender specific to every culture. Thus she claims that to describe both the fact of Pygmy women hiding in huts and the confinement of American women to the home as a consequence of childcare is to misdescribe both and to lose sight of the power dynamics in both.[19]

Rosaldo also argues that as an explanation the domestic/public thesis tends to reflect modern biases, particularly the nineteenth-century Victorian opposition of sexual spheres.[20] Nineteenth-century thinking construed the home and family in natural terms, fulfilling transhistorical individual needs, while viewing the public sphere as historical and constructed. In other words, it is within the context of our Victorian heritage that the explanation of the anthropologists makes sense to us. For Rosaldo, however, the alliance of the domestic/public explanation with this Victorian dualism is not healthy for feminist theory. It tends to reinforce a view of women as victims of their own biology, as opposed to seeing women as themselves social actors. The way out of this unhealthy alliance is to reject the search for "origins" which motivated the explanation initially:

> But asking "Why?" or "How did it begin?" appears inevitably to turn our thoughts from an account of the significance of gender for the organization of all human institutional forms (and, reciprocally, of the significance of all social facts to gender) toward dichotomous assumptions that link the roles of men and women to the different things that they, as individuals, are apt to do—things which for women in particular, are all too readily explained by the apparently primordial and unchanging facts of sexual physiology.[21]

Thus, as follows from these points, the gravest dangers that result from any appeals to women's biology or women's activity in the construction of feminist theory is that we read into these appeals assumptions from our own culture. There is nothing in itself problematic in the claim that in all human societies women bear children. That might be treated equivalently to the claim that in all human societies women and men urinate. Moreover, it may be that in all societies women have primary responsibility for early childcare. The important issue, however, is what significance we read into such universals and whether we project onto other cultures a significance borrowed from our own. Certainly within at least post-Victorian society women's association with childbearing *is* taken as a significant association and allied with the identification of women with the "natural." Also within our society childbearing and childrearing take place in a context where women are devalued. However, if only because of the strength of such associations of the biological or quasi-biological for us, we need to be careful against projecting them where they might not belong. In short, we need to be careful against too easily deducing the political from the biological.

It has not only been Rosaldo who has severely criticized domestic/public as a universal framework for analyzing gender. That framework has been attacked by many for a variety of reasons. For one, several anthropologists have pointed out that it is false on merely factual grounds, that women's lives have not been universally restricted to a household environment. Many women in different cultures travel widely in their effort to find wage employment or to trade.[22] Women have not only worked outside the home, they have also participated in positions of formal authority.[23] Moreover, the claim that it is men's "public" activities which have united individual household units into larger social units has been rebutted by the argument that women's participation in exchange transactions, informal women's communities, and kin networks have also been important in creating such larger social units.[24] It has been suggested that such counterevidence on women's nondomestic activity frequently has gone unreported because of the biases of Western investigators who merely fail to ask the right questions.[25]

It has also been argued that we need to be very careful in identifying the sphere of the public with the sphere of power and authority. Susan Rogers, for example, claims that since peasant societies are domestic-centered, the family here is the key social unit.[26] Thus in these societies to identify men with nonfamilial activities is not necessarily to identify men with authority. Moreover, she cautions that in deciding who has authority we must be sure that we question both women and men.[27] Not surprisingly, the answers women give may differ significantly from those of the men, a fact which can be overlooked when the anthropologist questions only men. This idea that in many societies a separation between men's and women's activities is not necessarily correlated with a unilateral devaluation of women is sometimes linked with the claim that events in human history, such as the growth of the state or colonization, transformed separate but equal female and male spheres into unequal spheres.[28] This is a position which many anthropologists sympathetic to Marxism have taken and which will be examined in depth later in this chapter.

One theme prominent in much of the critical literature on domestic/public, which had also been voiced by Rosaldo, is that women's status is indicated not by one measure but by a variety of different measures which do not necessarily correlate among themselves.[29] Martin King Whyte, for example, looks at a variety of different indicators of women's status, such as the gender of the gods that people worship, the degree of women's political and economic power, and views on sexuality and menstruation. His conclusion is that, with certain limited exceptions, such different indicators on women's place are not necessarily associated with one another.[30] Similarly, Ortner's claim that women have been universally devalued through an association with nature has been criticized on the grounds that nature is not always devalued and women are not always associated with the natural. Within modern Western culture there is the counterexample of Rousseau's concept of nature as that which is pure and noble. In the American frontier West there is also the association of masculinity with the natural and wild and femininity with the civilized and cultured.[31]

What is particularly important about this literature is that it has led to, and can be more fully developed into, new understandings of our own cultural presuppositions. The creation of the domestic/public framework may be viewed as a type of test by theorists who were highly sensitive to the fact of cross-cultural variation. Thus we might look at the development of the framework as a kind of experiment to try and generate what appeared most basic and common in human experience concerning gender. Insofar as the test has failed as a universal descriptor, it has also succeeded in helping to uncover the parameters of our own worldview on the nature of social organization.

This process of self-enlightenment becomes clear when we stop and think, as the domestic/public framework forces us to do, about what it is that *we* really mean by "domestic" and what are the differences between what our term signifies and what in other cultures may appear superficially to be the same. Rayna Rapp has suggested that in our society the distinction domestic/public primarily glosses the separation of private family life from the rest of society.[32] This accords with my belief that "private/public" is a more helpful set of terms for explicating modern Western culture than "domestic/public," since the issue of what is "private" versus what is "public" has represented and continues to represent a major societal concern in describing both economic activity and more recently interfamilial relationships. If, however, the modern Western meaning of "domestic/public" most primarily refers to a distinction between the familial and that which is outside the family, then such a distinction would have only a limited degree of similarity with divisions where the question of separating the familial from the nonfamilial may be less important than other concerns. Thus, for example, as Rapp suggests, our domestic/ public separation is significantly different from one evidenced in the Mediterranean. Here the distinction primarily has to do with the politics of state formation out of cultures where women's sexual purity had implications for male status and power. Thus the distinction in the Mediterranean is a result of different social tensions from those of our own society, where tensions in social organization make necessary an ideological separation between the two spheres of family and economy. Thus for us, "the distinction between private and public corresponds to the distinction between love and money—one is normatively the subject of the woman-centered family, the other is the focus of male-centered activities."[33]

An important reason why we in contemporary Western culture might tend to generalize from our own private/public separation to a universal domestic/public separation is that our notion of the private or family joins together two issues which seem to possess some significance in all societies: kinship, concerning whom one is genealogically related to, and domesticity, concerning whom one lives with. Related to this point is the claim that in contemporary America the concept "family" contains at least two meanings:

> For all classes of Americans, the word has at least two levels
> of meaning. One is normative; husbands, wives and children
> are a set of relatives who should live together (that is, the
> nuclear family). The other meaning includes a more extended

network of kin relatives which people may activate selectively. That is, the American family includes the narrower and broader webs of kin ties that are "the nuclear family" and all relations by blood and marriage.[34]

In other words, we can say that our contemporary concept of family has two components. On the one hand, it means something very similar to what is expressed in the concept of kinship. On the other hand, it adds to this concept an additional component of the domestic which is also normative. "Family" in this latter sense becomes those kinship members who "ought" to live together.

Thus while in all societies there may be rules concerning whom one lives with, and rules governing kinship, the union of kinship and domesticity which is expressed in one important meaning of our concept of family itself need not be universal; indeed, from a growing body of literature it appears very modern.[35] In ancient Rome, where the term originated, "family" originally referred to members of one household, be they relatives or slaves. Thus in its original meaning the component of domesticity figured more centrally than the component of kinship. This focus continued for much of its history, and for centuries the English word "family" included servants as well as people related by blood or marriage.[36] That the term for centuries did not discriminate between servants and kin living under one roof might be a function of the fact that an individual household functioned as a single economic productive unit, in ancient Rome and during much of early modern England.[37] With the decline of the household as an independent economic unit and the growth of the boundaries separating kin-related members living under one roof from the rest of society, there emerged the more modern meaning of family as certain kin living together.[38]

If, however, "family" means for us "kin who ought to live together," then we might ask the question, for which kin-members is there the strongest feeling that they ought to live together? Certainly a top candidate for an answer to this question in our own culture are mothers and children, perhaps followed by husbands and wives. The priority of the former is indicated by a greater willingness to accept spouse separation than mother/child separation (and to be noted, very little difficulty in accepting father/child separation). The point worth stressing again is that such norms are not universal to human society. There are many societies where husbands do not routinely live with wives. One example is the matrilineal Nayar, where the warrior lives of men kept them away from home and their wives were expected to take lovers.[39] That children do not always live with mothers is indicated by family practices among the aristocracy in the Middle Ages, continuing through the seventeenth century.[40] Moreover, and perhaps more obvious, are the examples of those societies where other kin members are also expected to live with the nuclear family, such as grandparents or unmarried aunts and uncles.

The ideas in the above can be further elaborated through the work of Sylvia Junko Yanagisako. Yanagisako argues that underlying our meanings of such related terms as domesticity, the household, the family, kinship, etc. is a belief in the centrality of the mother-child bond or most specifically reproduction. She claims that our idea of the family as a universal social unit is grounded in our conception of its primary task as reproduction.[41] Yanagisako also points to the emphasis contemporary theorists give to genealogy in explaining variations in domestic groups as an example of our contemporary focus on reproduction.[42] But if we grant her thesis here, we might conjoin it with the ideas raised previously to conclude that our modern concept of the family unites kinship and domesticity and links them through the idea of the centrality of the mother-child bond. At the core of our conception of domestic activities are mothers taking care of children; equally central in our idea of kinship is the mother-child relationship. Again, however, we need to ferret out that which is specific to our culture from that which might be truly cross-cultural. Merely because in all societies there are mothers and children does not entail that this relationship forms the central core in structuring either kinship ties or living arrangements or that it universally brings these two together, as it does for us, into a social unit describable as "the family."

We thus return to a question raised earlier, whether the domestic/public framework demanded that we read into the mother-child relationship a significance particular to our own society. It will be recalled that all the domestic/public theorists in some way invoked this relationship to explain the alleged universally inferior status of women. Rosaldo had argued that it was women's universal activity as mothers that kept them from participating in public activities. Ortner had claimed that it was women's identification with reproduction which caused women's identification with the natural as opposed to the cultural. Finally, Chodorow had argued that it was the fact of universal mothering that explained cross-cultural psychological differences between women and men which have been, at least in part, constitutive of male dominance. Before concluding this section I would like to return in more depth to the work of Chodorow, both because this work has been central in contemporary feminist theory and because it is one which has concentrated heavily on the mother/child relationship.

Chodorow maintains that mothering creates women with the psychological attributes appropriate to mothering, such as a willingness to take care of the needs of others. Conversely, it creates men with the psychological attributes appropriate to what we think of as public, nonintimate activities, for example, an ability to distance oneself from the feelings of others. Such differences for Chodorow stem from the fact that the adult who provides the primary caretaking for infants and young children possesses the same gender identity which girls but not boys must achieve. Young girls, in becoming female persons, experience a continuity with their mothers unavailable to young boys, who must, by contrast, distance themselves from their mothers in becoming male persons. In consequence, males tend to develop egos with more rigid boundaries than females and tend to see themselves as separate from others. Thus according to Chodorow, "the basic feminine sense of self is connected to the world, the basic masculine sense of self is separate."[43]

The above is an extremely simplified summary of a rich and insightful analysis. However, if merely because of its insight, we need to be cautious of its limitations. For example, one reading of Chodorow's account is that it is an explanation of universal personality differences between women and men which lay the basis for universal male dominance. Chodorow often cautions against such a cross-cultural reading. She stipulates, for example, that her analysis is of contemporary mothering, that it draws on psychoanalytic findings of the past hundred years, and that important structural features of her analysis, such as absent fathers and isolated women mothering, have all been accentuated in recent history.[44] However, that she does intend her theory to have at least some cross-cultural significance is indicated by other statements she makes, such as the following:

> But historically and cross-culturally we cannot separate the sexual division of labor from sexual inequality. The sexual division of labor and women's responsibilities for child care are linked to and generate male dominance. Psychologists have demonstrated unequivocally that the very fact of being mothered by a woman generates in men conflicts over masculinity, a psychology of male dominance and a need to be superior to women.[45]

This latter position is also repeated in a more recent reply to her critics:

> But also, I think there are important historical and cross-cultural continuities that feminists ignore at our peril. First, *women* mother (a fact not only in our society, where women and men have unequal incomes) and second, women's capacities for relationship and nurturance—as opposed to men's creation of a more separate and distanced ego that treats women as objects—do seem to develop in many different societies and are internal and psychological. These psychological qualities vary in degree and content and in relation to other aspects of personality. They also have varying effects on women's gratifications from mothering and desires to mother, and therefore their overall significance changes in different times and places. Nonetheless, these qualities retain

some elements of sameness and help to form male dominance.[46]

In part, Chodorow explicates mothering as a contributor to
"universal sexual assymmetries in the social organization of gender" by the fact that it creates "a basis for the structural differentiation of domestic and public spheres."[47] But we can question
the extent to which mothering lays such a basis by doubting, as
in the above, the universality of a domestic/public separation. If
mothering is universal, and a domestic/public separation is not,
then mothering must constitute only a partial basis for such a
separation. Moreover, as also noted in the above, even in societies
which do possess a separation roughly similar to our own, much
of the meaning of that separation is different. One difference is
that what we call "domestic," in at least some societies, is not
correlated with the same type of inferior status with which it is
associated in our own. This fact connects with an apparent cir-
cularity in Chodorow's explanation. On the one hand, Chodorow
wishes to explain male dominance as a consequence of female
parenting. However, to make her argument work she implicitly
must appeal to such dominance. Thus she notes that men, to
achieve gender identity, must renounce their early identification
with their mothers. However, is not the disdain that is a part of
this renunciation itself a consequence of existing ascribed inferiority? We could easily imagine a society in which boys were forced
to renounce their early identification with their mothers but where
this process was associated with a reluctant acceptance of male
inferiority. In such a society we might see young girls express the
same type of horror in being thought of as masculine that we
more frequently observe today in young boys being thought of
as a "sissy." Iris Young, noting the same point, has argued that
we need to separate the question of how gender identity is constructed from the question of how gender oppression is created.[48]
    There is a tendency to read Chodorow's account in the following
way. The infant develops a strong identification with the mother.
At a certain point in time, young boys, but not young girls, realize
that to achieve masculinity they must renounce this identification.

Thus young boys renounce femininity and become psychologically prepared for a male dominant society. The problem, however, is that what may appear as sequential stages in this account must in reality be interlocked. The child does not first see the "mother" as we see the mother, i.e., as a being with a different gender from someone else. The child's recognition of the gender of that being with whom she or he spends so much time must be interconnected with her or his growing recognition of gender per se, which means a recognition of her or his own gender as well. Moreover, it would appear strange that a child would *not* come to learn the values attached to the two genders as she or he was coming to learn their specific meanings.

Not only may mothering take place in a culture which does not devalue women; it may take place in a culture where mothering does not have the same importance as it has in our culture. One problem here is that our concept of mothering refers not only to the fact of biological mothers being responsible for the care of their young but also to the case where this relationship is interpreted as significant, and where the quality of the relationship is seen as constitutive of the character of the young. It would appear that how mothers perceive their activities as mothers, however, would also be a crucial variable affecting the nature of the mothering relationship.[49]

One way of summarizing these points would be to say that one cannot separate the social from the psychological, as one must do if one wishes to use the latter to explain the former. This would be a general problem of any explanation which attempted to explain social organization or values from psychological processes. One cannot deny, however, as the point has sometimes been interpreted to do, that family structure or early childhood experiences are an important component of both personality formation and social organization. As Chodorow correctly notes, it is a mistake to contrast psychological, or as she puts it, psychoanalytic, explanations with explanations which appeal to "social structures," since the family is itself a social structure, often denied its proper place in social explanation.[50] Rather, the family, as a social structure, is itself not universal. Moreover, the relationships constitutive of it, such as the mother-child relationship, do not possess the same importance and content either among cultures with different versions of the family or between these and cultures not containing families at all.

To put the same point in another way: there is nothing inherently unhelpful in explanations which focus on early childhood experiences. The problem is only in explanations which describe these experiences ahistorically. Certainly we could easily construe examples of psychological explanations which were self-consciously historical, describing, for example, such topics as early child development in the context of specific historical periods.[51] But the discipline of psychology in the nineteenth- and twentieth-century West, modeling itself after natural science, has tended to cast its explanations ahistorically. Unfortunately, so has Chodorow, at least at times. Without this aspect, her analysis might stand as an illuminating account of the gender construction of many in our own culture.

To return from Chodorow to the larger issue of domestic/public as an explanation of gender, we might say that all such accounts reflect biases of modern Western society. However, if only because these accounts were manifestations of an attempt to formulate that which appeared basic to human experience, in criticizing them, we can spotlight certain primary features of our own society: our separation of domestic from public activities; a devaluation of women associated with women's identification with domestic activities; our union of kinship and domesticity into a concept of the "family"; and an accentuation of the importance of the mother/ child bond. We are thus in a position to begin to understand the arbitrariness of what for so long in Western society has been taken as fundamental.

THE USE OF DOMESTIC/PUBLIC

It will be recalled that Rosaldo connected the methodological problems attendant on the domestic/public framework with the inclination of contemporary feminists to search for "origins." As she noted, a persistent tendency in contemporary feminist writing has been the attempt to uncover the roots of modern forms of male dominance in our far distant past. She claims that because of this tendency, feminists have tended to grant to anthropology an importance noticeably absent in much other social theory. She also states that feminists' views on what anthropology can contribute tend to reflect an old-fashioned nineteenth-century evolutionary approach:

> Few historians, sociologists or social philosophers writing today feel called upon—as was common practice in the nineteenth century—to begin their tales "at the beginning" and probe the anthropological record for the origins of doctors in shamans or of, say, Catholic ritual in the cannibalism of an imagined past. . . . Rather than probe origins, contemporary theorists will use anthropology, if at all, for the comparative insight that it offers; having decided, with good cause, to question evolutionary approaches, most would—I fear—go on to claim that data on premodern and traditional forms of social life have virtually no relevance to the understanding of contemporary society.
>
> Yet it seems to me that quite the opposite is true of the vast majority of recent feminist writing. If anthropology has been too much ignored by most contemporary social theorists, it has achieved a marked—though problematic—pride of place in classics like *Sexual Politics* and *The Second Sex*.[52]

In other words, Rosaldo appears to connect the methodological errors described earlier with the tendency in contemporary feminism to search for origins. Thus insofar as feminist anthropology, and presumably also other feminist theory, views itself as supplying answers to such demands as opposed to merely providing "comparative insights," feminist social theory will tend to commit those methodological errors she has discussed.

What I would like to claim in response here is that there is no necessary connection between the methodological errors Rosaldo has pointed to and a search for origins. A search for origins can be understood in a variety of different ways, not all of which need lead to an ahistorical methodology. If such a search were conceived of as finding the replicas of the present in the past, then it would be difficult to reconcile such a search with a sensitivity to historical diversity. However, the search for origins may be conceived of as the attempt to link our present with a past quite different from the present. According to this version of a search for origins, it would resemble the telling of a tale whose beginnings may be markedly different from its end.

How would we develop an account of origins which did not construe the present as a replica of the past but which also connected the present with the past? Following such a procedure, we would interpret our own forms of female devaluation as, at least in part, a product of our past but as not necessarily to be found in our past. In the modern period in the West, female devaluation and gender in general appear strongly linked to the separation of private and public. Thus, we could retain the use of private/public as an important tool for analyzing this period. Moreover, we might also say that our modern private/public separation has its roots in an older domestic/public separation as, for example, is to be found in medieval Europe and ancient Greece and Rome. Here we would have to be careful and recognize that the similarities which do exist between modern versions of this separation and earlier forms would have to be understood on the analogy of "family resemblances," i.e., as limited and changing similarities coexisting with differences. If we found versions of what may appear as somewhat similar separations in cultures even further removed from our own, we would need to be even more careful in recognizing the differences in conjunction with the similarities. However, if we kept such qualifications in mind, tracing the emergence and evolution of such forms of a separation could prove important in understanding our own construction of gender. We could thus explain our own construction of gender by viewing it as the most recent manifestation of a longer story, a story possessing for at least a certain amount of its existence changing versions of a separation of domestic and public spheres.

A second important caveat would have to be kept in mind. We would need to keep analytically distinct the issue of the specific content a domestic/public separation assumed at any point, i.e., the nature of the activities separated, from the issue of the differences in status ascribed to the separated activities. Theoretically we could imagine a history which evidenced forms of female devaluation present before the emergence of any version of a domestic/public separation comparable to our own, as well as one which located the origin of female devaluation in conjunction with the emergence of such a separation.

I believe that such a historical way of thinking about gender enables us to avoid methodological errors present in many of the contributions to contemporary feminist theory, while enabling us to retain many of their strengths. In the next chapter I intend to illustrate how this kind of approach is beneficial in analyzing the modern period in the West. I will show that when we think about the modern separation between private and public as historical, that is, as emergent out of an older form of social organization and as undergoing continuous change throughout its own history, we possess a means for understanding the nature of family, state, and economy and their relation in this period that does not commit us to certain errors in traditional political theory. For the conclusion of this chapter, however, I would like to sketch out roughly the kind of history we might construct for describing gender prior to the early modern period. To do so, I would like to look at the work of certain major contributors to contemporary feminist anthropological theory to see how some of their ideas could be plugged into such a history.

FRIEDRICH ENGELS:
THE ORIGIN OF THE FAMILY,
PRIVATE PROPERTY, AND THE STATE

One possible source of contribution to the construction of such a history would be from the theory of Friedrich Engels, if that theory were amended in certain ways. It will be recalled from chapter 1 that Engels claimed the existence of early communist societies in which there was a sexual division of labor but no sexual division of power. Since such societies operated at the level of subsistence, only a very small surplus was created which was transmitted through the mother. With the introduction of cattle breeding, metal working, weaving, and agriculture, a social surplus began to be produced. Men were primarily responsible for obtaining food, and thus it was men who had control over the means for producing this surplus. As the surplus increased, matrilineality became more contradictory in the context of masculine control over the means of production. Men in turn overthrew matrilineality in favor of patrilineality. For Engels, this change in inheritance procedure marked the "historical defeat of the female sex"; women became an instrument for ensuring the transmission of property from father to son.

Allied with this change in inheritance procedure was the breakup of the communist extended kin group. Private property undermined the collectivity of the group, breaking it down into more nuclearized families. Within these families, individual men assumed power over wives and children. The class divisions which emerged with the introduction of private property were also expressed and solidified in the first emergence of the state.

As is clear from this brief description of Engels' account, it differs markedly from the universalist position. Most notably, whereas the universalists saw the oppression of women as present within all human societies, Engels attributes its existence to a certain stage in human history, that which came into being with the emergence of private property. While Engels does appear to accept with the universalists some early connection of women with domestic activities, he believes that it was only because of certain contingent historical facts that this sexual division of labor in turn became associated with female devaluation. Thus Engels' account appears to avoid one of the important methodological problems which attended the universalist position: its failure to keep analytically distinct the issues of gender differentiation and gender devaluation.

However, Engels's explanation suffers from certain inadequacies. Since Engels' account, unlike the universalists', does not assume a necessary connection between female domesticity and female ascribed inferiority, he must account for the rise of such a connection. The problem is that the particular explanation Engels offers for this development is inadequate. Engels claims that in the early sexual division of labor it was men and not women who were in charge of food production. When that production began to produce a surplus it was therefore men who had control of that surplus, engendering a power difference between women and men. One weakness with this argument is that it is based on a false premise, that women were excluded from the primary production of food in early societies. This is contradicted by all available anthropological literature, which indicates women's important economic role in all premodern societies.[53]

Moreover, even if women were excluded from food production in early societies, Engels' assumption of a gender-based possessiveness on the part of men toward the social surplus is not explained. Why should men come to recognize their interests qua men as separate from women's, particularly from those individual women with whom they had sexual and familial connections? The difficulty with his move in the argument here replicates a more general problem in Marx's and Engels' theory, that of deducing the phenomenon of class divisions from the creation of an initial social surplus. Where did the initial motive for individual possession of the extra come from?[54] Similarly here, why should men come to see their interest in opposition to women's? Also why should men have come to link inheritance with biological paternity? Even assuming that men wished only other men to own property, why, for example, could not male owners of property have come to demand that their property be inherited by the sons of their wives, making unimportant the question of biological fatherhood? Why is there any necessary link between marriage as an economic institution and marriage as a sexual institution? Engels could not here respond that men have a "natural" sexual possessiveness or concern only with children they have biologically fathered, since neither phenomenon, according to Engels, was part of the early egalitarian societies he described. In short, is not Engels basing the concern of men in bequeathing their property to their biological offspring on the very attitudes that need to be explained? Similarly, given the existence of a gender-based possessiveness, why should not women also care and put up a struggle against the transformation of matrilineality to patrilineality? In Engels' analysis there is assumed no resistance on the part of women to the change. Is he assuming a universal feminine passivity? Or, as Isaac Balbus questions, is Engels assuming that very female subordination his account is supposed to explain?[55] In sum, is Engels not committing the same fallacy in his argument that Rosaldo earlier pointed to in the universalists, i.e., reading back into history present assumptions about gender?

Coexisting with these weaknesses in Engels' argument are also certain strengths. As already noted, his argument exemplifies certain methodological features, making it preferable, at least, to the universalist position. It describes the devaluation of women and their activities as a contingent historical phenomenon, not necessarily following from any specific characteristics of women's biology or from any particular tasks performed by women. Second, his account does make certain illuminating connections between specific forms of female devaluation and class society. There does appear an understandable link between the kind of social atomization he describes as occurring with the emergence of private property and the development of a more nuclear family. Thus when Engels claims that the accumulation of individual wealth undercut communal kin structures and brought about individual family units, his account makes a great deal of sense. If men as a class already had greater status than women, the specific form this difference in status would take in a society organized around such units would be that of head of family. Also, if it were men who were in control of the family's property and if they were concerned to make sure that it was passed on only to their biological offspring, then it makes sense that control of female sexuality and as a consequence control of many other female activities might follow.

One might retain such general strengths of Engels' argument, while avoiding some of its weaknesses, by maintaining the overall framework and altering aspects of the specific account. This indeed is the type of approach exemplified in the work of such theorists as June Nash, Viana Muller, and Martin Whyte. They all associate some change in forms of production related to a growing complexity of human social organization with a relative decline in women's status. Nash, describing early Aztec society, argues for the genesis of a state bureaucracy based on patrilineality as a consequence of the specialization of men in warfare. Nash notes that while women did play an important role in crafts, agriculture, and trade in early Aztec society, they were not part of that segment of the economy rooted in tribute from warfare. As that tribute became a more important aspect of the economy, a state bureaucracy developed, staffed by men and supported by an ideology of male dominance. Women in turn became part of the booty of warfare.[56] Similarly, Muller, using evidence from the Ganda kingdom in Central Africa, looks to the growth of a ruling elite associated with complex patron-client relationships as focal in the decline of women's status. Muller argues that women's biological involvement in childbearing and lactation prohibited their spending extended periods of time away from home. This fact explains their not becoming part of the new patron-client relationships from which a nascent state emerged.[57] Whyte also links the proliferation of extrafamilial roles dominated by men and the increasing hierarchical structure and ideology of political institutions with a relative decline in women's status. However, he associates these developments with the stratification and family property dynamics of intensive farming.[58]

Thus by employing some such explanation as the above we could elaborate our history. We could argue that prior to our own modern private/public separation arose a much earlier domestic/public separation associated with the rise of some type of state or prestate formation. This domestic/public separation itself brought about, or was correlated with, a devaluation of women. Thus, similarly to the universalists, this elaboration would link the emergence of a domestic/public separation with female devaluation. However, unlike the universalists, it would situate both at a certain point in human history associated with the emergence of changes in social organization.

THE EXCHANGE OF WOMEN

The only problem with such an elaboration would result from evidence which found female devaluation even in very early societies. Noteworthy in this regard is an argument put forth by Collier and Rosaldo. These two anthropologists analyze marriage and kinship relations in preclass societies, finding in such relations a form of sexual assymetry. They focus in on societies marked by "brideservice" exchange, rather than by "bridewealth"; the former depicting most hunter-gatherers and some horticulturalists, the latter describing most horticultural tribal groups. They note that in brideservice societies marriage has a quite different meaning for men and women as a consequence of the sexual division of labor and the rules governing the social distribution of food. Whereas both the products of women's daily gathering and men's more occasional hunting provide needed sustenance, they are distributed in very different ways. Women are required to feed their more immediate family group members with the products of their gathering, whereas men distribute the meat of the animals they kill among the social group as a whole through rules favoring the eldest members.[59] In consequence, while marriage results in decided advantages for men, particularly access to the products of female labor, marriage for women produces no gain, and indeed results often in a loss of personal and sexual freedom.[60] These differences are manifest in the attempts of many young women to avoid marriage and in the "fiction that men, through their gifts or exchanges, 'win' something to fight for and value, in coming to live with a wife."[61] Through the complex rules associated with the distribution of men's meat, men but not women emerge as the creators of social ties. Moreover, "As a man with recognized interests to protect, he can speak up and expect to be heard in public gatherings. And, as an individual whose basic needs are provided, he can devote his time to building the exchange networks that enhance social influence and prestige."[62]

Collier and Rosaldo's argument provides grounding for an analysis which has played a major role in contemporary feminist theory, that offered by Gayle Rubin. Rubin has argued, employing ideas from Lévi-Strauss, that the exchange of women in marriage in prestate societies acts to establish kinship structures. Since in prestate societies kinship serves as the principal means by which all activities, including those we would label "economic," "political," "sexual," and "religious" are organized, the exchange of women can be said to structure, in kinship-organized societies, the very basis of society. It also expresses a difference in power between men and women in such societies:

> If it is women who are being transacted, then it is the men who give and take them who are linked, the woman being a conduit of a relationship rather than a partner to it. The exchange of women does not necessarily imply that women are objectified in the modern sense, since objects in the primitive world are imbued with highly personal qualities. But it does imply a distinction between gift and giver. If women are the gifts, then it is men who are the exchange partners. And it is the partners, not the presents, upon whom reciprocal exchange confers its quasi-mystical power of social linkage. The relations of such a system are such that women are in no position to realize the benefits of their own circulation. As long as the relations specify that men exchange women, it is men who are the beneficiaries of the product of such exchanges—social organization.[63]

We might interpret Rubin's analysis as supplementing an account of origins by adding the claim that men and their activities are evaluated differently from women and their activities, whatever the specific content of those activities, as a function of men's and women's different roles in structuring kinship. Thus as I read Rubin, what her description of the 'exchange of women' suggests is most fundamentally a fact of symbolism built into the principles of kinship. The exchange of women does not imply that women, unlike men, necessarily change their geographical location in marriage. Nor does it imply, as I read Rubin, that individual men necessarily have more power in choosing a marriage partner or leaving a marriage than individual women. Rather it appears to suggest a difference in the ways in which women as a class are perceived in the structuring of marriage and thus as Rubin suggests, following Lévi-Strauss, in the structuring of society. This difference in perception is well expressed in the following statement of a Northern Melpa man which Rubin quotes:

> "What woman," mused a young Northern Melpa man, "is ever strong enough to get up and say, 'Let us make moha, let us find wives and pigs, let us give our daughters to men, let us wage war, let us kill our enemies!' No indeed not! . . . they are little rubbish things who stay at home simply, don't you see?"

Rubin comments:

> What women indeed! The Melpa women of whom the young man spoke can't get wives, they *are* wives, and what they get are husbands, an entirely different matter. The Melpa women can't give their daughters to men, because they do not have the same rights in their daughters that their male kin have, rights of bestowal (although *not* of ownership).[64]

Again we need to be careful what we read into this symbolism. As Rubin notes, it should not be equated with rights of ownership. Nor, as I noted above, need it imply that individual men necessarily have more power in choosing or leaving a wife than an individual woman has in choosing or leaving a husband. Rather it suggests a very general difference in perceived power between men and women in kin-organized societies from which, in later historical periods, might follow a greater power of individual men to choose or leave marriage partners when individual choice becomes an option.

The symbolic power that Rubin is attributing to men in kin-organized societies is a power of men as a class over women as a class, as expressed in the meaning of marriage. It is thus not the power that is suggested by the term "patriarchy," i.e., the power of an individual man over a household which might include one or several women, children, slaves, property, etc., or even over an extended family unit. Moreover, it is not the power that an institutionalized public sphere, such as the state, may possess over individual household or family units. Rubin's account, however, does provide us with the means of understanding how, insofar as these last forms of power opposition arise, it is men and not women who emerge as the class from whom the powerful are represented. In other words, from Rubin's analysis we might construct a continuum in gender relations between societies organized by kin with no predominant public sphere to those with such a public sphere to prestate or state societies. Her analysis would allow us to explain the differences in status and power between men and women in state societies from the differences in status and power between men and women in kinship societies. Insofar as it is men with whom power and authority reside in kinship-organized societies, then when the state replaces kinship as the means by which social life is organized, men would also be associated with the power residing in the state.

The above analysis, like the analysis suggested by Engels and his elaborators, would therefore construe the separation between domestic and public associated with female devaluation as a product of historical evolution. The only difference would be that this approach would interpret its component of female devaluation as a product of an earlier devaluation rather than as a result of historical factors associated with the emergence of the separation. Of course, these two kinds of approaches are not necessarily in conflict. One could theorize that in early, prestate societies elements of a female devaluation are to be found, but that they become accentuated with the emergence of a state and a strict separation between domestic and public spheres. One reason might be that the newly emerging state further devalued spheres of activity separate from itself as a means of legitimating itself.[65]

Another reason why we ought not to feel compelled to have to choose between the above types of arguments is that there may be kinds of prestate societies which devalue women and those which do not. What is abundantly clear from Peggy Sanday's *Female Power and Male Dominance* is that there is enormous variation in the extent and forms of female devaluation among "simple" societies.[66] While I have been arguing for a type of evolutionary approach in thinking about male dominance, this does not mean that I am advocating a simple "one story" approach such as tended to predominate amongst the nineteenth-century evolutionists. Since the roots of modern society are diverse rather than singular, there seems no reason why we need insist on a singular account of the origins of our own constructions of gender.

This latter point further illuminates a problem with the early radical feminist/Marxist debate, as a debate between the universality of male domination versus its origins in class, state societies. Radical feminists have tended to respond to the Marxist position on the link between private property and female devaluation by noting the existence of female devaluation in preclass societies. That argument may be valid, if we interpret it as claiming that the emergence of private property is not *the* cause of female devaluation. On the Marxist side, however, the emergence of private property, or as Whyte qualifies the point, stratified society, could have been *a* cause of accentuating any devaluation which already existed. In short, to analyze the origins of female devaluation, we may need to construct more than one story.

IDEOLOGY AND REALITY

Before concluding, I would like to resolve one possible source of confusion concerning my meaning of the opposition domestic/public. An important contribution of contemporary American feminism has been to question those social divisions which I would claim represent the modern forms of this opposition, i.e., the separation of family from work, the private from the public, the personal from the political. Some contemporary feminists have argued that these divisions are ideological in that they obscure the unity and commonalities in social life. Thus feminists have claimed that to separate the personal from the political is to obscure the common existence of power dynamics in both. Similarly, many have argued that to think of the family as a sphere separate and apart from the work world is to ignore the ways in which the social dynamics in the two spheres affect each other. This demand to transcend contemporary social divisions so as to understand the unitary nature of social life is present in the following remarks of Rosalind Petchesky:

> This, in turn led to a further analytical insight: that "production" and "reproduction," work and the family, far from being separate territories like the moon and the sun or the kitchen and the shop, are really intimately related modes that reverberate upon one another and frequently occur in the same social, physical and even psychic spaces. This point bears emphasizing, since many of us are still stuck in the model of "separate spheres" (dividing off "woman's place," "reproduction," "private life," the home etc. from the world of men, production, "public life," the office, etc.). We are now learning that this model of separate spheres distorts reality, that it is every bit as much an ideological construct as are the notions of "male" and "female" themselves. Not only do reproduction and kinship, or the family, have their own historically determined products, material techniques, modes of organization, and power relationships, but reproduction and kinship are themselves integrally related to the social relations of production and the state; they reshape those relations all the time.[67]

The confusion which might arise concerning my use of the opposition domestic/public, or for the modern period, private/public, is that it might be interpreted as merely reflecting an ideologically divided world. To avoid this confusion, it is important to note the difference between a theory describing a reality and reflecting a reality. A distinguishing feature is the degree to which the theory assumes as inevitable that which it describes. As I will argue in a later chapter, what makes Locke's theory ideological is not that he describes political interaction differently from familial interaction as that he does not see the differences between the two as historical and thus not inevitable. Similarly, many contemporary understandings of our own components of a domestic/public separation, i.e., as between family and state and household and work, assume these separations as natural. This assumption mitigates against viewing such separations in historical terms. However, as we shall see in the following chapter, *because* these separations are historical, the separated spheres share common origins and interrelations which the very fact of separation has helped to obscure. A feminist perspective has brought to light many of these commonalities and interrelations. The task is to reconcile these insights with the reality of the separations, a task, I believe, made possible only through a historical understanding.

CONCLUSION

The major thesis of this chapter is that we need to think about gender and female devaluation historically. There has been a tendency among feminist theorists to employ a causal model for analyzing the origins of such devaluation. By translating questions of origins into questions of causes, the tendency has been to search for cross-cultural factors generating a supposedly cross-cultural phenomenon. But as female devaluation is not one fact but many, interlinked with specificities of culture, so also should we abandon the search for one cross-cultural cause. Such a search was present in the early postulation of a domestic/public separation as such a universal cause, as well as in Chodorow's related theory, which looks to universal female parenting as such an ultimate factor.

One reason why radical feminists and the early domestic/public theorists were attracted to this type of explanation is that they were impatient with the widespread tendency to minimize the persistence of female devaluation. This latter tendency was present, for example, among many Marxists. But, as I hope to have shown, one does not need a universal cause to admit of this persistence or indeed even of the universality of such devaluation. One could argue that such devaluation or oppression began very early in human history, for reasons not present in later periods. Persisting, it took on new forms. This kind of account would be similar to an explanation of twentieth-century racism of whites against blacks which traced its history in eighteenth- and nineteenth-century slavery. Such a type of explanation need not deny that the oppression of women, like contemporary racism, serves some function for some people long after the reasons which originally generated both have disappeared. It is only that it would be a mistake in both cases to look for one single, cross-cultural cause.

It is not only gender, or female devaluation, which needs to be understood historically, but also the separation of domestic and public. I have argued that the early domestic/public theorists, in searching for those features of social organization which were basic and possibly explanatory of gender, did hit onto something fundamental in pointing to the separation of domestic and public activities. However, I have claimed that this separation, while fundamental to our contemporary organization of gender, and indeed to that of long stretches of our past, has to be understood as emerging at a certain point in human history and as changing its nature over time. Moreover, we also need to keep analytically distinct the issue of the emergence of such a separation as a separation of activities from the issue of a devaluation attached to such activities. If, however, such conditions were satisfied, we would possess a framework helpful in illuminating our own history of gender. We could envision such a separation emerging out of forms of social organization which possessed either some sexual division of labor or some form of female devaluation, to form that type of separation roughly comparable to what we know today, i.e., where women have primary responsibility for childrearing and household-related tasks and both women and such tasks are devalued. This very general social division could then be seen as the source out of which evolved an early modern public/private division, when the family as a social unit became seen as a separated unit from the rest of society.

One important outcome of such an approach is that we could come to generate an awareness of the historical specificity of our own modern version of this general division. We could then begin to see that many features which we take to be central in social organization, such as the family or the importance of the mother/child bond, have indeed been products of history. This is a direction that several contemporary feminist theorists have begun to take, not only in anthropological theory, as an outcome of criticism of the early domestic/public framework, but in other disciplines as well.

This last outcome possesses exciting potential for illuminating modern Western history. It also enables us to rethink basic cultural assumptions of this period. I would now like to turn to the modern period and new historical work on it.

CHAPTER FOUR

GENDER AND MODERNITY: REINTERPRETING THE FAMILY, THE STATE, AND THE ECONOMY

THE METHODOLOGICAL APPROACH for feminist theory outlined in the last chapter embodies the prohistorical, antiscientific model advocated for social theory in general by such nineteenth-century philosophers as Hegel and Dilthey, and by those scholars in the twentieth century associated with "critical theory" and the Frankfurt school. As a means for understanding social life, it is also, at least implicitly, represented in the work of practicing historians. The feminist version of this position deviates from the one of the German philosophers and many historians in its insistence that the histories which we have inherited have ignored, for the most part, the issue of gender. Thus while we have well-developed histories of government, religion, and culture, we have little in the way of the history of the relations between women and men. Moreover, this omission distorts the histories we do possess, which often falsely suggest that historically important turning points for men had the same meaning and consequences for women. However, as Joan Kelly-Gadol has noted, such widely recognized historical changes as the emergence of Athenian civilization, the Renaissance, or the French revolution cannot be understood equivalently for both genders. For example, "there was no 'Renaissance' for women—at least not during the Renaissance."[1] In sum, the methodological position I am arguing for demands of feminist theory that it become more historical and demands of historically oriented social theory that it become more feminist, that is, more concerned with the issue of gender relations. A historically oriented social theory which focuses on gender can provide, I believe, a new and powerful means for understanding our past.

In this chapter I wish to show the implications of employing a historical method for analyzing women's oppression, and the implications for social theory of focusing on gender, by turning to the modern period, i.e., from 1500 on in Western Europe. An examination of this period reveals an important pattern: the progressive decline of kinship as a principle of organizing social life. In the first two chapters I noted the steady decline of the family over the past two centuries as many of its functions have been taken over by the state or have become commoditized. I now wish to suggest that such changes are only the most recent manifestations of the declining importance of kinship which extends beyond the past two centuries to at least the beginning of the breakdown of feudalism. A point worth emphasizing, however, is that while the declining importance of kinship over the past two centuries may be described as a decline in the importance of the institution of the family, this very decline in the importance of kinship in the early modern period caused the *emergence* of the institution of the family. In this period the decline in the importance of kinship meant the emergence of a public sphere, or state, unstructured by relations of kinship, and the increased restriction of kinship to the sphere of domestic life. Thus, in the early modern period, while the link between kinship and politics increasingly disappeared, the link between kinship and household organization increasingly grew. One consequence is the emergence of the modern family which unites kinship and domesticity. A second consequence is a growing separation of the family from the external society, as expressed in the idea of the family as the sphere of the private. Thus, it is in the early modern period that a distinction between domestic and nondomestic activities takes the form of a distinction between the private and the public.

At the start of this period, the family/private sphere is a sphere of economic production, in the context of a growing nonfamilial sphere of economic exchange. This heritage of economic production within the familial is marked even in the twentieth century by its description by many as "private" activity. With the onset of industrialization, production moves outside the home and becomes itself a nonfamilial activity. In consequence, there emerges a sphere of social life, the economy, which is viewed as distinct from both the family and the state.

Describing the modern period in this way makes possible the articulation of the following thesis: that some of the basic categories we have traditionally employed to explain social life, particularly the categories of family, state, and economy reflect historical, and not natural, social divisions. By this I do not mean that the categories of particularly family and state can only be applied to one period in history, such as the modern period. As there are types of states in ancient society, similar in many ways to the modern nation state, so also are there types of families in at least classical Greek and Roman society similar in many, though not all, respects to the modern family. A point to note, however, is that while the category of "family" is not limited to the modern period, it is not universal either. Again, comparable to the recognition that there are types of states beyond the modern nation state and also types of societies, such as tribal societies, where the concept of the state is not usefully applied, so also are there types of families outside the modern family, and types of societies where the concept of family is not helpful either.[2]

The distinctiveness of such a thesis, particularly with regard to the concept of the family, needs elaboration. Few would argue with a definition of the family as "those members of the same kin who live together under one roof."[3] More controversial is the claim that this joining together of kinship and domesticity into a significant unit requiring a label is an historical process, occurring in some periods but not in all. As a thesis it is stronger, for example, than the claim that there are many types of families, at least when this latter claim is not also supplemented by the point that in some societies there are no "families" at all. However, this stronger point must be articulated, to counteract the tendency present in much of modern Western social theory to think of "the family" as a naturally demarcatable social unit, analytically distinguishable from political or economic spheres. Using philosophical language, we can say that social theorists tend to "ontologize" or "reify" such categories, meaning that they tend to see that which these categories differentiate as inherently differentiatable. This is not a minor problem.

Moreover, without a recognition of the historically created nature of such spheres as "family," "state" and "economy," we have no means for understanding important components of gender relations. A problem with social theory which assumes the demarcation of these three is that it presupposes that which must be accounted for and analyzed in terms of its effect on gender. Thus theorists who assume that the state is naturally differentiated from the familial also tend to assume women's exclusion from the political and do not raise such questions as when and why this happened. Moreover, not to be cognizant of the historical creation and separation of the family, state, and economy, is to be handicapped in understanding the interconnections among these separated spheres which are a function of their common origins. For example, insofar as we cannot see the emergence of the state and the family out of societies where both the political and the familial are interconnected in principles of kinship, it becomes difficult to comprehend the nature and origins of patterns of power and hierarchy within the family, which feminists have claimed constitute the family as a political institution. Similarly, to the extent we do not perceive the historical emergence of the economy out of the household, it becomes that much harder to comprehend the ways in which interfamilial relations themselves are economic relations and how interfamilial relations have affected the economy. For such reasons feminist theorists have frequently sensed that it is crucial to denaturalize such categories as "family," "private life," etc. in order to explicate gender.[4] In the following, I hope to expand and validate this suspicion.

THE FAMILY

While many feminist theorists have been cognizant of the need to "denaturalize" the family, it is from the relatively recent work of many historians, not necessarily feminist, that much of the justification for such denaturalization can be found. That schol-

arship arising from the field of history substantiates certain suspicions of feminist theorists is not coincidental. The changing
nature of the family and its changing relation to other spheres of
society has brought into being a widespread focus on the family.
Indeed, part of what has changed about the contemporary family
is that it has become a very public institution, an appropriate
object for analysis and discussion. Thus it is not surprising that
within the relatively recent past, the discipline of history has
engendered a new subfield, family history, which in turn has
contributed to new ways of thinking about the family.[5]

There are a variety of ways of describing what has been new
in such work. At one level it has involved a reperiodization of
the family. Before the last twenty years, many believed that for
most of human history people were members of what might be
called "extended" families which included a number of relatives
outside the immediate core.[6] It was believed that as a consequence
of industrialization, the extended family gave way to the nuclear
family. The new family history challenged this periodization. Particularly, it pushed the emergence of the nuclear family back from
the recent past to the preindustrial or early modern period, at
least in Europe and colonial America. A major contributor to the
debunking of the earlier model was Peter Laslett, working with
a group of historians and anthropologists in Cambridge, England.
This group initially looked at census data in England from the
latter part of the sixteenth century to the early part of the nineteenth
century and found strikingly little variation in mean household
size over this period, not deviating significantly from the figure
of 4.75. This finding was expanded by work done in other countries
of Europe and in colonial America which brought forth similar
figures.[7]

A problem, however, was that this research, while useful in
debunking earlier myths, did not itself provide a helpful model
for thinking about Western family history. Two issues are particularly significant. For one, the data did not differentiate among
classes. Jean-Louis Flandrin, looking at one of the villages used
as an example by Laslett in *The World We Have Lost*, found the
following problem.[8] Flandrin noted that while the village of

Goodnestone next-Wingham in Kent in 1676 did possess a small median household size (4.47), the median figure obscured important differences in class. It was the households of the lower social classes—which formed the majority of households—that were predominantly small, averaging under three persons. However, the membership of such households constituted only just over one-third of the population, the rest living in the larger households of the yeomen and gentry. Some of these households were indeed quite large; the one, for example, of Sir Edward Hall and his wife, comprising 23 persons: himself, his wife, their 6 children, and 15 domestic servants. Among the 26 households of the yeomen, there were 12 large families, accounting for about a hundred people. Thus as Flandrin concluded: "The lord of the manor and these dozen yeoman—who owned almost all the land, gave employment to other families and were the political as well as the economic leaders of the village—accommodated in their great households over half the population of the village. Can it be said, in these circumstances, that large households were non-existent or without importance?"[9]

Related to the issue of class differences was the adequacy of numbers alone in providing significant indicators. Laslett and the Cambridge group concentrated on demography and specifically on the number of persons, related or not, who formed a coresident group. Such a focus ignores how such persons perceive each other in relation to their perception of persons outside the group. For example, if such a group includes servants, as well as kin-related members, what is the relation between the members' perception of the group and their perception of the kinship bonds they, as individuals, possess with persons residing outside the group? Laslett skirted over this issue by speaking of the family in a particular sense, "as a group of persons living together, a household, what we shall call a coresident domestic group."[10] Such a stipulative definition of the family neglects the important question of the relative significance of either domesticity or kinship in constituting the family and also the question of which kin members are perceived of as most centrally core.

One reason, of course, for the appeal of numbers was the promise of objectivity and the avoidance of bias on the part of the researcher. A means of countering such bias while incorporating the question of significance is to pay particular attention to the meanings and language of the subjects of study. Two authors who have relied heavily on this kind of approach in recent family history have been Flandrin and Philippe Ariès.

Ariès work *Centuries of Childhood* has become most famous for its claim that the concept of childhood has been historically specific to the modern period. More relevant to the present purposes, however, is his assertion that this has been true also of the concept of the family. Ariès argues that the concept of the family was unknown in the Middle Ages and only originated in the fifteenth and sixteenth centuries.[11] He does not take this change to imply that there was no such entity as the family, meaning the conjugal unit of parents and children, before the early modern period. Rather his argument is that the premodern family was at least very different from its progeny in regard to the silence which surrounded it:

> It would be vain to deny the existence of a family life in the Middle Ages. But the family existed in silence: it did not awaken feelings strong enough to inspire poet or artist. We must recognize the importance of this silence: not much value was placed on the family. Similarly, we must admit the significance of the iconographic blossoming which after the fifteenth and especially the sixteenth century followed this long period of obscurity: the birth and development of the concept of the family.
>
> This powerful concept was formed around the conjugal family, that of the parents and children. This concept is closely linked to that of childhood.[12]

If the family existed in silence before the early modern period, what evoked "noise" or the kind of importance which later became associated with the family was, at least for the aristocracy, the "line." The line, as Ariès notes "extended to the ties of blood without regard to the emotions engendered by cohabitation and intimacy."[13] This description emphasizes a feature which was to importantly differentiate "family" from "line": its union of kinship and domesticity into a significant association.

The joining together of kinship and domesticity into this construction of "family" was a gradual process. Indeed, a definition of family as mother, father, and children living together did not firmly emerge as the primary definition of the family until the nineteenth century.[14] In earlier centuries the word possessed several different and distinct meanings. There is first a definition of family which has to do primarily with coresidence and includes servants as well as kin. Thus Flandrin quotes Samuel Pepys writing in 1660, "I lived in Axe yard, having my wife and servant Jane, and no more in family than us three."[15] "Family" here both in word and sense derives from the ancient Latin where "familial" includes slaves, wife, and children under one head of household. There is a second sense of family used in the seventeenth and eighteenth centuries which refers to the wider kinship network of people of a certain class. It was most frequently, though not unambiguously, used of the bourgeoisie rather than the aristocracy, members of the latter more properly being referred to as of a given "house"; it was clearly not, however, a term used of the common people.[16] There is finally a sense of "family," appearing in late seventeenth- and eighteenth-century French dictionaries and not until the nineteenth century in England, which is used more democratically and refers to close kinship. The evolution of "close kinship" to mean, however, mother, father, and children does not become definitive even in France until after the mid-eighteenth century with the conflation of the two older meanings of domesticity and kinship.[17] In short, *our* primary meaning of family, as mother, father, and children living together is an evolutionary composite of earlier meanings: one of which had as its core domesticity, and the other, kinship. Over the course of the modern period these two components became conjoined, while eliminating on the side of domesticity, servants, and deemphasizing (though not eliminating) the more extended kinship network. This growing focus on the more nuclear kinship core was also linked with its spread to all classes.

An important observation to derive from the above is the minimal place of biology in the ancestry of our meaning of family. Because of the centrality of the parent-child bond in our conception, we tend to think of family as primarily a biological unit. However, in looking at the history of the term, its political and economic aspects become more prominant. In its meaning as the bourgeois analogue to "house" or "lineage" there is certainly an element of biology, insofar as "blood" is a component of that which unites. However, it is clearly only one component, given its class associations and the fact that sexual alliances, particularly among those of property, needed to be legitimized to count as constituting family connections. The political and economic aspects of the term are also obviously present in the other older meaning of "family" as domestic unit.

Indeed, the political and economic aspects seem to tie together the two meanings of family as domestic unit and family as comparable with "line." We might even speculate that the latter meaning of "family" arose later in time than the former to suggest for the head of the early modern household of conjugal unit plus servants the same kind of legitimized connection between his position as head with his position in an elite kinship network that was made for the aristocracy in the concept of "good lordship." As Lawrence Stone notes, " 'lordship' embraced not only the wider ramifications of the kin, but also the household retainers and servants, the client gentry and the tenants on the estates, all comprising a collective 'affinity'."[18] Similarly, "family" connects position within a household with position within a kinship system, thus uniting these two different kinds of social relationships.

THE FAMILY AND THE STATE

If the emergence and transformation of the family has largely to do with political and economic issues understood broadly, i.e., with changing obligations of people to one another and changing relations to property, then we might expect a close interconnection between the history of the family and political and economic history. Here I would like to focus specifically on the interconnection of family and state, particularly in terms of origins. Before proceeding it will be useful to elaborate that cultural perspective which the methodological stance I am advocating contradicts. According to the dominant view of the modern period, the family is seen as a quasi-natural institution, a rational solution to the problem of the perceived inability of women to provide for themselves and children during their childbearing years. This conception of the family is clearly articulated in the writings of John Locke, whose work also elaborates a position often conjoined with it: that in human history at a much later date than the creation of the first families, many families came together to form larger social units for the prevention of interfamilial conflict. Such larger units were the beginnings of what we know as the state. Thus, according to this story, families and states originated not only at different points in time but to solve different kinds of problems.

This account will be further elaborated in the next chapter, where I specifically focus on the work of John Locke. For now, however, I want to put forth the following theses: that the family and state arose in conjunction with each other and that their very structures are interdependent. These, to be sure, are not original theses. Most prominently, Marx articulated a related point in his early insistence on the interconnection of the creation of the private and the public: "the abstraction of the *state as such* belongs only to modern times because the abstraction of private life belongs only to these times. The abstraction of the *political state* is a modern product."[19]

We can give this insight further elaboration through much of the concrete anthropological and historical work which has been done in the century since Marx's death. For one, there is a literature in the field of political anthropology which, while disagreeing over the reasons for the emergence of the state, achieves consensus around the point that its growth is coeval with the decline of kinship as a principle of social organization.[20] Kinship can serve as such an organizing principle, either insofar as kinship ties operate in structuring a society per se or because a larger society is broken down into units organized by kin relations, i.e., as clans or lineages.[21] Since I have been claiming in the above that what distinguishes the "family" from "kinship" is that the former represents a conjunction and restriction of kinship to coresidence, then it would follow that those societies which make such a restriction would develop principles alternative to kinship for relating such kinship/domestic units. What we mean by the "political" or the "state" constitutes an example of one such set of alternative principles.

The above discussion is analytic. We can give it empirical instantiation by looking at two periods in Western history which evidence the emergence of "families" and "states": archaic Greece and medieval Europe. One historian whose work is directly relevant to the former period is Marilyn Arthur. Arthur relates the growth of the Greek city state to certain economic changes occuring in the archaic period. She notes particularly the transition from a society dominated by a relatively small group of landholding families to one characterized by a more broadly based class of small property holders. She argues that, "At this point in history the small household emerged as the productive unit of society, and any head of a household (who was simultaneously a landowner) automatically became a citizen or member of the state. Conversely, the state itself, the polis, was defined as the sum of all individual households."[22] Thus for Arthur, the rise of the Greek city state, the polis, was directly related to the emergence of the oikos or household as a productive unit. She describes the oikos as "a small holding corporation composed of its male head, his wife, their children, and the slaves who served it and worked the land that was its economic base."[23] What is interesting about this description of the oikos is that it employs a small business metaphor which, as we shall see, also becomes helpful in understanding the early modern family. One clear difference is the inclusion of slaves, though the inclusion of servants in the families of the very early modern period illustrates also a similarity.

From the emerging importance of the oikos as a productive unit in preclassical Greece, Arthur relates its new importance as a political unit. Political power in the emerging democratic state became more widely shared among the diverse constituents of the new "midddle-class," whose claim to political representation lay in possession of the amount of property capable of supporting an individual household. In this context the integrity of each individual household took on an importance not present in the older tribal or kin-based society. New laws concerning marriage, inheritance, and adultery reflected these changes.[24]

Arthur believes her analysis applicable also to later periods, particularly to the transition from feudalism to capitalism.[25] The claim that there may be certain parallel developments in preclassical Greece and early modern Europe appears supported in the similar emergence in both cases of the household unit as a productive unit. Moreover, while the political form characteristic of the Greek polis is not repeated in Western Europe, certainly there is a parallel move toward democratization rooted in household/ property ownership. Most relevant, however, to the purposes of the present point is the idea that in both preclassical Greece and early modern Europe there appears a similar opposition between kinship or tribal forms of social organization and the state. This thesis finds support in the work of others. Hannah Arendt, for example, long ago pointed out that the foundation of the polis was preceded by the destruction of all organized units resting on kinship.[26] In reference to the early modern period, Stone has argued that the forms of social organization which had structured medieval aristrocratic life, specifically kinship, lordship, and clientage were antithetical to the functioning of the modern state:

> The modern state is a natural enemy to the values of the clan, of kinship, and of good lordship and clientage links among the upper classes, for at this social and political level they are a direct threat to the state's own claim to prior loyalty. Aristocratic kinship and clientage leads to faction and rebellion, such as the Wars of the Roses or the Fronde, to the use of kin loyalty and client empires by entrenched local potentates to create independent centres of power and to make the working of the jury system of justice impossible by the subordination of objective judgment to ties of blood or local loyalty.[27]

During the Middle Ages there existed a seesaw relationship between loyalty to the kin and to the state, with loyalty to the latter being in effect loyalty to the most powerful kin network of all, headed by the king.[28] In the sixteenth century in England, the state enhanced its reign, increasing its control over property, crime, and punishment. Later, it changed the nature of the loyalty it demanded. Particularistic notions of obligation and allegiance became transformed into a more universalistic moral code.[29] This transformation in the extent and nature of the relation between subjects and their king entailed that existing, more particularistic allegiances be undermined. As Stone notes, one of the tools used by the emerging state in its battle for power with such allegiances was to transfer the idea of good lordship from its association with the head of an extended kinship and clientage unit to the individual male head of household. The new state thus encouraged patriarchy within the *family*—claiming that allegiances within it were analogous to allegiances of all to the king—while undermining patriarchy in its more traditional sense. Thus, as Stone concludes, the principle of patriarchy was transformed by the state from a threat to its existence into a formidable buttress to it.[30]

In short, contrary to the picture which Locke and others have given us, of the family preceding the state in time, the above analysis suggests a mutual emergence. The family as that institution which focuses on kinship ties in the conjugal, domestically centered unit arises as an understandable component of a form of society whose overarching organizational principles become now based on criteria antithetical to kinship. Moreover, also antithetical to the received picture of families creating states for reasons different from those generating families, is the fact of families and states originating together and containing common features as a function of their common origins. For example, that the governmental bodies were primarily made up of men and that families/household units were perceived as headed by men, two facts crucial in understanding gender relations in the modern period, can be seen as two interrelated consequences of the origins of both the family and the state in patriarchal kinship structures. Thus families and states can be understood as institutions not inherently different in kind but with important features in common in the context of simultaneously increasing differences in function.

I claimed earlier that a recognition of the separation of family and state as historical and not analytic provides us with clues for comprehending women's changing status not available from the dominant view. This point can be substantiated by both Arthur's and Stone's work. Arthur, for example, after noting the status of women as objects of exchange in the period prior to the one with which she is concerned, argues that the transformations which resulted in the rise in the importance of the household as a political unit in ancient Greece in turn added a new dimension to this status. In a context in which the integrity of each individual household came to possess political significance, so did the bio-logical activities of women which could potentially violate that integrity take on political significance. Adultery, for example, when practiced by women became seen as a crime against society.[31] The corollary to the legal sanctions against adultery by women was the idealization given to the citizen wife who produced legitimate heirs. This idealization has caused some to argue that the overall status of women in classical Athens was not all that bad.[32] Arthur's position, like that of some others, is that the idealization given to the citizen wife does not mitigate against the fundamental misogynistic attitude of classical Athens. True, the proper Athenian housewife may have been praised when she acted as she ought; beyond the praise stood the recurrent fear that she might not:

> This praise of women in the marriage relationship does not invalidate the idea that the fundamental attitude of the Greeks toward women remained misogynistic. As social beings, women in the polis entered into a partnership with men that fostered civilization, and only in this relationship did women gain favor. As we have seen, the misogyny of the Greeks originally sprang from the association of women with the world of instincts and passions, which was hostile to civilized life. Unlike man, the woman of the polis was regarded as a hybrid creature, a domesticated animal who could be adapted to the needs of society but whose fundamental instincts were antagonistic to it.[33]

Insofar as the polis depended upon the autonomy and inviolability of the individual household and thus the legitimacy of each man's heirs, it is understandable that women's sexuality would be highly feared. Women, as those beings whose sexuality had the power to disrupt the political order, would be idealized for doing right while being hated and feared for their power to do wrong. What also follows in such a context is that women's activities generally would be closely watched. This deduction is supported by other accounts of the situation of women in classical Athens such as that of Sarah Pomeroy. Pomeroy's work dovetails Arthur's by documenting the manner in which women's lives were closely supervised in classical Athens.[34]

As noted, Arthur intends her analysis to serve more than as an explanation of the situation of women in classical Athens. Rather she makes a broader historical claim: that the democratic state based on power distributed among male heads of households has specific consequences for women. Thus she argues that in the Hellenistic period which followed, women's position in certain respects improved as a consequence of the decline of both the polis and household at the expense of the empire. Since in the Hellenistic city, citizenship no longer depended upon one's membership in a family, the laws ceased to concern themselves with women's childbearing activities.[35] Women gained more control over property, and the range of their allowed activities generally increased. Arthur's claims about the improved position of women in the Hellenistic period are not without a cynical edge:

Our evaluation of the position of women in this world must ultimately be informed by the same cynicism. Women were free to own property, but property ownership no longer led to citizenship; women were citizens and officials of the polis, but the polis was no longer the dominant political form; women were no longer a testimony to the gods' hatred of mankind, but it was the gods who ceased to hate men, not men who ceased to hate women.[36]

Arthur's argument that the emergence of a more individualized household unit as a significant political/economic entity was on the whole bad for women finds certain parallels in Stone's work on early modern England. As earlier noted, Stone claims that one of the tools used by the state in its battle for power with existing feudal lords was to transfer the idea of good lordship to the individual male head of household. Thus the state proclaimed the subordination of the wife to her husband as a principal "guarantee of law and order in the body politic."[37] Stone notes other social transformations besides the emergence of the state which occurred in the early modern period and which both reflected and reinforced this increased power of the individual male head of household. One such change was an attack on entailment which occurred in the late fifteenth century, an attack whose consequence was to give greater power to the male head of household to dispose of his property according to his personal inclinations. Stone also points to the Lutheran Reformation in increasing the spiritual authority of the father and husband. The wife lost a source of external appeal in the priest and church, a loss which paralleled the more general decline in the influence of external countervailing influences, such as her kin, over the rule of her husband.

While both Stone's and Arthur's analyses are suggestive, it would be wise to recall an earlier discussion of the complexity of the issue of status before we derive any immediate conclusions on the status of women in state societies organized around individualized household units. To raise again a reminder from Rosaldo: "women's status" does not describe a singular variable which can be isolated and then correlated with any given social form. How women are perceived in any given society is always a complicated issue involving a variety of factors. Some of the complexity involved is illustrated in the work of another historian of the early modern period, Roberta Hamilton. Hamilton's work certainly supports the claim that there did exist a high degree of control over women's activities in this period and also a dominant view of women's inferiority and necessary subordination to men. However, she also notes the importance of the new ideology of marriage as a partnership which entailed a certain degree of equality between women and men. One manifestation of this new ideology was the Protestant rejection of women as Eve:

> But for the family to be so elevated meant that attitudes towards sex and women had to be substantially changed. For how were men to live morally impeccable lives capitulating with the evil seductress who populated Catholic treatises? Perhaps the Protestant preachers were not consciously motivated. None the less, they went about the task of rescuing sex and women from what they perceived as the worst slurs of Catholicism.[38]

Thus from the work of such scholars as Stone, Arthur, and others I do not want to derive specific conclusions on the status of women under particular social forms. Rather I wish to draw on their arguments to underline my more general thesis: that only through an awareness of the family as a social institution, that is, as created and in interaction with other social institutions, can we even begin to take the first steps toward reaching satisfactory conclusions on the issue. In sum, to answer the questions feminism raises, we need to reject a social ontology which views modern social configurations as immutable.

THE FAMILY AND THE ECONOMY

The belief in the family as a quasi-natural institution and as necessarily distinct in purpose and origins from the state has, since the nineteenth century, become associated with a corollary assumption: that home and family are also necessarily distinct from the sphere of "the economy." Thus in our contemporary worldview, a description of "worker productivity" does not normally include household tasks unless these tasks are performed for a salary. This belief that activities performed outside the home and particularly outside the system of familial relations are "naturally" different in kind from those performed within the home and family is so endemic to our cultural ideology that it has sometimes been found even among the most radical critics of that ideology, such as Marxists. Thus in a later chapter we shall see how this latter assumption, though antithetical to much in Marx's social theory, also surfaced in significant ways within that theory.

Here I would like to counter this belief by making a similar kind of claim as I did earlier: that the separation of the family and the economy, like the separation of the family and the state, needs to be comprehended as occurring within history. Since what we now perceive as separate spheres have common origins and interrelated histories, we should expect to find important connections between them. Thus, in preindustrial societies kinship embraces much of what we mean by the "economic." This point sometimes gets lost as a function of a prevailing contemporary convention that economic relations revolve primarily around interactions of trade or exchange. However, even as we use the term "economic," a use which reflects its history, economics is most fundamentally about the production and distribution of social resources, of which trade and exchange are only one means. Thus kinship relations, which organize the production and distribution of resources among members of social groups (as well as organizing sexuality, religion, and other human practices) are at least in part about "economics." Following from this point, gender relationships, as historically structured by kinship, have always been at least in part economic relations, a point with important implications for the relation of Marxism and feminism. Moreover, it is not only intersex relations which are economically structured through kinship rules; intergenerational relations are also so structured, as, for example, in inheritance procedures.

The above claims, on the face of it, seem obvious. They require emphasis only as a consequence of the fact that since at least the early modern period (and indeed beginning much earlier), many of the interactions around the production and distribution of resources have become structured increasingly outside the domain of kinship. Before industrialization, this meant primarily a growing sphere of trade governed by principles of exchange. The early modern family/household unit was, however, until industrialization a productive and thus "economic" unit. After industrialization this ceased to be the case. In conjunction with the growth of an "economy" outside of the household, there also developed a more limited meaning of the term "economic," so that it came primarily to refer to the production and exchange of commodities. As a result, it has become increasingly difficult to keep in sight the common origins and interconnections of the familial and the economic. As with the family and the state, these two spheres now appear to exist as worlds apart, with different and unrelated histories and concerns.

Moreover, as with the analogous view on the relation of the family and the state, this latter perspective has raised large obstacles in explicating women's history and women's lives, perhaps because it has been women who have been most strongly affected by the separation. Thus to take this separation for granted and not to focus explicitly on the how and the why of its occurrence has been to overlook a process crucial in understanding women's history. In consequence, comprehending women's history and the changing dynamics of gender has entailed throwing off this belief in necessarily separate spheres and beginning to examine the very history of the separation. Two pathbreaking works on the changing relation of the family and the economy have been Alice Clark's *Working Life of Women in the Seventeenth Century*, published in 1919, and Louise Tilly and Joan Scott's *Women, Work, and Family*, published in 1978. What is revealed in both works is the necessity, for explaining women's history, of developing an organizing framework which traces the changing relation of the familial and the economic. Clark, in explaining the early modern period in England, makes a tripartite distinction between domestic industry, family industry, and capitalist industry. She defines the three as follows:

(a) Domestic Industry is the form of production in which the goods produced are for the exclusive use of the family and are not therefore subject to an exchange or monetary value.

(b) Family Industry is the form in which the family becomes the unit for the production of goods to be sold or exchanged.

(c) Capitalist Industry or Industrialization is the system by which production is controlled by the owners of capital, and the labourers or producers, men, women and children receive individual wages.

Tilly and Scott, in explaining the period from the eighteenth to the twentieth centuries in England and France, employ somewhat different categories, defined as follows:

> In the household mode of production typical of the preindustrial economy, the unit of production was small and productivity was low. All household members worked at productive tasks, differentiated by age and sex. We have called this form of organization the family economy. . . . During industrialization the size of productive units grew and productive activity moved out of the household to workshops and factories. Increasingly, people worked for wages. Early industrialization, particularly in the textile industry, relied heavily on the labor of women and children. Families adapted older expectations about work and strategies of reproduction to the new circumstances. The result was the *family wage economy*. Under this organization the family continued to allocate the labor of its members. Now the household's need for wages rather than for labor determined the productive activity of women when they were daughters as well as wives and mothers. . . . Technological change, the growth of heavy industry, and the increased scale of industrial organization led to increased productivity and greater prosperity by the end of the nineteenth century. . . . The family economy became a *family consumer economy*, as households specialized in reproduction and consumption. Nonetheless, the family continued to allocate the labor of its members. . . . Family needs thus allocated the mother's time away from wage earning and toward domestic responsibilities and child care.[39]

These frameworks enable us to comprehend aspects of women's lives invisible from a perspective which analytically separates family history from economic history. For example, from Clark's work we can understand the consequences for women's lives of the capitalization of the guilds in the context of existing familial relationships. Whereas women as junior partners under family industry could share in their husband's work when he passed from journeyman to master, such status entailed their departure from that work when the crafts became capitalized and he became a wage earner:

> Under family industry the wife of every master craftsman became free of his gild and could share his work. But as the crafts became capitalized many journeymen never qualified as masters, remaining in the outer courts of the companies all their lives, and actually forming separate organizations to protect their interests against their masters and to secure a privileged position for themselves by restricting the number of apprentices. As the journeymen worked on their masters' premises it naturally followed that their wives were not associated with them in their work, and that apprenticeship became the only entrance to their trade. . . . As the journeyman's wife could not work at her husband's trade she must, if need be, find employment for herself as an individual.[40]

Tilly and Scott similarly illustrate the consequences on women's lives of the preindustrial gender division of labor in conjunction with industrialization:

> Under the family wage economy married women performed several roles for their families. They often contributed wages to the family fund, they managed the household, and they bore and cared for children. With industrialization, however, the demands of wage labor increasingly conflicted with women's domestic activities. The terms of labor and the price paid for it were a function of employers' interest, which took little account of household needs under most circumstances. Industrial jobs required specialization and a full-time commitment to work, usually in a specific location away from home. While under the domestic mode of production women combined market-oriented activities and domestic work, the industrial mode of production precluded an easy reconciliation of married women's activities. The resolution of the conflict

was for married women not to work unless family finances urgently required it, and then to try to find that work which conflicted least with their domestic responsibilities.[41]

Moreover, an analysis which focuses on the historical separation of the economic from the familial enables us to see both the economic nature of gender relations within the family and the gendered aspect of economic relations outside it as a consequence of the emergence of the economy out of kinship. This point runs against a liberal perspective which conceptualizes the market as an autonomous realm governed only by forces internal to itself. It also runs counter to the orthodox Marxist dictum that in the interrelation of the economic and the familial, it is always the former and never the latter which is causally prior. However, again from works such as Tilly and Scott's, among others, we can provide counter evidence to both points of view.[42] For example, Scott and Tilly note that young, unmarried women becoming primary workers in many industries in the early stages of industrialization is poorly described as capitalism invading and changing previous familial patterns. Rather they argue that this phenomenon needs to be explained at least in part in terms of preindustrial familial relations which saw women as necessary contributors to family subsistence. They describe the ways in which the conditions in the early factories replicated conditions at home, with factory owners even on occasion taking responsibility for arranging suitable marriages for their female workers.[43] They point to the persistence of the expectation that the wages of these girls would be sent to their families, noting that in some cases the factories sent the girls' wages to their parents while in other cases the girls merely sent most of it themselves.[44]

Of course, industrialization did radically affect kinship relations. Most fundamentally it entailed a general distancing of the household from the productive sphere. This accentuated the development of the idea, discussed in chapter 2, of "separate spheres" for men and women. This idea cannot be described as mere ideology; the lives of many middle class women did conform to the ideal. Moreover, even among the working class, where the ideal was often contradicted, the norm affected, as earlier noted, the perceptions of married women's labor.

Thus the point is not that industrialization and market forces had no effect on preindustrial values and practices; it is rather that the story is poorly understood as one where the causal arrow moves in only one direction. That, for instance, a nineteenth-century woman would become a prostitute to support the rest of her family is a story not only about the commercialization of sex but also about the persistence of familial loyalties in new contexts.[45] This methodological point becomes a political point in our own day as preindustrial values and practices of kinship and gender continue to affect market relationships in the context of a political ideology which denies that possibility. According to this ideology, with the establishment of true equality of educational opportunity, and the abolition of old prejudices about women's capabilities, the criteria of merit and effort alone determine women's participation in the economy. However, as feminists have been pointing out, the problem is not merely one of overcoming old prejudices, but rather of recognizing and coming to alter a contemporary economy long structured by values and practices of kinship and gender. Thus, for the ideology of the free marketplace to become in any way a reality for women requires a recognition of the ways in which that marketplace has been determined by aspects of human existence supposedly localized outside itself.[46]

Moreover—and now I want to take the argument to what I perceive as its most extreme conclusion—comprehending the separation of the economic from the familial as a historical phenomenon enables us to see certain very basic structural components of our economy as rooted in kinship and some of the basic categories we possess for describing it as "familial." In consequence, the connection between the familial and the economic has to be understood as more than causal, but at least in part as analytic. For example, one important category we use in describing our modern economy is the category of "private property." This concept, however, is partially a familial concept, referring to ownership by family units. Thus the increased privatization and alienability of property, usually hailed as a defining component in the rise of capitalism in the early modern period, is also analytically connected with what we mean by the rise of "family" in this period, at least for those of property.

A similar point can be made about many of our categories of class, often generated from the Marxist tradition, which also should be seen as joining together both familial and economic components.

To illustrate this point, let us focus on one element of Lawrence Stone's description of "The Restricted Patriarchal Nuclear Family," the family type he identifies as becoming prominent in England during the period 1550–1700. He notes as an important feature of this family type the increasing tightness of the bonds drawing together parents and children. At first this tightening did not necessarily entail a greater emotional attachment, though it did by later centuries. Rather, at least in its initial form, this drawing in of the family was associated with a growing sense of the family as an active entity internally controlled in the pursuit of the common good.

Natalie Zemon Davis similarly describes what was new:

> Let me begin by noting a central concern of many families in the sixteenth and seventeenth centuries: They want to plan for a family future during and beyond the lifetimes of the current parents. . . . This is not, it should be remembered a "natural" or inevitable way for families to act. It implies a situation unlike that in the early Middle Ages when wives in some landholding families might have closer ties to their family of birth than to their husbands; when family identity might well extend horizontally out to third and fourth cousins with whom one consulted about immediate issues of vengeance and alliance rather than about distant prospects. It implies a situation in which the family unit, whatever its spread, conceived of its future as requiring intervention and effort rather than simple reliance on traditional custom and providence.[47]

A phrase we could use to capture this new family type might be "private enterprise"; that we could do so, however, suggests more than a peripheral connection between the change in family type and what we also associated with the rise of the "bourgeoisie" in this period. The point here is not only that the bourgeoisie, as that class which made its fortunes through trade, evidenced such features as a concern for regulating its future and a focus on a more nuclear family core, but also that such features seem importantly connected with the type of economic activity in which it was engaged.

CONCLUSION

In the previous chapter I argued that an explicitly historical methodology was the only one able to tie together what was most fruitful in contemporary feminist anthropological discussions on the origins of women's oppression. In this chapter I have focused on a further consequence of such an approach: that it gives coherence to feminism's suspicion that contemporary understandings of the necessary distinctiveness of family, state, and economy are mistaken. If we recognize these spheres of society as historical creations, we can comprehend how the family would contain economic and political aspects—since such aspects were inherited from the family's origins in kinship—and we can see the familial components of our political and economic spheres, as these both evolved out of kinship and the family.

We can also see, in addition to certain methodological implications, certain historical patterns. One pattern that appears to emerge is the declining importance of kinship in structuring social life. The very growth of the state in conjunction with the emergence of the modern family attests to the decline of kinship in governing political functions. Similarly, both the development of trade and the decline of production as a domestic activity can be described as constituting the growth of the economic sphere as a non-kinship-governed sphere. Indeed, a major claim in the above, that the social divisions of family, state, and economy need to be understood as modern, might be viewed as a weaker version of the claim that all these forms represent the modern manifestations of the decline of kinship in structuring society. This historical pattern I will also draw on in the next two chapters as I attempt to historically situate the theories of Locke and Marx and further elaborate on the historical context of contemporary feminism.

PART THREE
POLITICAL THEORY

THE EARLIER PART of the book was devoted to analyzing contemporary feminist theory. The purpose was to generate, through both synthesis and criticism, a framework for thinking about gender. I argued the desirability of a historical approach both for dealing with the issue of "origins" and in thinking about our more recent past. To think about origins historically means rejecting the equation of origins with cause and reinterpreting origins as early elements in a long story. To be historical in thinking about our more recent past means seeing that the social divisions described by the categories of family, state, and economy are not natural to the human condition but the product of changes in social organization in the modern period and continuously in flux in the course of this period.

For feminist theory to adopt such a perspective on the categories of family, state, and economy would place it in a distinct relation to modern political theory. As I shall show in this section, two major political theories of the modern West, liberalism and Marxism, have rested on a reification of these categories, that is, they have tended to treat what these categories demarcate as inherently demarcatable. Moreover, this tendency within both theories is not marginal to either. Liberalism at its base is founded on a reification of the categories of family and state, and Marxism is equally founded on a reification of the category of the economic. These constitutive features can be related to changes in Western society occurring in the periods in which both theories arose. Liberalism as a theory reifying the separation of family and state originated in a period when family and state had newly emerged as separate institutions. Similarly, Marxism as a theory reifying the economic was generated in concurrence with the emergence of the economic as a separate sphere out of the household. Both sets of social changes can be understood as manifestations of the gradual decline of kinship in the modern period discussed in the previous chapter. The emergence of family and state meant the depoliticization of kinship and its restriction as a governing principle to such matters as sexuality, inheritance, and household activity. Similarly, the emergence of the social sphere of the economic meant that many forms of labor were no longer organized by rules of kinship.

By adopting such an approach, feminist theory becomes capable of explaining components of gender relations which liberalism and Marxism lack the means to explain. As I shall claim, it is precisely liberalism's and Marxism's reification of the categories of family, state, and economy which make their respective analyses of gender inadequate. To make these arguments I will examine in the following two chapters the work of two theorists central in the exposition of liberalism and Marxism: John Locke and Karl Marx.

CHAPTER FIVE

JOHN LOCKE:
THE THEORETICAL SEPARATION OF
THE FAMILY AND THE STATE

Radical feminism recognizes the oppression of women as a fundamental political oppression wherein women are categorized as an inferior class based upon their sex. It is the aim of radical feminism to organize politically to destroy this sex class system. . . . The oppression of women is manifested in particular institutions, constituted and maintained to keep women in their place. Among these are the institutions of marriage, motherhood, love and sexual intercourse (the family unit is incorporated by the above).
—"Politics of the Ego: A Manifesto for N. Y. Radical Feminists"

To this purpose, I think it may not be amiss, to set down what I take to be Political Power. That the Power of a *Magistrate* over a Subject, may be distinguished from that of a *Father* over his Children, a *Master* over his Servant, a *Husband* over his Wife, and a *Lord* over his Slave.
                              —John Locke, *Two Treatises of Government*

PERIODICALLY in the history of ideas, a theorist appears whose position becomes so widely accepted that the very terms of the debate in which he or she had been a part become changed. That John Locke is such a figure is revealed by contrasting his writings with *Patriarcha*, a work of Sir Robert Filmer to which Locke responded. On reading *Patriarcha*, whose purpose was to defend absolute monarchy on the basis of divine dispensation, one is sharply reminded that not all people have at all times believed in the natural rights and equality of all men. A less obvious though similar kind of transformation between pre- and post-Locke political debate concerns the place of the family in such debate.

While within the period in which Locke was writing, the family served as a central issue for political theory, later this ceased to be so. In part the transformation must be viewed as a consequence of Locke's writing. It is not because Locke did not spend much time discussing the family and the relation of familial to political authority; on the contrary, he spent much time on both. Rather it follows from his conclusions on the necessary distinctiveness of political and familial authority that further political theorists should not continue to conceive of the family as relevant to political analysis. So thoroughly has post-seventeenth-century political theory accepted his conclusion that little attention has even been given to this component of Locke's work. Several centuries before Wittgenstein, Locke was successful in having the ladder upon which his argument rested abandoned after he had reached the conclusion to which it led.

Recently, this ladder has begun to be raised again. Of key importance has been a new attention on Filmer's role in setting the terms for Locke's theory. Underlying Filmer's defense of the divine right of kings was an identification of familial and political authority extending back to Adam. Thus a new focus on Filmer entailed also a new focus on Locke's attack on this identification. Peter Laslett's republication of Filmer's work in 1949, the first republication since 1696, coupled with Laslett's arguments that it was Filmer and not Hobbes who served as Locke's opponent in the important *Second Treatise* as well as in the tedious *First*, must account for some of this change.[1]

A new emphasis on the relation between familial and political authority in Locke has also come from contemporary feminist political theory. When the contemporary women's movement claimed that "The personal is political," sympathetic political theorists recognized the necessity of uncovering the origins of the belief that it is not. Many correctly recognized the importance of Locke as an early exponent of the modern separation of the familial and the political.[2]

Much of this new scholarship by feminist political theorists and others will provide substantiation for claims I wish to advance in this chapter. However, more work is still needed to uncover the full dimensions of the abandoned ladder of Locke's position. In particular I believe that what is yet to be fully elaborated is the nature of Locke's contribution to what is in effect a drastically new conception of social organization, best characterized as a change in social ontology. The new social ontology is one where society is seen as fundamentally demarcated into two necessarily distinct institutions: the family and the state.

Part of the difficulty which we post-Lockeans have in understanding what is new about such a way of dividing up society is that it is so embedded in our own view of social organization as to appear universal to the human situation. Certainly on one level there has been a recognition of Locke's contribution to very basic components of a modern worldview, particularly a recognition of his role in making articulate some of the basic premises of methodological and political individualism. Thus it has been recognized that Locke's theory contributed to a new way of dividing up the world which emphasized the physical and moral inviolability of each individual. Less sufficiently recognized is that connected to this change was another in which the physical and moral inviolability of each family was stressed. As liberalism has been credited with constituting the individual, in all the senses in which we understand that term, so too must it be credited with constituting the family in the most fundamental sense in which we understand that term, specifically as a separate and distinct unit related to a more inclusive governing body. One obstacle which prevents us from fully understanding this change is that we tend not to sufficiently distinguish the concept of family from the concept of kinship. Since kinship seems to be a universal of social organization, and since we tend to equate kinship with family, we tend to view all human societies as possessing families. We fail to see that a central feature of our concept of family is that it is one unit within a larger social whole, and not, as with kinship, a principle governing a social whole. We thus fail to grasp what is unique in our concept of family.

Before proceeding directly to Locke, it might be helpful to briefly clarify some of the components of our concept of family and specifically the idea of the family as a singular unit related to a

larger governing body, such as the state. What is entailed by
viewing the relation of the family to the state in this manner? For
one, such a view entails that one perceive the purposes and needs
which motivate individuals in becoming members of families to
be necessarily different from the purposes and needs which motivate families in becoming members of states. This point can be
illustrated by looking at the issue of needs. Since the early modern
period, it has been widely believed that the needs which motivate
individuals to become members of families are of a fundamentally
different nature from the needs which motivate families to unite
into states. The basic human needs which have been thought to
motivate the creation of families typically include intimacy, affection, sexuality, and mutual care and support. Of course, over the
last several centuries there has been much variability in the exact
specification of such needs and the designation of who possesses
which in what amounts. For example, the need for intimacy and
affection on the part of all family members begins to be stressed
only during the eighteenth century. Also historically variable is
the extent to which sexual needs are attributed to women. However, whatever the particular specification and allocation of needs,
a consistent claim has been made that there are some needs which
underlie the creation of families and which are fundamentally
different from those which underlie the creation of states. Thus,
when the origin of states is discussed, reference is not often made
to needs for sexuality, aid, support, care, or affection. Rather the
quite different need for protection from attack on one's property
has been frequently mentioned. As this point illustrates, and as
we shall see in analyzing Locke, besides assumed differences in
needs, there are also postulated distinctions in how people relate
to nonfamily as opposed to family members.

   This view that human beings are motivated by two quite different
sets of needs to form the necessarily distinct institutions of family
and state reflects the changes in social organization occurring in
the early modern period which were discussed in the preceding
chapter. There it was argued that an older principle of kinship
had become replaced by the dual institutions of family and state,
the former as well as the latter being significantly different from

the common ancestor. In this chapter I would like to analyze Locke's theory as one which reflected and helped to make explicit some of the basic features of this new view of social organization. In so doing, I do not want to imply that Locke was alone in this endeavor. Much in Locke's writings was also being articulated by other theorists of his century. However, as Locke is widely and rightly recognized to be one of the most forceful and consistent representatives of classical liberalism, understood as a theory of the state, so also is he one of the most forceful and consistent representatives of classical liberalism understood as a theory of the family.

Another reason exists for focusing on Locke as a spokesperson of the new worldview. Locke made certain important contributions to a methodological position which has helped obfuscate the very historical nature of this worldview. Locke, in responding to Filmer, did more than challenge Filmer's identification of familial and political authority; he also challenged the relevance of history in justifying political obligation.[3] Whereas Filmer claimed that the origins of government in the family argued for its noncontractual nature, Locke made the issue of origins irrelevant. By so doing, and by employing the heuristic device of a "state of nature," Locke contributed to an important methodological aspect of liberal social theory, its discrediting of history as relevant not only to political justification but more generally to political analysis at all. This book is fundamentally opposed to this latter methodological position. Of course, also here, it is not Locke alone who represents an early exponent of this position. Hobbes, for example, also stands as an important contributor.[4] However, what is most interesting about Locke for our purposes is that, because of his debate with Filmer, his very defense of the new role of the family as an institution separate from the state is connected with his discreditation of history. Thus by focusing on that debate we can see the connection in Locke's theory between the separation of family and state and a particular methodological position on social theory. Moreover, Locke's commitment to both positions shows how he *reified* the separation of family and state, that is, failed to comprehend it as a historical phenomenon.

Thus the argument of this chapter is not only that Locke helped make explicit certain important components of what was in effect a drastically new view of social organization, but also that his methodological contributions to social theory aided in the obfuscation of this very accomplishment. In other words, Locke's discrediting history as a relevant factor in political analysis made it difficult to challenge his own description of social organization as historical. The difficulty continues in our own time, as many of the features of social organization described by Locke continue to be accepted as "natural" and as many theorists continue to accept the position that history is fundamentally irrelevant to political analysis. Both positions prevent an adequate comprehension of gender. To begin to challenge them I would now like to focus explicitly on Locke's debate with Filmer.

LOCKE AND FILMER

For those not familiar with Filmer's position, a brief summary may be helpful. Filmer argued for the absolute sovereignty of monarchs through both a positive position and a negative attack. His positive position rested upon the claim that the authority of kings followed from their authority as heads of families, which could be traced back to Adam. Thus Filmer thought of human society not as resembling one big family but literally as being one big family. Adam as the first father was also the first sovereign, and this sovereignty was passed on through a succession of eldest sons until Noah. Noah divided the world among his sons, and its further division following Babel laid the basis for the emergence of the different states which could be found in the seventeenth century. In his account, Filmer recognized that history did not necessarily reveal neat successions of eldest son succeeding eldest son. Revolutions and lost lines occurred frequently. Filmer argued that in these instances God directly intervened to restore legitimate authority. Thus as Laslett notes, "Filmer nowhere tried to show how Charles I was a direct heir of one of the sons of Noah, but he obviously assumed it. . . ."[5] Noteworthy about this defense of the sovereignty of kings is that it appeals both to an assumed recognition of the authority of fathers and to a story, linked with that found in the Bible, about the history of the world. An account of origins, associated with one which was widely accepted, was thus tied to a moral claim about paternal authority.

Filmer also put forth an attack against a contractarian position. He argued against those who would justify popular rights by an appeal to an original social contract by asking the question, "When and how was such a contract made?" His claim was that for such a contract to be binding a simultaneous and unanimous vote had to be obtained from all those bound by it. He pointed out the difficulty of such conditions ever being fulfilled and indeed impossibility if one took into account children and those yet unborn. However, he argued, one could not avoid the issue of children and the unborn by justifying their allegiance through the votes of their fathers without in turn acceding to the principle of paternal authority.

Filmer's attack against social contractarianism is important, and was given serious attention by Locke. I shall examine Locke's response later. For now, I would like to look more closely at Filmer's positive position. What kind of a position was it and what historically did it represent?

To answer these questions we need to focus on the term "patriarchy." While the term has often come to be used broadly to refer to any situation where men have power over women and children, its original meaning is narrower. In a strict sense the term refers to a type of social organization where power is given to one male figure who claims it by virtue of being the eldest son of the existing head. The model from which the term derives is the ancient Hebrew tribes.[6] The principle of "lordship" in medieval Europe, exemplifying also a transmission of rule to the eldest son, is similar in some respects though different in others. One difference is that "patriarchy" here is allied with a system of vassalage and serfdom. The principle of monarchy, allied to that of lordship, also contains certain similarities with and differences from a pure principle of patriarchy. Like lordship, the rule of monarchs is based on a certain pattern of succession within a kinship network.

However, also like lordship, this basis of rule has been, historically, augmented by other factors, such as vassalage, conquest, and treaty.

The significance of Filmer's position was that it attempted to identify the rule of monarchs with their position as heads of families and thus to ignore the nonpatriarchal basis of monarchical rule. Filmer's move here had certain similarities with other political positions of his time. While few might have been claiming that the king was the literal father of his people, many at least accepted the position that he was *like* a father to his people. Indeed, as many writers have pointed out, familial metaphors were basic to seventeenth-century political thinking. As R.W.K. Hinton, quoting Laslett, notes:

> Thus the family figured in early modern political thinking both as the model of political thinking and also as its actual, if remote, origin. 'All writers,' as Mr. Laslett says, 'shared this preoccupation with the family as the fundamental unit of social relationships.' The family provided them with an insight into what seemed to them to be real and natural in political relationships, in contrast to the artificiality of man-made regulations. What strikes us as metaphor and myth, they turned to as the world of historical reality.[7]

The familial metaphor was used to justify a wide variety of political positions. Thus Hinton remarks on the work of Sir Thomas Smith, *De Republica Anglorium*, written in the reign of Elizabeth I, to make the point that use of the analogy of the family did not even necessarily lead to patriarchalism. Smith supported a voluntarist political position by describing marriage as a partnership.[8] This appeal to the contractual nature of marriage was, however, then used by Royalists to justify *their* position, as supporters of Charles I appealed to the irrevocable and hierarchical nature of the marriage contract to justify the irrevocable and hierarchical relation between a sovereign and his subjects.[9] They in turn were answered by seventeenth-century liberals such as William Bridge, Henry Parker, and Herbert Palmer, who began to question the irrevocable and hierarchical nature of the marriage contract to justify a more

revocable and egalitarian relation between subjects and sovereign.[10]
The point is that, whether it eased their position or made it more
difficult, many political writers of the period felt the need to deal
with a familial metaphor concerning the king's relationship to his
subjects.

Of course, what is distinctive about Filmer's position is that the
relation between sovereign and subjects for which he argues does
not rest upon a familial *metaphor*; rather, he claims the sovereign
is the father of his people in some quite literal sense. Thus we
cannot account for Filmer's position by claiming that a familial
metaphor was then in vogue, since the metaphor as metaphor is
what his position rejects.

To account for the distinctive character of Filmer's position and
its difference from other contemporary political appeals to the idea
of family, we need to turn back to the distinction between the
idea of kinship and the idea of family. Earlier I noted that one
important factor which differentiates the newer concept of family
from an older concept of kinship is that the family is one institution
among many. Allied to this difference, as I remarked earlier, is
the fact that "family," unlike "kinship," describes more what we
understand as the "nuclear family," insofar as it focuses on ties
between spouses and between parents and children rather than
on ties among cousins, between grandparents and grandchildren,
etc., as does kinship. I would claim that Filmer's position in effect
is a defense of the kinship basis of monarchy in a period in which
kinship had already been replaced to a significant extent by the
newer institution of the family. Therefore, as others were using
the analogy of a father's relation to his children when speaking
of the king's relation to his subjects, Filmer was speaking of the
king's relation to his subjects as if they were all one extended
kinship system.[11]

Filmer's position can be seen as a reaction to the new separation
of family and state occurring in his time. It was simultaneously
an attempt to justify the power of the king by appeal to older
principles of social organization which, however, even in their
time had not been about monarchy. By applying the principle of
patriarchy to kings, he thus gave the principle an extension it had

not previously held.[12] In effect, he was putting forth a very antitraditional conception of patriarchy in a period when patriarchy was itself being undermined. In consequence, his position was subject to attack, both as a description of the past and as at odds with his present.

John Locke used both tactics to discredit Filmer. Part of Locke's attack was based on showing that Filmer's account of history could not possibly be valid. For example, Locke rightly took issue with Filmer's description of true patriarchs as monarchs. Filmer frequently drew on the tribes of Israel as representing the best example of monarchy founded on paternal authority. However, Locke remarks that there were no kings to be found within the history of the Jews until "many years after they were a people."[13] Locke also claims that it takes some stretching of the Bible to describe Abraham as a king.[14] Finally, he notes that such kings as Filmer does point to, such as Moses and Joshua, possessed no title of fatherhood.[15]

More relevant for the purposes of this book are Locke's criticisms of Filmer which drew on inconsistencies between Filmer's position and features of the time. By noting those features of Locke's social world he drew on in criticizing Filmer, we can begin to see the historical aspect of Locke's own position.

For example, Locke criticizes Filmer's justification of paternal power as following from the fact that fathers beget their children. Locke notes that mothers also beget their children and therefore ought to be entitled to the same authority over children as fathers.[16] A weakness of Filmer's position is that it attempted to attach to paternal begetting a significance it no longer had, and indeed never had as merely *paternal* begetting. Filmer was looking to the significance of begetting within a traditional patriarchy, where the act of begetting of the patriarch does confirm and pass on the power he possesses as patriarch. But even within a traditional patriarchy, that power does not stem merely from the fact of fatherly begetting but rather from the patriarch's position within a stipulated order of succession. Within a true patriarchy, a father may beget but neither confirm nor pass on any power if, for example, that power is possessed by an older brother. Moreover, within the period in which Filmer was writing and Locke was responding, fatherly power no longer held the political component it had occasionally held. Nor did it possess the same economic significance it had also sometimes held. In the Middle Ages, the passing on of power was also connected with the passing on of property. Thus among the aristocracy, a major purpose of marriage and children was maintaining a proper succession of power and an undivided succession of property. This points to another important difference between the medieval "line" or "house" and the modern "family" which was noted earlier. The modern family increasingly came to be seen as a mutual survival unit, with the existence of the institution possessing little meaning apart from this purpose. This idea of the family is revealed in many of Locke's arguments throughout the *Two Treatises.* For example, Locke argues that since the major function of the family is to raise children, once this function is fulfilled there appears no reason why husbands and wives cannot divorce.[17] Similarly, he claims, attacking primogeniture, that given this function of the family, all children ought to have equal rights of inheritance.[18] One might contrast both claims with the very point of the "line" in the Middle Ages, whose very meaning spoke to an unbroken connection linked with an undivided property.

Another argument Locke makes against Filmer is that the authority of the sovereign cannot be identical to the authority of the father because the sovereign possesses a type of power over his subjects not possessed by the father over his family, the power of life and death. Here again, what Locke could draw on to reinforce his position was a modern distinction between paternal and political power not always present in previous times. Medieval lords certainly did possess the power of life and death over their kin and subjects. True, this power was mitigated, as typically it is with sovereigns. For example, a lord who killed his wife was liable to military revenge on the part of her kin. The point, however, is that in his own way, the lord was once as supreme as kings and as later universal laws were to become. The nature of this supremacy is indicated in the following passage from Lawrence Stone, describing the idea of "kin":

Its psychological manifestation was a particularistic system of values, by which personalized loyalty and lordship was the highest and most prized of qualities taking precedence over those of obedience to the Ten Commandments, of submission to the impersonal dictates of the law, and of deference to the personal authority of the King. It was a bounded, localized, highly personal world, which had yet to be affected by wider notions of loyalty to more universalistic codes and ideals.[19]

Of course, even here the power of the patriarch could not merely be identified with his position as father, as Filmer would have it. It was only *some* fathers who had the power of life and death over kin and subjects. Thus Filmer's problem again was that of attempting to conjoin an older concept of patriarchy with the more modern concept of fatherhood.

One of the most devastating arguments Locke raised against Filmer, which can be described as the problem of "the one and the many," can be similarly explained. Locke correctly raised the following dilemma about Filmer's position: if political sovereignty and fatherhood are identical, then in any given nation there should be as many political sovereigns as there are fathers. This, however, is clearly absurd. Moreover, given Filmer's justification of sovereignty on the basis of succession from Adam, why should there be many kings? As Locke puts it:

If there be more than one heir of Adam, every one is his Heir, and so every one has Regal Power. For if two Sons can be Heirs together, then all the Sons are equally Heirs, and so all are Heirs, being all Sons, or Sons Sons of Adam. Betwixt these two the Right of Heir cannot stand; for by it either but one only Man, or all Men are Kings.[20]

Locke notes that if in fact there is one true heir to Adam, "no body can be obliged to pay obedience to him, till he be known and his Title made out."[21] Obviously, Locke did not believe this last theoretical possibility raised much of a practical objection to his own political views.

The problem of "the one and the many" results from the attempt to conflate patriarchy and fatherhood, or to put the same point in another way, to attempt to apply principles from one form of social organization, patriarchy, to another governed by monarchy and fatherhood. In the latter there is no conflict between there being many fathers and one monarch, since monarchy and fatherhood are independently defined. Nor in a true patriarchy would the problem arise. While here there is a union of political power with principles of kinship, it is not fatherhood alone, in the sense of biological male parenthood, that defines the patriarch. The problem of "the one and the many" only results from attempting to apply the union of kinship and politics to a society possessing monarchs and fathers.

In sum, we might say that a fundamental weakness of Filmer's position, which Locke never explicated but certainly used against Filmer, was that of conjoining principles of an outdated form of social organization with modern institutions. Filmer tried to apply the once real union of kinship and politics found in medieval lordship to a society where lords had become replaced by fathers and kings. Locke could use the inconsistencies which resulted to discredit not only Filmer's position but the general principle of unity of kinship and politics.

While Filmer's position may have suffered from the inappropriateness of connecting principles of the past with institutions of the present, his position was at least strengthened by containing some aspects of the past within it. Locke, on the other hand, could not appeal to the past to justify his own position. What Locke did instead was to eliminate appeals to the past as relevant for political analysis.

LOCKE AND HISTORY

That Locke did not have history on his side was a liability he shared with other Parliamentarians of the sixteenth and seventeenth centuries. The rights of the Commons they were arguing for were innovative. To admit this, however, would have given their opponents a decided debating advantage, for to a very strong degree in the seventeenth century tradition carried moral force. As Pocock points out, in consequence, these Parliamentarians often rewrote English history:

> When Elizabeth I's parliaments began to claim rights that were in fact new, they indeed produced precedents but they did much more. They made their claim in the form that what they desired was theirs by already existing law—the content of English law being undefined and unwritten—and it could always be claimed, in the way that we have seen, that anything which was in the existing law was immemorial. The common lawyers began to rewrite English history on parliamentary lines in the Elizabethan House of Commons. . . . and by the time of the Apology of 1604 the Commons were already insisting that the whole body of their privileges should be recognized as theirs by right of time immemorial.[22]

Locke made such rewriting unnecessary by making history irrelevant. Explicating how Locke did this, however, is complicated. For one, Locke does not specifically elaborate on the issue. Even Locke's often quoted point on the impossibility of deriving normative claims from claims about what has been is inserted parenthetically in a sentence apparently granting history at least some weight:

> For if they can give so many instances out of History, of *Governments begun* upon Paternal Right, I think (though at best an Argument from what has been, to what should of right be, has no great force) one might, without any great danger, yield them the cause.[23]

More seriously, the issue is complicated by the fact that Locke himself employs history, at least in some fashion, in constructing his own substantive position. Thus one cannot say that Locke merely abandons history as a component of political analysis; his position is more ambiguous than that. To cut through some of this ambiguity requires that we turn for the moment to the means by which Locke ultimately justifies his entire political position. With that accomplished, we will then be able to understand the nature of his justification of the separation of the familial and the political as a logical and necessary, and thus not historical, separation.

As is well known, the principal means by which Locke justifies his position is elaboration of a "state of nature." Locke argues that the problems which result from such a state mandate certain responses. However, as commentators on Locke have asked, how do we interpret such a state? Does Locke intend his readers to believe that the state of nature actually existed, or is it sufficient for his arguments that we understand such a state as a hypothetical construct? If Locke's state of nature is interpreted as referring to an actually existing state, then Locke makes his position susceptible to certain criticisms raised initially by Filmer. On the other hand, a reading of Locke's state of nature as a logical construct, while more internally consistent, demands that Locke universalize certain historically specific features of his time. In reference to the major concerns of this chapter, it demands that he universalize the separation of the familial and the political.

Let us begin by interpreting Locke's state of nature as historical. Following from this interpretation, and from certain specific remarks he makes, we could view Locke as holding the following view of history. In the beginning there was just one or a sprinkling of families. At a certain early point, the members assigned political authority to the father. Paternal rule at a later stage in history became supplanted by political societies in the true sense of the word, meaning that political rule did not rest in the hands of one man but was at least partly located in a representative body such as a legislature. Following this reading of Locke, one might claim that Locke's position is not all that different from Filmer's. Like Filmer, Locke would locate paternal rule in the early stages of human history. One difference is that Locke, unlike Filmer, would argue that human societies have, or ought to have, grown out of this earlier mode. A second difference is that Locke would claim that the changes were made possible by compacts entered into by members of the society.

Filmer, since he was writing many decades before Locke, was not responding to such an interpretation of Locke. He was, however, responding to this type of position. Thus Filmer raised the following question of it: if human beings left paternal rule through an act of compact or consent, when did such an act take place? Moreover, as previously noted, how could such an act be binding if not incorporating the unanimous assent of all future as well as present persons subject to it?

These objections of Filmer's would not hold as objections to Locke's position if we interpret the *Two Treatises of Government* as embodying a different relation to history from that represented in the above. According to an alternative reading, while for Locke, all the above stages may be found in history, such historical existence is not necessary to prove his case. Rather we might describe Locke's position as an account of logical possibilities and their relation, and thus his state of nature can be interpreted as a logical construct. This would not entail denying that Locke believed these stages were in fact to be found within history but only that his argument had to rest on such a case.

This reading of Locke, that actual history stands to his stages as representing possible though not necessary instances of them, can be elaborated to incorporate his doctrine of consent. In this elaboration, actual acts of consent in history would be viewed as the occasions on which persons came to embody that which was justifiable independent of such acts. This elaboration is in accord with a reading of Locke suggested by John Dunn, which interprets acts of consent as serving as the occasion by which political obligation is incurred but not that which grounds political obligation.[24] Expanding on this point, Dunn suggests an analogy in Locke between acts of consent and acts of assent:

> There is an illuminating analogy between the way in which Locke talks of consenting to authority in this way and his conception of assenting to the truth of beliefs about the world. Occasionally he even uses consent and assent inter-

changeably. The notion of a truth is not contingent on whether individuals *do* assent to it—but the only way in which it can be known to be true is in such an assent. Men have a responsibility to "regulate" their assent; they have cognitive duties and they have a duty not to assent to false ideas. There is an order of potentially recognized legitimacy and potentially apprehended truth; the order of nature. There are also orders of authorized legitimate governments and systematically apprehended truths: the orders of political society and of science.[25]

Dunn's use of the phrase "an order of potentially recognized legitimacy and potentially apprehended truth," conjoined with his analogy of science and society, suggests that we ought to interpret the different social stages of Locke's in parallel with an evolutionist theory of science: as precursors to the truth, not completely wrong but not completely right either. Elaborating on this model, we might say that as the limits of a scientific law can be shown by extending the conditions under which it is tested, so also the limits of the earlier forms of social organization have been revealed as their conditions of application have been broadened. Thus for Locke, in the beginning of human history when land was plentiful enough and the earth's population small enough so that families could remain apart, people did not need to distinguish political from familial authority and placed political rule in the father. For Locke, this was an understandable as well as a rational arrangement. It was understandable in that the children of the father were accustomed to obeying him, and it was rational in that they could justifiably rely on his paternal affection to secure their property and interest.[26] Also, Locke claims that the presence of mutual affection and a low standard of living, which made checks against internal conflict less necessary than defenses against foreign invasion, further argued for the rationality of this type of rule.[27] Using even stronger language, Locke defends the wisdom of paternal rule in such circumstances:

And unless they had done so, young societies could not have subsisted: without such nursing Fathers tender and careful of the public weale, all Governments would have sunk under the Weakness and Infirmities of their Infancy; and the Prince and the People had soon perished together.[28]

The problem, however, is that while paternal rule might be a rational form of government in certain circumstances, those which we might reasonably, though again not necessarily, attribute to the early stages of human history, it does suffer from certain fundamental liabilities. These become evident when, analogously to a scientific law, the range of circumstances under which paternal rule is applied are enlarged. When such circumstances come to include "Ambition" and "Luxury" and those which "taught Princes to have distinct and separate Interests from their People[,] Men found it necessary to examine more carefully *the Original* and Rights of *Government*."[29] What they found or could find under such circumstances was the truth that government which is in the hands of one man contains a fundamental weakness: that there is no means of resolving conflict between the interests of the ruler as an individual and the interests of those over whom he rules. Also that which they found or could find under such circumstances was the truth that political and paternal authority are distinguishable, even when embodied in one man.[30]

One might argue in response to this reading of Locke that while it may be preferable to read his series of stages as representing logical possibilities and thus his state of nature as a theoretical construct, it is mistaken to read the relation among the stages as representing logical, or more accurately described, epistemological, advance. One might claim that the truths which are uncovered with the advent of ambition and luxury hold only when ambition and luxury are to be found and are not therefore to be understood as universal. In short, one might advance a relativist reading of Locke.

I believe, however, that such a reading will not hold. For one, there are the many passages in Locke's writings where he claims that what is explicitly discovered with the advent of greed and ambition has always been true, for example, as previously referenced, that paternal and political rule are always distinguishable.

Moreover, langauge such as that which was earlier quoted—"Men found it necessary to examine more carefully *the Original* and Rights of *Government"*—strongly suggests that for Locke what history provides are the circumstances in which people come to see certain truths, not the circumstances in which certain propositions become true. Thus Locke would argue that the fundamental weakness of monarchy, that there is no means of separating the interests of the monarch as individual from his interests as ruler, exists even when other factors make monarchy highly rational.

However, if, in spite of the above, a sufficiently strong case could be made for interpreting Locke as a relativist, my response would be positive. The argument of this chapter is directed against Locke as a universalist and as committed to defending as universal certain claims, particularly the necessary separation of the political and the familial. If Locke's universalism is itself abandoned, so is the need for this argument. However, my belief is that what has made Locke so fundamental as a modern theorist follows from a reading of his work which is not relativistic. Thus it is against a universalist reading that this chapter is directed, and it is of such a reading that I would now like to ask: do the theses which the theory reveals in fact represent universal truths, or are they theses true only in certain circumstances?

The question I am raising may be described in a different way. Sometimes when Locke's state of nature is described as a logical construct, what is meant is that this state describes general problems of human existence to which his theory of government can be viewed as a solution. If, however, the conditions described by his state of nature could be shown to be of limited applicability, and were themselves historical, then the generality and ahistoricity of his solution could also be called into question. In short, the following argument would in effect be made: that Locke's theory was essentially historical in spite of an interpretation deliberately designed to avoid history.

This type of criticism of Locke has been made by others. Most prominently, C. B. Macpherson has argued that Locke's state of nature is in effect a very bourgeois world, populated by persons with bourgeois values, needs, and attitudes toward self and others.

Macpherson argues that some of the contradictions within the bourgeois conception of human nature surface within Locke's state of nature, particularly the contradiction between the belief that all men are rational and social beings, capable of living without a state, and the belief that some men are not so rational and not so social.[31] Given such premises, Locke's conclusions follow. The issue, however, concerns the generality of the premises. Similarly, I wish to argue that Locke's contentions in *Two Treatises* on the relation of familial and political authority follow only given the acceptance of certain premises which are of limited historical applicability.

THE FAMILY AND THE STATE

When Locke discusses the relation of familial and political authority, his tone becomes stipulative. Frequently at these points, Locke does not so much provide reasons as merely assert the distinction. The following passages reveal this tendency:

> That the Power of a *Magistrate* over a Subject, may be distinguished from that of a *Father* over his Children, a *Master* over his Servant, a *Husband* over his Wife, and a *Lord* over his Slave.[32]

> But these two *Powers, Political* and *Paternal, are so perfectly distinct* and separate; are built upon so different Foundations, and given to so different Ends, that every Subject that is a Father, has as much a *Paternal Power* over his children, as the Prince has over his. . . .[33]

Of course, as this last quotation illustrates, Locke believes that the necessary distinctiveness of political and paternal authority follows from the different ends which are embodied in political and conjugal society. The end of political society is most basically the preservation of property. This end is jeopardized where there exists no common judge to regulate controversy.[34] The primary end of conjugal society, on the other hand, is procreation and the raising of children. For Locke, because the female of the human species is capable of bearing a child before older children can care for themselves, she needs the help of another during her child-bearing years. For this reason, the ties binding males and females are longer than among "other creatures."[35] As a consequence of this primary purpose of conjugal society, other secondary purposes develop such as "mutual Support, and Assistance and a Communion of Interest too, as necessary not only to unite their Care, and Affection, but also necessary to their common Off-spring, who have a Right to be nourished and maintained by them, till they are able to provide for themselves."[36] Locke on some occasions also speaks of the family as providing the means for regulating inheritance, though he is ambiguous on whether this is primarily for the benefit of the father or the children.

In the earlier discussion on Filmer I noted some of the connections between this type of position and those social changes occurring in the early modern period which were described earlier. For example, it was noted that Locke's views on the family as being concerned with mutual support and the raising of children and not, for example, with the regulation of crime and punishment, reflected real changes in the meaning and province of kinship in the early modern period. Not noted earlier but also important is the connection between such views and the increasing "privatization" of property which was an important feature of the early modern period; that social unit under whose control property rested had grown smaller. Given a social organization composed of relatively small property units, whose members saw their interests in common and opposed to the interests of those outside such units, the kinds of distinctions Locke draws follow easily.

In this section I would like to further elaborate this type of argument but through a different means. Here I would like to reveal the historical embeddedness of Locke's position by focusing on certain features of his descriptions of political and conjugal society which from our vantage point must appear inconsistent. As I have argued, Locke's position reflects a change in social organization wherein a relatively nuclearized family unit was emerging out of older, more extended kinship systems in conjunction with the growth of the modern state. This nuclearized family unit was both modern in many respects and contained certain inherited features from the past. It was modern in that it evidenced within itself aspects of the individualism, instrumentalism, and egalitarianism which were increasingly characterizing social relations in the political and economic realms. It also contained features from past principles of kinship which were anti-individualistic, anti-instrumental and antiegalitarian. In part, we in the twentieth century can now see many of these tensions in the seventeenth-century family and between it and the political realm as a consequence of the fact that the family has become in the intervening centuries more consistently individualistic, instrumental, and egalitarian, and thus more in synchrony with social relations in the political and also the economic sphere. As a result we tend to see as outdated many of the patriarchal features of the seventeenth-century family. Insofar as these features reveal themselves in Locke's writings, we tend to see them as unfortunate historical baggage of his time, in distinction from the more individualistic, and the more frequently perceived as "universal," components of his writings. In the following I will show the connection between the nature of the distinction Locke makes between the familial and the political and such obviously outdated features of his writings. I also will note the inconsistencies between the grounds he provides for this distinction and the more individualistic components of his theory, which have become an even more integral part of our own society than they were of Locke's. Thus the point of this argument is to show that Locke's separation of the familial and the political is connected with a specifically seventeenth-century "dual vision." This dual vision, while ancestral to one remaining today, is not the same as the one of today. Our contemporary dual vision, as more thoroughly individualistic, rests on different and indeed more precarious grounds. Thus while we might look to Locke's arguments as supporting a form of a separation of the familial and the political ancestral to our own, we cannot look to Locke's arguments to support our own version of this separation. In sum, if the point of the earlier discussion on Filmer was to begin to reveal the historicity of Locke's position by contrasting it with a more ancient one, the point of the present discussion is to reveal this same historicity by contrasting that position with a more modern one.

I would like to begin by focusing on that within Locke's arguments which must appear to us as obviously outdated. It is helpful to look at two of the conditions Locke believes are necessary to take men out of the state of nature:

> *First,* there wants an *establish'd,* settled, known *Law,* received and allowed by common consent to be the standard of Right and Wrong, and the Common measure to decide all Controversies between them. . . .
>
> *Secondly,* In the State of Nature there wants a *known and indifferent Judge,* with Authority to determine all differences according to the Established Law.[37]

For Locke neither of these conditions is required in the governance of the family. He admits possible conflicts of interest between husband and wife, but claims that in these instances the ultimate determination should rest with the husband, as "the abler and stronger."[38] He points out that the authority of the husband covers only matters of common concern and does not entail any powers of life and death. Despite such qualifications, an obvious problem remains: why are strength and ability sufficient grounds for allocating authority in conjugal but not political society? As Lorenne Clark notes, whereas Locke does not believe differences in men concerning their strengths, abilities, ages, etc., override their equality with respect to the right of autonomy, he does believe such differences between women and men override their equality with respect to this right.[39]

Even if we ignore Locke's arguments giving authority to the husband rather than the wife, there remains the separable issue of why he does not believe that some "common judge" is also required within the family. One possibility is that, for Locke, property is "common" within the family but not within the state. Thus he explicitly notes that it is only over common property that the husband does have authority. Moreover it is this belief in the "communality" of property within the family but not within the state which underlines the differences in the ends of both, as previously described. It is the lack of common property in the state but not the family which makes preservation of property the purpose of the former but not of the latter. It is because property is common within the family that the raising of children is made possible. In short, it appears that Locke's description and arguments on the differences between the family and the state rely heavily on a belief in the communality of property in the former but not the latter.

That Locke believes in the communality of property within the family is, of course, not surprising. It is not until the nineteenth century that the issue of married women retaining control over property becomes a significant political issue. A point, however, that has been insufficiently noted about Locke's theory of the communality of family property is that it conflicts with the individualistic assumptions underlying his labor theory of property. Throughout Locke's elaboration of that theory he assumes that labor is primarily an individual activity and that the fruits of labor are individually owned. Both assumptions are illustrated in the following passage:

> The *Labour* of his Body, and the *Work* of his Hands, we may say, are properly his. Whatsoever then he removes out of the state that Nature hath provided, and left it in, he hath mixed his Labour with, and joyned to it something that is his own, and thereby makes it his *Property*. It being by him removed from the common state Nature placed it in, hath by this *labour* something annexed to it, that excludes the common right of other Men. For this Labour being the unquestionable Property of the Labourer, no Man but he can have a right to what that is once joyned to, at least where there is enough, and as good left in common for others.[40]

Locke on one occasion extended his position to include the labor of women. In speaking of the rights of women and children to the estate of the father in the event of conquest, Locke argues:

For as to the Wife's share, whether her own Labour or Compact gave her a Title to it, 'tis plain, Her Husband could not forfeit what was hers.[41]

However, nowhere does Locke reconcile this latter claim, which rests upon an individualistic theory of property ownership, with his more frequently asserted one that the husband has control over that part of his wife's property which he jointly shares with her. This latter position is only made possible through a view of property ownership which is not individualistic; why, given any consistent individualism, would one person hand over the control of their property to another?[42]

This ambiguity in Locke between a communal and individualistic theory of property ownership is related to another ambiguity in his theory, that concerning women's political representation. One can find good grounds in his writings in support of either side of this question. In part the ambiguity here stems from an ambiguity in his use of the word "property," noted by C. B. Macpherson. Sometimes by property Locke means "life, liberty, and estate"; sometimes he means only goods or land. Macpherson concludes that since it is for the sake of the protection of property that civil society is formed, men without goods or land are, for Locke, both in and not in civil society.[43] The point here obviously holds also for women. Insofar as they are not owners of property, their property being for the most part that of their husbands, they are not members of civil society. Insofar as they too have "life and liberty" which requires protection, they too then ought to be entitled to membership.

The point of discussing these inconsistencies and ambiguities in Locke is not to show the weaknesses of a theorist so many have admired. At least some of the problems noted in the above could be resolved in ways which have been employed by liberalism in succeeding centuries. Locke could explicitly define property to include "life and liberty" and extend the suffrage to all adults. He could make joint property within marriage a function of explicit contract and under equal control of husband and wife. He could extend the rule of the "common judge" in the state to cover many conflicts within the family, taking authority away in these cases from the male head of household. He could in short make his theory more consistently individualistic in the same manner in which Western European and American society has itself become.

The point, however, is that if Locke were to amend his theory to reflect twentieth-century as opposed to seventeenth-century Western society, he would be defending a separation of the familial and the political that would be different from and, in many ways, more problematic than his own. Since he could not assume that control of property rested with the husband, he would have to bring in the state to regulate conflicts of interest within the family in regard to such property, in the same way it regulates conflicts among nonfamily members. This need for state intervention to resolve conflicts within the family would extend also beyond matters of property, since in regard to any issue, without an assumption that strength and ability provide justifiable grounds for resolving conflict, there emerges the need for a "common judge." Thus, if Locke were to abandon the patriarchal components of his writing, the line separating issues which are the province of the family from issues which are the province of the state must shift. However, it is not only that the line separating the familial from the political need be drawn differently if Locke's theory were to be made more consistently individualistic, but also that the grounds offered for the purpose of this line would have to be changed. Locke argues that the purpose of the family is to support women through the rearing of children. As Lorenne Clark cogently remarks, this purpose only arises once women's control over property has already been denied.[44] If we conjoin the possibility of women having independent control of property with modern methods of birth control, or alternatively raise the possibility of a form of social organization where women's sustenance is provided by other means, then Locke's argument loses much of its force. This is not to say that other grounds for and other versions of Locke's separation of the familial and the political cannot, and indeed, have not been developed to reflect changing conditions and a more widespread individualism. One can, of course, talk about the family as a place of equals, regulated by explicit contract, for the purpose of the sharing of affection and the raising of children. One would in consequence, however, be talking about a type of family with a type of relationship to the state which is not that of Locke.

This is not a trivial claim. It goes against a very widespread tendency to view the family, the state, and their relation ahistorically, i.e., as uniform over time. This tendency is reinforced by certain beliefs we have inherited from Locke regarding the origins or foundations of these institutions. Following Locke we tend to see the family and the state as products of a social contract, explicitly or implicitly continually renewed. History becomes irrelevant following such a position insofar as the terms which make up the contract are viewed as the best or only ones possible to solve problems endemic to the human condition. If we recognize that the problems such terms respond to are historical, so also must we recognize the historicity of the institutions of family and state, as institutional solutions.

In other words, in accord with the argument of the previous chapter, there is no cross-cultural family, no cross-cultural state, and no cross-cultural relation between the two. Both the family and the state are primarily modern institutions, whose internal content and external relation with each other have been in continuous flux during the course of this period. Certainly there have been other periods in history which have created institutions somewhat similar to certain versions of the modern family and state. As previously noted, classical Greek society might be one such example, making understandable a similarity between Locke's and Aristotle's separation of the political and the familial.[45] The historical specificity of these institutions does mean, however, that when theorists such as Locke or others claim that the political is distinct from the familial, one is justified in responding, yes, for certain periods in history, though even then we need to know "which political" and "which familial" the theorist means to determine the specific import of the claim.

FEMINIST POLITICAL THEORY

I have been arguing that Locke's political theory expressed a dual vision of its time. That dual vision surfaced not only in his separation of political and conjugal society but also within his account of conjugal society. That account contained both features of the family's medieval, anti-individual, and antiegalitarian past and also features of its more modern present. Before concluding this chapter, I would like to suggest ways in which the above analysis might resolve and supplement certain discussions within current feminist theory on Locke.

For one, I believe it might help us to see the difficulties involved in trying to answer a question often raised in this literature, whether Locke's position was "feminist" or not; we might become inclined to suspect the usefulness of the question. Some theorists, such as Zillah Eisenstein, have rightly wished to stress the patriarchal, medieval component of Locke's treatment of the family. Eisenstein claims that ". . . Locke differentiates between family and political rule in order to free the market from paternalist, autocratic relations, rather than to free the family from paternal rule."[46] Lorenne Clark appears to articulate a similar position. Clark recognizes that Locke's depiction of familial relations is much less patriarchal than might be expected, given the views of his time. However, her argument suggests that this results only from his need to undermine the concept of patriarchal government.[47] Both Eisenstein and Clark may indeed be correct. That fact need not, however, undermine the type of position represented by other theorists, such as Mary Lyndon Shanley and Melissa Butler, who have wished to stress the contractual and thus antipatriarchal aspect of Locke's treatment of the family.[47] Any inclination to see an inconsistency in these positions, in determining the extent of Locke's feminism, is countered by the recognition that the new family Locke's theory was describing was both being affected by new social relations in the state and economy and was, as a product of its past, antithetical to such relations.[49]

The above emphasis on the historical context of Locke's position may help us see that, for our purposes, what is important about

Locke has less to do with his specific stances on women and more to do with the nature of his articulation of the separation of the familial and the political. While the changes in society this articulation reflected were in many respects liberating for women, the grounds which Locke and others have used to justify it now serve as a very real impediment.

For one, basic to the Lockean position is a conception of the relatively nuclearized family as transhistorical, as a rational solution to biological dictates. Thus Locke justifies the family on the grounds that human infants need care for long periods of time. That women are able to bear successive children even when younger children are still dependent places individual women, according to Locke, in a necessarily dependent position on individual men. Some of the fallacies of this argument were earlier noted, for example, that even if infant dependency entails adult female dependency, it does not entail female dependency on one man; an individual woman could be dependent on other nonchildbearing women or any combination of males and nonchildbearing females. Most generally, what is wrong with this appeal to biology to explain the family is that it prevents us from understanding the family in historical terms. Such a dehistoricization is fatal for comprehending gender, since it is importantly through understanding the history of the family and its relation to nonfamilial institutions as well as the prehistory of the family in institutions of kinship, that we will be able to comprehend that history of gender which has brought us to our present. Moreover, such a biologization of the modern family serves to freeze those gender relations expressed in it, to conceptualize them also as grounded in biology. Thus Locke could not comprehend the dominance of men over women in the family of his time as an inheritance of older patriarchal kinship patterns, but instead sought out biological explanations, such as that men are "stronger" and "abler." When similar arguments are used today, the effect is to rule out the possibility of change.

Also basic to the Lockean view we inherit today is a conception of the state or politics as nongendered. As with the family, the state is perceived of as a rational solution to certain problems endemic to the human condition, though in the case of the state, such problems only become manifest in later, complex societies. On the Lockean view, there is no account of why one gender rather than another has predominated in its governance. Insofar as this issue has been addressed, appeals to biology, again, have often been made. Here, as in the account of the family, the problem stems from a failure to understand the state as a product of history.

A historical perspective on the state strengthens some aspects of Filmer's critique of Locke. For example, Filmer was correct in noting a major fallacy of Locke's contractarian justification of the state, that it is impossible to envision any point in time when such a contract could be or could have been made which would make it a genuine contract for all past, present, and future citizens.[50] Filmer's alternative, to justify a patriarchal state by appeals to the claim that a patriarchal state has always been found in history, is, of course, equally problematic. We in the modern period long ago abandoned appeals to the past as sufficient grounds of justification. Unfortunately, however, with the abandonment of history as sufficient grounds of justification we also have abandoned it as a component of analysis. This abandonment serves, in our own time, the same conservative function as Filmer's position served in his. Certainly, this is true for our understanding of gender.

Thus more important for contemporary feminist theory than Locke's specific position on women's place is the kind of argument he advances for thinking about social theory. Certainly the ramifications for explicating gender by countering his type of method through an explicitly historical approach are enormous. Not only would such an approach transform predominant conceptions of the family and the state, but it would also transform our understanding of a set of psychological characteristics and modes of behavior which have become associated in the modern period with the private world of the family and the public world of the state. The significance of this point may be noted by looking at certain suggestions made by Jean Elshtain on this separation. Elshtain, drawing on the work of Roberto Unger, makes an interesting connection between Locke's distinction between private and public and the liberal epistemological distinction between reason and desire. Thus following from her arguments, both Locke's epistemology and political theory represent a complimentary contribution to an emerging worldview where rationality becomes joined with that which is public and desire becomes separated from both in the sphere of the private:

> The presumption that human beings are rational, metaphysically free, prudential calculators of marginal utility—and all think alike in this regard in the public sphere of politics and understanding—is used as a contrast model for the qualities and activities in a private world from which the public sphere is bifurcated theoretically. The public realm and "public mind" exist as defenses against the private sphere in which desire, conceived as uncontrolled and arbitrary, is held to rank supreme. Again, Unger: "In our public mode of being we speak the common language of reason, and live under laws of the state, the constraints of the market and the customs of the different social bodies to which we belong. In our private incarnation, however, we are at the mercy of our own sense impressions and desires."[51]

Elshtain comments on this epistemological view, noting that it is plausible to argue that "human beings differ from one another less by what they desire and need . . . than by what they 'understand' in an abstract and formal sense, but may neither need nor desire."[52] In criticizing liberalism's separation of reason and desire, Elshtain joins a prominent twentieth-century epistemological movement which one might plausibly attribute to the breakdown of the separation of private and public in twentieth-century society. The point I wish to stress is that this separation of reason and desire might be interestingly elaborated to historically explicate modern notions of masculinity and femininity. Insofar as the public world of the state became associated with both reason and masculinity and the sphere of the family with desire and femininity, so were the conditions established for the modern association of reason with masculinity and desire with femininity. Indeed, the separation of public and private in the modern West can be correlated with a variety of gender-coded psychic separations, pitting reason not only against desire but also against emotion in general. This contrast reflects the different types of concerns which came to dominate the respective spheres of private and public. As Larry Blum argues:

> The male world of work in corporate and governmental bureaucracies requires a *certain* kind of 'universalistic' outlook (though this outlook is ultimately compatible with serving private or parochial interests), a suppression of personal emotion, and adherence to procedures which abstract from personal attachment, inclination, concern for particular others. Similarly love, personal attachment, emotional attachment, emotional support and nurturance are appropriate to the distinctive tasks of the family. To the extent that men are allotted to the former realm and women to the latter, different sorts of attributes and characteristics will be required of the different sexes. And society will have to provide a form of sex-differentiated socialization which prepares men and women for their societal roles.[53]

In sum, to see private and public historically provides us with the initial framework for creating a history of gender in the modern period, a history we have only begun to write.

CONCLUSION

For feminist theory to reject that conceptualization of the family, the state, and their relation found in classical liberal theory would be to take a position toward which it is already strongly inclined. The type of position on family and state I have argued for in this chapter and in the one preceding represents only a fuller articulation of a position already found in various forms in both the women's movement and feminist theory. But from the arguments in the preceding we might also see why this might be the case, that is, we might relate our own social context which has produced a women's movement inclined to be suspicious of inherited conceptions of family and state with the social context which created a theorist such as Locke who contributed to the articulation of these conceptions.

As argued, Locke's theory expressed a dual vision. One component of this vision was a new stress on the individual with an accompanying belief in equality, autonomy, and social relations of competition and exchange. The other component was that inherited from the past and was expressed in a partial view of the family as communal, hierarchical, and based on social relations of obligation and concern. This duality of Locke's vision was not an incidental component of his theory. To justify a new political sphere based on individual autonomy or the "rights of man" necessitated that Locke separate, as the world in which he was writing was itself separating, the political and the familial.

Liberalism from the seventeenth to the twentieth century has become more pervasively individualistic. This has reflected changes in the family and in the relation of its members to the state. In most Western countries the male head of household no longer "represents" the family in the state; both husband and wife possess suffrage and relate to the state as individuals. That the individual has replaced the family as the primary political unit parallels the succession of an economy based on rural households to one based on individual wage earners.

However, the duality of Locke's vision is still with us, in our own twentieth-century version. Our version is in many ways more precarious and problematic than the one of the seventeenth century, particularly for women. As I argued in chapter 2, because it is women whose identity has been more closely tied to the family, it is women's lives, particularly over the past two centuries, which have more acutely expressed the conflict between an expanding individualism and an older conception of the family. I argued that this conflict underlies the emergence of the women's movement in the nineteenth century. In the twentieth century, an important manner in which the conflict has expressed itself has been in a self-conscious questioning of the separation of the personal and the political. This questioning became most articulate in the expression "The personal is political" and through radical feminism, which created the expression. Thus in one sense, twentieth-century radical feminism might be seen as the contemporary rejoinder to a view of social organization first importantly articulated by Locke.

CHAPTER SIX

KARL MARX:
THE THEORETICAL SEPARATION OF
THE DOMESTIC AND THE ECONOMIC

In other words, the system of political economy does not produce only the individual as labor power that is sold and exchanged; it produces the very conception of labor power as the fundamental human potential. More deeply than in the fiction of the individual freely selling his labor power in the market, the system is rooted in the identification of the individual with his labor power and with his act of "transforming nature according to human ends." . . . *And in this Marxism assists the cunning of Capital.*
—Jean Baudrillard, *The Mirror of Production*

As LOCKE'S WRITINGS in the seventeenth century expressed the historical separation of kinship and state taking place in his time, so also in the eighteenth and nineteenth centuries a new branch of study arose, economic theory, which expressed a comparable separation of the economy from both the state and kinship taking place in these centuries. While nascent versions of an "economy" can be traced back at least to the Middle Ages, it was only by the eighteenth century that this sphere became independent enough to generate its own body of theory, constructed in the writings of such figures as Smith, Ricardo, and Marx.

Distinguishing Karl Marx in this list, not only from Smith and Ricardo but even more strongly from economic theorists who were to come later, was his recognition that the seemingly autonomous operation of the economy belied its interdependence with other aspects of social life. Marx, more than most economic theorists, had a strong sense of history and in consequence was aware of the origins of contemporary economic relations in older political and familial relations and the continuous interaction of state, family, and economy even in the context of their historical separation. However, while Marx more than most economic theorists was aware of the interconnection of family, state, and economy, his theory did not consistently abide by this awareness. Most important, the assumption common to much economic theory, that there is cross-culturally an economic component of human existence which can be studied independently from other aspects of human life, exists as a significant strand within his writings, and most prominently in what might be called his philosophical anthropology or cross-cultural theory on the nature of human life and social organization. Indeed, Marx, by building a philosophical anthropology on the basis of this assumption, developed and made more explicit that very perspective in much other economic theory which in other contexts he criticized.[1]

This inconsistency makes Marx a crucial figure for feminist theory. In the previous chapter I argued that Locke, by obscuring the separation of family and state as historical, contributed to a perspective on the analytic distinctiveness of these realms which has been harmful for understanding gender. Similarly, I would claim that feminist theory needs to challenge that prevalent modern assumption on the autonomy of the economic which has been equally harmful for comprehending gender. Yet in this respect feminist theory has in Marx both a strong ally and a serious opponent. As we shall see, feminists can employ much of the historical work of Marx and many Marxists in comprehending both the evolution of the separation of family, state, and economy and their interaction. On the other hand, Marx's philosophical anthropology raises serious obstacles for Marxism's understanding of gender, and thus its ability to become an ally of feminism.

MARX'S MATERIALISM

A concept which lies at the center of Marx's views on human life and social organization is the concept of materialism. It is a concept around which there has been much controversy in the various interpretations of Marx. The earliest interpreters, such as Engels, Plekhanov, and Lenin, developed a reading of Marx, labeled "dialectical materialism," which emphasized the continuities between human and natural phenomena and their common comprehension in scientific law.[2] This interpretation was in turn challenged by a variety of writers who found components in Marx's writings which stressed the distinctiveness of human thought and action. An example here is Jürgen Habermas, who, within the tradition of critical theory, has described his project as the creation of a "reconstructed materialism."[3] Many socialist feminists, in the attempt to integrate aspects of Marx's theory with a feminist approach, have stated their intent to build a "feminist materialism."[4] Thus it appears that any adequate analysis of Marxism must come to grips with this concept and answer the question: what is Marx's materialism?

Part of the difficulty involved in answering this question, and one of the reasons why a variety of answers has been given to it, is that there are very few passages in Marx's works where he explicitly elaborates the meaning of this very basic concept in his theory. Moreover, those passages where he does so are highly ambiguous. The ambiguity is illustrated in the well-known description of his theory in the preface to *The Contribution to the Critique of Political Economy*:

> The general conclusion at which I arrived and which, once reached, became the guiding principle of my studies can be summarized as follows. In the social production of their existence, men inevitably enter into definite relations, which are independent of their will, namely relations of production appropriate to a given stage in the development of their material forces of production. The totality of these relations of production constitutes the economic structure of society, the real foundation, on which arises a legal and political superstructure and to which correspond definite forms of social consciousness. The mode of production of material life conditions the general process of social, political and intellectual life. It is not the consciousness of men that determines

their existence, but their social existence that determines their consciousness.[5]

In this passage there are five phrases which appear to be key in indicating what Marx considered primary for explaining social life: (1) "the social production of their existence," (2) "the development of their material forces of production," (3) "the economic structure of society," (4) "the mode of production of material life," and (5) "their social existence." The specific meaning of many of these phrases is unclear, and their relationship to each other also is not clear. Particularly problematic is the last sentence claiming that social existence "determines" consciousness.

Following the death of Marx, many of his early interpreters chose to interpret such passages as the above and particularly its last sentence as indicating a commitment of Marx to an ontology composed of two elements: the material and the mental, being and consciousness. The accompanying belief was that Marx's materialism could at least partly be defined in terms of giving causal priority to the former as opposed to the latter. Thus Marxism as social theory came to be viewed as spotlighting the material or physical conditions of human existence: the physiological conditions of human behavior, the natural environment upon which the behavior acts and the physical aspect of such behavior itself. What was seen as differentiating Marx from earlier materialists was that he was also "dialectical," meaning that he viewed such conditions in interaction with each other. Because of this stress on interaction, Marx appeared to be following a certain tradition set by Hegel. Marx, however, was said to "stand Hegel on his feet" by giving his dialectics a natural content. This interpretation was well supported by much in Marx's writings:

Since we are dealing with the Germans, who are devoid of premises, we must begin by stating the first premise, namely, that men must be in a position to live in order to be able to "make history." But life involves before everything else eating and drinking, a habitation, clothing and many other things. The first historical act is thus the production of the means to satisfy these needs, the production of material life itself.[6]

This interpretation of Marxism contains a number of problems. To posit a dichotomy between "social being" and "consciousness" leaves one with the difficulty of explaining how the conscious element can be removed from social existence. Moreover, as is clear from many passages in Marx's writings, Marx himself did not believe this was possible. He states, for example, that human activity is conscious activity, as manifested in the universality of its object.[7] He also frequently argues that human needs are historically variable. It is difficult understanding this latter claim without attributing to human needs at least a partial cognitive content.

Many of the writers in sympathy with a more humanistic Marxism have attempted to avoid such difficulties through what might be labeled a "praxis" or "instrumentalist" elaboration of materialism. It is well represented in Shlomo Avineri's *The Social and Political Thought of Karl Marx*. In this work Avineri interprets the dichotomy that Marx creates between foundation and superstructure or life and consciousness not as a distinction between "matter" and "spirit" but rather as a distinction "between conscious human activity, aimed at the creation and preservation of the conditions of human life, and human consciousness, which furnishes reasons, rationalizations and modes of legitimization and moral justification for the specific forms that activity takes."[8] This reading of Marx thus draws on Marx's claim that social agents may not necessarily provide the most adequate descriptions and explanations of their activity to salvage his commitment to the position that human existence is conscious existence.

The instrumentalist reading of Marx, found in varying forms in Avineri and other scholars, agrees with the earlier dialectical materialist account in recognizing the centrality for Marx of human activity in interaction with its environment. The differences lie in how this activity is described. The instrumentalist approach differs from that of the dialectical materialist in ways similar to early twentieth-century instrumentalists' differences from empiricist and stimulus-response accounts of human behavior.[9] At stake in both challenges is an emphasis on the role of consciousness in distinguishing human from other forms of natural existence. Thus Avineri and others have tended to point to those passages in Marx's writings where Marx notes the role of consciousness in guiding behavior. A frequently noted passage, useful because it is found in Marx's later work, is one in *Capital* where Marx distinguishes the behavior of humans from animals by noting that for humans the goals which motivate behavior need not be physically present:

> We presuppose labour in a form that stamps it as distinctively human. A spider conducts operations that resemble those of a weaver, and a bee puts to shame many of an architect in the construction of her cells. But what distinguishes the worst architect from the best of bees is this, that the architect raises his structure in imagination before he erects it in reality. At the end of every labour process we get a result that already existed in the imagination of the labourer at its commencement.[10]

Similarly, Avineri and others have tended to draw on Marx's *Theses on Feuerbach* where, as in the following, Marx stresses the active role of consciousness in giving content to the objects of perception:

> The chief defect of all hitherto existing materialism (that of Feuerbach included) is that the thing, reality, sensuousness, is conceived only in the form of the *object or of contemplation,* but not as *sensuous human activity, practice,* not subjectively.[11]

The instrumentalist reading of Marx is powerful; it is both more sophisticated conceptually than the previous account and truer to at least one significant strain within Marx. It does not, however, resolve an important ambiguity within Marx which contemporary feminists have recently identified.

Both the dialectical and instrumentalist interpretations of Marx recognized the centrality for Marx of human activity engaged in satisfying the conditions of human life. The two interpretations differed only in that the former tended to view such activity and such conditions in biological terms. From a feminist perspective both theories contain a common deficiency. While neither theory provides any grounds for differentiating, for "scientific" Marxists among biological needs, and for "humanistic" Marxists among historically constituted needs, both theories in fact end up giving priority to certain needs—those which can be satisfied by the use or consumption of physical objects. Similarly, both accounts do in fact, though without explanation, stress one type of activity as central for Marx in satisfying the "conditions of life"—that activity which results in procuring or producing such objects. Thus those human activities associated with the gathering, hunting, or growing of food and the making of objects become central and other activities such as childrearing or nursing become marginal. To be sure, this elimination of certain needs and activities is not universally present in either interpretation. Engels, for example, on at least one occasion describes activities as childrearing as equivalent in importance to those activities involved in the production of food and objects:

According to the materialist conception, the determining factor in history is, in the final instance, the production and reproduction of immediate life. This, again, is of a twofold character: on the one side, the production of the means of existence, of food, clothing and shelter and the tools necessary for that production; on the other side, the production of human beings themselves, the propagation of the species. The social organization under which the people of a particular historical epoch and a particular country live is determined by both kinds of production: by the stage of development of labor on the one hand and of the family on the other. The lower the development of labor and the more limited the amount of its products, and consequently, the more limited also the wealth of the society, the more the social order is found to be dominated by kinship groups. However, within this structure based on kinship groups the productivity of labor increasingly develops . . . , the old society founded on kinship groups is broken up. In its place appears a new society, with its control centered in the state, the subordinate units of which are no longer kinship associations, but local associations; a society in which the system of the family is completely dominated by the system of property.[12]

Even in the above Engels is somewhat ambivalent regarding the equivalence of what has been described in the feminist literature as "reproductive" and "productive" activities. Engels in this quote locates "reproductive" activities in the institution of the family or kinship. He argues that while in early societies with low productivity of labor the family "dominates," in later societies the system of the family is itself dominated by the system of property. This would seem to imply that whether productive or reproductive activities are basic varies historically. However, since he argues that the factor deciding this variation is itself the productivity of labor, it would appear that production is always the ultimate "determining" factor. This implication of his argument is indeed further elaborated in other sections of the work from which this passage was taken.

The same ambiguity, also culminating in a focus on activity aimed at the creation of food and objects, can be found in writers in the instrumentalist tradition. For example, Avineri elaborates the concept of "material base" in Marx to mean "conscious human activity, aimed at the creation and preservation of the conditions of human life." From this elaboration there would appear to follow no differentiation between productive and reproductive activities. However, a few pages later, Avineri goes on to claim, without explanation, that for Marx "the concrete expression of this human activity is work, the creation of tools of human activity that leaves its impact on the world."[13] A reasonable question to ask, which has recently been asked by feminists, is why this should be so, i.e., why should the concrete expression of human activity be work as so elaborated?

The source of this unclarity in the interpreters of Marx regarding the relation of reproductive to productive activities has its source in Marx. In particular, it stems from an ambiguity in Marx's use of the term "production." This ambiguity is illustrated in the following passage (emphasis added):

> The production of life, both of one's own in labour and of fresh life in procreation now appears as a double relationship: on the one hand as a natural, and on the other as a social relationship. By social we understand the cooperation of several individuals, no matter under what conditions, in what manner and to what end. It follows from this that a certain mode of production, *or industrial stage,* is always combined with a certain mode of co-operation, or social stage, and this mode of co-operation is itself a 'productive force.' Further, that the multitude of productive forces accessible to men determines the nature of society, hence, that the 'history of humanity' must always be studied and treated in relation to the *history of industry and exchange.*[14]

In the first sentence "production" refers to all activities necessary for species survival; by the middle of the passage its meaning has become restricted to those activities which are geared to the creation of material objects (industrial). While from the meaning of "production" in the first sentence, Marx could include family forms under the "modes of cooperation" he describes, by the middle of the paragraph its meaning has become such to now include only those "modes of cooperation" found within the "history of industry and exchange." In effect, Marx has eliminated from his theoretical focus all activities basic to human survival which fall outside a capitalist "economy." Those activities he has eliminated include those identified by feminists as "reproductive" (childcare, nursing) and also those concerned with social organization, i.e., those regulating kinship relations or in modern societies those we would classify as "political."[15] Marx's ability to do this was made possible by his moving from a broad to a narrow meaning of "production."

This ambiguity in Marx's use of "production" can be further understood in terms of the variety of meanings the word possesses. First, in its broadest meaning it can refer to any activity that has consequences. More narrowly, it refers to those activities that result in objects. Finally, in an even more specific sense, it refers to those activities that result in objects that are bought and sold, i.e., commodities. Similarly, if we look at such related words as "labor" and "product" we can find a confusion between respectively (1) activity requiring any effort and the result of such activity, (2) activity resulting in an object and that object, and (3) activity resulting in a commodity and that commodity.

Marx and many of his later followers often do not make clear which of these meanings they are employing when they use these and related words. For example, when Marx claims that labor is the motor of historical change, does he mean all human effort which changes the natural and/or social environment, only that effort which results in objects or effort which results in commodities? Similarly, Marx's concept of the "economy" often becomes confusing, in part as a consequence of ambiguities in his use of "production." To illustrate this point it is helpful to refer again to the passage quoted earlier from the preface to the *Contribution to the Critique of Political Economy*:

> In the social production of their existence, men inevitably enter into definite relations, which are independent of their will, namely relations of production appropriate to a given stage in the development of their material forces of production. The totality of these relations of production constitutes the economic structure of society, the real foundation, on which arises a legal and political superstructure and to which correspond definite forms of social consciousness. The mode of production of material life conditions the general process of social, political and intellectual life.

In the above, Marx equates the "economic structure of society" with its "relations of production." Since a reasonable interpretation of "mode of production of material life" would be all activities conducive to the creation and recreation of the society's physical existence, the "relations of production" should reasonably include all social interaction having this object as its end. Thus the family should count as a component of the "economy." Even if we interpret the phrase "mode of production of material life" to refer only to activities concerned with the gathering, hunting, or growing of food and the making of objects, the family, in many societies, would still be included as a component of the economy. Neither of these two meanings of "economy," however, is the same as its meaning in postindustrial capitalism, where the "economy" comes to refer principally to the activities of those engaged in the creation and exchange of commodities. Thus Marx's concept of economy in the above is ambiguous as a consequence of the ambiguity in his concept of production.

Such ambiguities in the meaning of key words in Marx's theory in turn make possible certain serious problems within the theory. In particular, they enable Marx to falsely project features of capitalist society onto all societies. This point is illustrated by examining Marx's claim that "the changes in the economic foundation lead sooner or later to the transformation of the whole immense superstructure." This claim is intended as a universal claim of social theory, i.e., it is meant to state that in all societies there is a certain relation between the "economy" and the "superstructure." If we interpret "economy" here to refer to "all activities necessary to meet the conditions of human survival," the claim is nonproblematic but trivial. More frequently, "economy" is interpreted by Marx and Marxists to refer to "those activities concerned with the production of food and objects." Here, while the claim ceases to be trivial, it now contains certain problems as a cross-cultural claim. While all societies have some means of organizing the production of food and objects as well as some means of organizing sexuality and childcare, it is only in capitalist society that the former set of activities becomes differentiated from the latter under the concept of the "economic" and takes on a certain priority. Thus by employing the more specific meaning of "economic" in his cross-cultural claims, Marx projects the specialization and primacy of the "economic" found in capitalist society onto all human societies.

A Marxist might respond that yes, there is this ambiguity in many of the texts of Marx and his followers, but that it can be avoided by careful attention to the following distinctions: that only the most general meaning of "production," "labor," and "economic" can be employed cross-culturally; that the more specific meaning of these terms applies only to class societies and the most specific meaning only to capitalist societies. The point might be made that Marx is accomplishing a variety of different tasks in his writing: (1) he is developing a general, cross-cultural theory of human existence and social organization; (2) he is articulating a theory of class societies; and (3) he is offering a specific analysis of capitalist society. For these different tasks, he needs different meanings for the above terms.[16] Thus cross-culturally, Marx would define "labor" very generally as that process by which human beings regulate the material reactions between themselves and nature. In class societies this general activity is developed most strongly in the activity of producing food and physical objects. Finally, in capitalist society, the latter activity becomes most predominantly the even more narrowly circumscribed activity of producing commodities.

This response, while forceful, contains certain weaknesses which can be seen when we attempt to translate the above distinctions into actual theoretical claims. Most important, the interpretation of the most general meaning of "labor," as "that process by which human beings regulate the material reactions between themselves and nature" remains ambiguous. If we translate this phrase to incorporate activities we would describe as familial, political, *and* economic, we have differentiated it from the more narrow meanings but have emerged with a very trivial cross-cultural theory whose specific import is difficult to see. On the other hand, if we mean it to include only activities concerned with the making of food and objects, we have a theory more theoretically interesting but still subject to the preceding charges.

Moreover, it is the latter option which in the literature has almost always been followed; Marx and Marxists most always interpret "labor," "production," and "economic" to refer to those activities concerned with the making of food and objects. The following represent only a few examples:

Production is always a *particular* branch of production—e.g. agriculture, cattle-breeding, manufacture etc.—or it is a *totality*.[17]

The obvious, trite notion: in production the members of society approximate (create, shape) the products of nature in accord with human needs. . . . Production creates the objects which correspond to the given need.[18]

Assume a particular state of development in the productive forces of man and you will get a particular form of commerce and consumption.[19]

The response could perhaps be made that Marx employs this more narrow meaning of production because of the implicit assumption that he is speaking only of class societies where, according to the above response, this meaning would be appropriate. But even here the objections raised previously still hold: why should we assume that even in all class societies that those activities concerned with the making of food and objects are primary or even that they are sufficiently differentiated to make such a claim? Are we not again merely projecting features of capitalist society backward?

Let us look first at the idea of an economic component of society as a separable sphere. This idea is built into Marx's statements on determinacy, for to argue that anything is a determinant one must be able to separate it from that which is being determined. In Marx's case, the assertion that the nature of production or the "economic" structures all other aspects of society commits him to the point that the "economic" can be differentiated from other aspects of society. But as many commentators on Marx have pointed out—such as Georg Lukács or the group of theorists writing in *Socialisme ou barbarie*—such a claim is relatively true only for capitalist societies.[20] In precapitalist societies, economic aspects of life are more clearly intertwined with the religious, the sexual, and the political.

One means which Marxists have employed in responding to this point has been to distinguish economic functions from economic institutions. Thus the argument has been made that it is only in capitalist society that the economy, the state, and the family are separated as institutions. However, this does not mean that the theorist cannot differentiate the "economic" as a societal function even in societies which do not differentiate it as an institution. An example of this type of response is to be found in the writings of Maurice Godelier. Godelier argues that in many early societies it is the dominant institution of kinship through which the economic function is expressed. Thus, while here the economic does not determine as an institution, it does as a function.[21]

Isaac Balbus has argued that the above reinterpretation of Marxism makes the theory into a tautology. As he claims:

> for Godelier, what activity can be demonstrated to predominate over all the other activities in a society becomes, by definition, the mode of production! The theory of determination by the mode of production, then, becomes true by definition and does not lend itself to possible falsification. Nor is it a terribly useful tautology because it in no way helps us to understand which social activities become determinative—and thus function as the mode of production—under what conditions. We are back to where we started, because this was exactly what the theory of the determinative power of the mode of production was supposed to tell us![22]

An even more fundamental question can be raised: what grounds do we have for believing that it is important to focus on the economic component of kinship in kinship-organized societies as a separable social component? The argument that we need to separate out an economic function even in societies which themselves do not separate out the economic as an institution rests ultimately on the belief that such a function is basic and thus must receive specialized attention. We are back to the issue of primacy.

Thus, let us look more closely at this issue. Marx, by asserting the primacy of the economic, cannot merely be arguing that the production of food and objects is a necessary condition for human life to continue. That certainly is true, but the same can be said about many other aspects and activities of human beings: that we breathe, communicate with each other through language and other means, engage in heterosexual activity which results in child-bearing, create forms of social organization, raise children, etc. Rather Marx appears to be making the stronger and more interesting claim that the ways in which we produce food and objects in turn structure the manner in which other necessary human activities are performed. But the force of this claim, I would argue, rests upon a feature true only for capitalist society: that here the mode in which food and object production is organized to a significant extent does structure other necessary human activities. This is because in capitalist society, the production of food and objects takes on an importance going beyond its importance as a necessary life activity.

To express the same point in another way: insofar as capitalist society organizes the production and distribution of food and objects according to the profit motive, those activities concerned with the making and exchanging of food and goods assume a value which is relatively *independent* of their role in satisfying human needs. The ability of such activities to generate a profit gives to them a priority which can be mistakenly associated with their function in satisfying such needs. As Marshall Sahlins has noted, this priority makes credible a kind of reflectionist or economic determinist theory where the system of production and exchange appears basic:

> Since the objectives and relations of each subsystem are distinct, each has a certain internal logic and a relative autonomy. But since all are subordinated to the requirements of the economy, this gives credibility to the kind of reflectionist theory which perceives in the superstructure the differentiations (notably of class) established in production and exchange.[23]

Thus, if in capitalist society such activities as raising children or nursing the sick had been as easily conducive to making a profit as activities concerned with the production of food and objects became, we might in turn believe that the manner in which human societies raise children or nurse their sick structures all other life activities in which they engage.

This priority given to the making of food and objects in capitalist society has had many diverse ramifications. One was a transformation in prevailing attitudes toward labor. In precapitalist societies, such as that of ancient Greece or medieval Europe, labor was held in contempt. It was recognized that some humans must necessarily engage in it, as it was recognized that all human beings must eat, sleep, defecate, etc. But all these activities were viewed as that which expressed the lowest and most animal-like aspects of human existence, and not those in which humans should take any pride.

This negative stance toward labor began to change in the early modern period. Labor or industriousness became a sign of one's saintliness and no longer a sign of one's beastliness.[24] In association with this change arose also a fundamental alteration in motivation: the rise of the acquisitive motive. R. H. Tawney describes the shift involved by way of contrast with the medieval attitude toward gain:

> But economic motives are suspect. Because they are powerful appetites, men fear them, but they are not mean enough to applaud them. Like other strong passions, what they need, it is thought, is not a clear field but repression. There is no place in medieval theory for economic activity which is not related to a moral end, and to found a science of society upon the assumption that the appetite for economic gain is a constant and measureable force, to be accepted, like other natural forces, as an inevitable and self-evident *datum* would have appeared to the medieval thinker as hardly less irrational or less immoral than to make the premise of social philosophy the unrestrained operation of such necessary human attributes as pugnacity or the sexual instinct. The outer is ordained for the sake of the inner; economic goods are instrumental. . . .
> At every turn, therefore, there are limits, restrictions, warnings

against allowing economic interests to interfere with serious affairs.[25]

In an earlier chapter I argued for the specificity of the "family" to the modern period on the grounds that while some of the features we associate with the family may have existed before this period, they did not possess the same significance which they later acquired. Similarly, we might say here that while an acquisitive motive may have existed before the early modern period, it too existed with a different significance; it existed within the context of shame and silence. This context began to disappear in the modern period and the acquisitive motive became the basis upon which the economy—meaning those activities concerned with the production and distribution of food and objects—became organized. With the rise of prominence of the acquisitive motive attendant upon the emergence of capitalism came a change in how these activities, and the conditions which make them possible, were viewed. Activity concerned with the making of food and objects became "labor" and acquired a new evaluative standing. The soil, an important physical condition to such activity, became "land." Finally, with land, the tools conducive to the productivity of labor became "capital." What distinguishes "labor" from "work," "land" from "soil," and "capital" from "tools" is the motive of accumulation.[26]

Marx, in many respects, assumes these values and assumptions of capitalist society within his cross-cultural theory. Thus he assumes that labor is the prime manner in which human beings express and define themselves:

> Men can be distinguished from animals by consciousness, by religion or anything else you like. They themselves begin to distinguish themselves from animals as soon as they begin to *produce* their means of subsistence, a step which is conditioned by their physical organization. . . . What they are, therefore, coincides with their production, both with *what* they produce and with *how* they produce.[27]

As Jean Baudrillard comments on the above: why must our vocation always be to distinguish ourselves from animals, and moreover, why must this be in the form of production?

> On this dialectical base, Marxist philosophy unfolds in two directions: an ethic of labor and an esthetic of non-labor. The former traverses all bourgeois and socialist ideology. It exalts labor as value, as end in itself, as categorical imperative. Labor loses its negativity and is raised to an absolute value. . . . A spectre haunts the revolutionary imagination: the phantom of production. Everywhere it sustains an unbridled romanticism of productivity.[28]

It is not only the idolization of labor that Marx takes over from bourgeois society. It is also at times, and more surprisingly, an assumption of natural acquisitiveness. For example, Marx and Engels explain the emergence of the first class division on the basis of the creation of an initial social surplus. An implicit premise is that any surplus over what is required for bare subsistence will be sought after and struggled over. But why should we assume this to be the case without an assumption of acquisitiveness?[29] This same reliance on an assumption of acquisitiveness seems also present in Marx's claim that in the conflict between expanding modes of production and existing relations of production, the outcome is, if not determined, at least prejudiced on the side of the expanding productive forces. At least part of the effectiveness of this argument for modern readers rests on the force of the shared assumption of acquisitiveness.

Similar questions can be raised about Marx's dictum on the perpetuity of human need creation. Marx argues that in the process of humans acting on the natural world to satisfy their needs, they create new needs which in turn demand satisfaction. Thus he claims in *The German Ideology:* "The satisfaction of the first need (the action of satisfying, and the instruments of satisfaction which have been acquired) leads to new needs; and this production of new needs is the first historical act."[30] This, however, appears a valid description of human behavior only in capitalist societies.

Such societies have as an important basis the perpetual creation of need. However, there are many examples of societies which after laboring to satisfy their needs, stop working. Marx is aware of societies where needs are not being continually created. In his work he frequently draws on a distinction between societies which consume their surplus and remain stable for long periods of time and societies which invest their surplus and have histories. However, Marx does not appear to have reconciled this historical awareness with the above more general, anthropological claim.

Most significant for the purposes of this book is Marx's projection of the autonomy of the economic into his cross-cultural theory. To illustrate how that projection may be a function not merely of the embeddedness of Marx's work in capitalist values and assumptions but even more specifically of certain unique features of his time, I would like now to look more closely at the historical context in which Marx wrote.

THE HISTORICAL CONTEXT OF MARXISM

One theorist whose work can provide us with useful tools for understanding the historical context of Marxism is Karl Polanyi. One of the major theses of his book *The Great Transformation* is similar to a point stressed here: that while it is true that all societies must satisfy the needs of biology to stay alive, it is only true of modern society that the satisfaction of some of these needs in ever increasing amounts becomes a central motive of action. This transformation Polanyi identifies with the establishment of a market economy whose full development, he argues, does not occur until the nineteenth century. Polanyi acknowledges the existence of markets, both external and local, before this century. However, he makes a distinction between what he describes as external, local, and internal trade. External and local trade are complementary to the economies in which they exist. They involve the transfer of goods from a geographical area where they are available to an area where they are not available. The trading that goes on between town and countryside or between areas different in climate represent such types of trading. Internal trade differs from both the above in that it is essentially competitive, involving "a very much larger number of exchanges in which similar goods from different sources are offered in competition with one another."[31] Polanyi claims that these different forms of trade have different origins; in particular, internal trade arose neither from external nor from local trade, as common sense might suggest, but rather from the deliberate intervention on the part of the state.[32] The mercantile system of the fifteenth and sixteenth centuries established its initial conditions, making possible the beginnings of a national market.

While state intervention was necessary to establish the initial conditions for a national market, the true flourishing of such a market required the absence of at least some of the kinds of state regulation found under mercantilism.[33] A market economy is one where the movement of the elements of the economy—goods, labor, land, money—is governed by the actions of the market. Under feudalism and the guild system, nonmarket mechanisms controlled two of these elements, land and labor. This nonmarket control over labor and land did not disappear under mercantilism; it merely changed its form. The principles of statute and ordinance became employed over those of custom and tradition.[34] Indeed, as Polanyi claims, it is not until after 1834 in England, with the repeal of the Speenhamland law which had provided government subsidies for the unemployed and underemployed, that the last of these elements, labor, was freed to become a commodity. Thus it was not until the nineteenth century in England that a market economy could be said to be fully functioning.

A market economy has certain distinctive features. Of key importance is the dominance of the principle of price as the mechanism for organizing the production and distribution of goods. This means that not until all the elements necessary to the production and distribution of goods are controlled by price can a market economy be said to be functioning. A market economy demands the freeing of the elements comprising the economy from the governance of other social institutions, such as the state or the family. Polanyi does not discuss the decline of the family in governing such elements. He does, however, stress the separation of the political and the economic as a necessary condition of a market economy:

> A self-regulating market demands nothing less than the institutionalized separation of society into an economic and political sphere. Such a dichotomy is, in effect, merely the restatement, from the point of view of society as a whole, of the existence of a self-regulating market. It might be argued that the separateness of the two spheres obtains in every type of society at all times. Such an inference, however, would be based on a fallacy. True, no society can exist without a system of some kind which ensures order in the production and distribution of goods. But that does not imply the existence of separate economic institutions; normally, the economic order is merely a function of the social, in which it is contained. Neither under tribal, nor feudal, nor mercantile conditions was there, as we have shown, a separate economic system in society. Nineteenth century society, in which economic activity was isolated and imputed to a distinctive economic motive was, indeed, a singular departure.[35]

Polanyi goes on to argue that not only does a market economy require the separation of the elements of the economy from other spheres of social life, but that this means in effect the dominance of the principle of the market over other social principles. Since two of the elements of the economy, land and labor, are basic features of social life, to subordinate them to market mechanisms is in effect to subordinate society to the market:

> But labor and land are not other than the human beings themselves of which every society consists and the natural surrounding in which it exists. To include them in the market mechanism means to subordinate the substance of society itself to the laws of the market.[36]

We might qualify Polanyi's argument by saying that not all labor becomes subordinate to the laws of the market when the economy becomes a market economy; domestic labor does not, at least in any simple sense. Since, however, *some* of the labor essential to human survival does become subordinated to the market, we can still accede to this point of the growing dominance of the market. Moreover, we might also agree with his further claim that the organization of the economic system under a market mechanism means also the dominance of the economic. He argues that this occurs because "the vital importance of the economic factor to the existence of society precludes any other result. For once the economic system is organized in separate institutions, based on specific motives and conferring a special status, society must be shaped in such a manner as to allow that system to function according to its own laws. This is the meaning of the familiar assertion that a market economy can function only in a market society."[37] Such an argument can be supplemented by the earlier claim that the alliance of the production of goods with the acquisitive motive means the rise in importance of the production of goods over other life activities. The acquisitive motive is such so that to allow it as a motive means to allow it as a dominant motive.

Thus, a thesis often thought of as central to Marxism, the separation and dominance of the economic, is in effect a defining condition of a market economy. Moreover, as follows from Polanyi's analysis, it is just this condition which only becomes true within the nineteenth century. Thus one can conclude that Marxism as social theory is very much a product of its time, insightful as an exposition of that which was becoming true, and false to the extent that the limited historical applicability of its claims was not recognized.

Polanyi provides us with another claim about the origins of a market economy which also might shed some light on the historical context of Marxism. Occasionally Marx's materialism has been given a technological interpretation. Following from such a reading, the degree of a society's technical competence in producing food and objects is taken as the primary fact in explaining that society. There is much evidence in Marx's writing for such an interpretation. It is consistent with the previously quoted preface to *The Contri-*

bution to the Critique of Political Economy where Marx does appear to treat "the development of their material forces of production" as the most basic fact about a society to which even the "relations of production" must be "appropriate." G. A. Cohen convincingly argues for such a reading and also provides examples of many other passages in Marx's work which support it.[38] One often quoted instance is the following from *The Poverty of Philosophy:*

> Social relations are closely bound up with productive forces. In acquiring new productive forces men change their mode of production; and in changing their mode of production, in changing their way of earning a living, they change all their social relations. The hand-mill gives you society with the feudal lord: the steammill society with the industrialist capitalist.[39]

However, again we might interpret as historically specific this claim about the socially causal role of technological development. Polanyi points to the importance of technological developments in the eighteenth century for bringing about the rise of a market economy. He notes that as long as the machinery used in production was simple and inexpensive, production remained an accessory to commerce, engaged in only as long as it produced a profit. However, once machinery became more complex and expensive, its purchase demanded steady use to pay back the initial investment. It thus became necessary to ensure the steady supply of the necessary elements of production: labor, land, and money. In consequence, these elements had to be brought within the market system itself.[40]

However, a thesis of technological determinism, while perhaps more true for the eighteenth and nineteenth centuries than for others, even here needs qualification. As the above example indicates, technological developments can only be socially efficacious when the social conditions allow them to be such. A concern with producing goods more efficiently and in greater amounts makes sense only in a society which both values the increased production of goods and has no means other than technological advance for accomplishing it. As Robert Heilbroner points out, there have been many societies where such a concern was lacking. Neither the societies of antiquity nor of the Middle Ages showed much interest in technological development, at least as this applied to the production of goods. Even societies such as the Egyptians, Greeks, and Romans, who created an impressive technology of architecture, showed no interest in developing a technology of production.[41] Thus technological development, even when socially efficacious, itself requires explanation.

As noted, Polanyi claims that a defining condition of a market economy is a separation of the economic and political. Not noted by him, but also essential, is the separation of the economic from the domestic and familial. Indeed, when we think of what is pivotal about industrialization it is that the production of goods ceases to be organized by kinship relations and to be an activity of the household. The creation of goods by members of the household for the purpose of use by the household and organized primarily in accordance with family roles becomes replaced by the creation of goods by members of many different households for the purpose of exchange and organized in accordance with the profit motive. The commoditization of the elements of production means not only, as Polanyi notes, a withdrawal of control on the part of the state over these elements but also a withdrawal on the part of the family. When labor remained at home, its content and organization were primarily family matters; when it left only its consequences, wages, remained such.

Thus from the above analysis we can comprehend the emergence of the "economic" as separate from both the family and the state as the outcome of a historical process. This kind of analysis, I have repeatedly suggested, is one most in sympathy with the requirements of feminism. It is also one which might be used to challenge and explain the tendency among Marx and his followers to employ the category of the "economic" cross-culturally. The irony, however, is that such a historical analysis could itself be described as Marxist. Polanyi's work builds on the kinds of historical investigations Marx himself carried out in studying the emergence of capitalism out of earlier social forms. This irony reinforces a point suggested earlier—that while in Marx's concrete historical analysis there is much from which feminism can draw in comprehending the changing relation of family, state, and economy, it is most strongly in Marx's cross-cultural claims that the theory becomes unhelpful.

However, one point of qualification needs to be made even to this distinction. It is not only in Marx's actual historical investigations that he avoids the problems found in his cross-cultural theory. Also at times in his reflections on theory he becomes cognizant of the dangers of ahistoricity. Precisely on such grounds, he himself criticizes other social theorists. For example, in *The Poverty of Philosophy* he accuses Proudhon of falling into the mistake of bourgeois economists who fail to recognize the historical specificity of economic categories.[42] Similarly, as Anthony Giddens notes, one of the two principal criticisms which Marx makes against political economists in the Paris Manuscripts is that they assume that the conditions of production present within capitalism can be attributed to all economic forms.[43] In *Capital* Marx frequently notes that what he is describing is true only of a particular society. For example, he claims that "definite historical conditions are necessary that a product may become a commodity."[44] Thus, many of the distinctions Marx makes in *Capital*, such as that between use value and exchange value, are distinctions applicable only for certain societies.

The problem, however, is that Marx does not offer clear guidelines for avoiding the mistake of historical projection. He certainly does not want the social theorist to employ only those categories available to the social agents whom the theory describes. Marx, on at least one occasion, argues for the useful application of categories which have arisen in later societies to explain earlier societies:

> Bourgeois society is the most advanced and complex historical organization of production. The categories which express its relations, and an understanding of its structure, therefore, provide an insight into the structure and the relations of production of all formerly existing social formations the ruins

and component elements of which were used in the creation
of bourgeois society. Some of these unassimilated remains
are still carried on within bourgeois society, others, however,
which previously existed only in rudimentary form, have
been further developed and have attained their full significance, etc. The anatomy of man is a key to the anatomy of
the ape.[45]

Marx explicitly states that the above does not entail that we see
"in all social phenomena only bourgeois phenomena," for, as he
claims, the earlier phenomena always exist in a different form.[46]
However, what he does not further remark on is the always difficult
decision of determining for any particular case whether the phenomena being studied are sufficiently similar to be granted an
identical label.

Even if Marx's methodological remarks provided us with clear
guidelines, this would not remove the possibility that he himself
occasionally failed to follow such guidelines and falsely generalized
phenomena from his own society onto others. This latter tendency
is a feature of his work, and the problems which result, exemplified
most strongly in his cross-cultural theory, make that work frequently unhelpful for explaining gender. To elaborate this point,
that is, to show that it is precisely Marx's ahistoricity which
accounts for the theory's weaknesses in analyzing gender, I would
now like to focus specifically on the consequences of these problems for Marxism's analysis of gender.

MARX ON WOMEN, GENDER RELATIONS,
AND THE FAMILY

In comprehending Marxism on gender it is first important to
note that Marx's concept of class relies on the narrow translation
of "production" and "economic"—i.e., as incorporating only those
activities concerned with the making of food and objects. Thus
the criterion which Marx employs to demarcate class position,
"relations to the means of production," is understood as relation
to the means of producing food and objects. For Marx, the first

class division arose over the struggle for appropriation of the first social surplus, meaning the first surplus of food and objects. A consequence of such a definition of class is to eliminate from consideration historical conflicts over other socially necessary activities, such as childbearing and childrearing. A second consequence is to eliminate from consideration changes in the organization of such activities as components of historical change. The theory thus eliminates from consideration activities which have historically been at least one important component in gender relations. But again we can ask of the theory questions similar to those raised earlier: why ought we to eliminate or to count as less important in our theory of history changes in reproduction or childrearing practices than changes involved in food- or object-producing activities? First, does it even make sense to attempt to separate the changes involved, prior to the time when these activities were themselves differentiated, i.e., prior to the time when the "economy" became differentiated from the "family"? Furthermore, is not the assumption of the greater importance of changes in production itself a product of a society which gives priority to food and object creation over other life activities?

Many feminist theorists have noted the consequences for Marx of leaving out reproductive activities from his theory of history. Mary O'Brien, for example, argues that one effect is to separate historical continuity from biological continuity, which one might note is particularly ironic for a "materialist":

> Thus Marx talks continuously of the need for men to 're-produce' themselves, and by this he almost always means reproduction of the self on a daily basis by the continual and necessary restoking of the organism with fuel for its biological needs. Man makes himself materially, and this is of course true. Man, however, is also 'made' reproductively by the parturitive labour of women, but Marx ultimately combines these two processes. This has the effect of negating biological continuity which is mediated by women's reproductive labour, and replacing this with productive continuity in which men, in making themselves, also make history. Marx never observes that men are in fact separated *materially*

from both nature and biological continuity by the alienation of the male seed in copulation.[47]

Similarly, though from a different perspective, Marx's lack of consideration of reproductive activities enables him to ignore, to the extent that he does, the component of socialization in human history. In other words, the failures in Marx's theory which result from his attraction to a narrow interpretation of "materialism" might have been alleviated had he paid more attention to the activity of childrearing.

As O'Brien points out, there is a tendency for Marx to negate the sociability and historicity of reproductive activities, to see such activities as natural and thus ahistorical.[48] Alternatively, he occasionally treats changes in the organization of such activities as historical effects of changes in productive relations. Thus she notes that in *The Communist Manifesto*, Marx treats the family as a superstructural effect of the economy.[49] This is evidenced also in a letter to P. V. Annenkov of December 28, 1846, where Marx states: "Assume particular stages of development of production, commerce and consumption and you will have a corresponding social constitution, a corresponding organization of the family, of orders and classes, in a word, a corresponding civil society. . . ."[50] Here again, such tendencies in Marx can be explained by looking to the role and ideology of the family in an industrial society. When "productive" activities leave the household and in turn come to constitute the world of change and dynamism, then activities of "reproduction" become viewed as either the brute, physiological, and nonhistorical aspects of human existence or as byproducts of changes in the economy.

One important problem which specifically follows from seeing "reproductive" activities as universally the consequence of "productive" activities is that we are thereby prevented from comprehending the integration of production and reproduction in precapitalist societies. Godelier has come closest to this awareness in his claim that in many precapitalist societies the institution through which the "economic" determines is kinship. But, in societies organized through kinship, sexual and economic relations are integrally linked. An important consequence is that women and men in such societies occupy very distinctive relations to those activities concerned with the making of food and objects *in connection with* those rules regulating marriage and sexuality. Moreover, this distinctive relation to "productive" activities cannot be described solely in terms of a "division of labor." While some gender division of labor even in relation to the making of food and objects appears consistent throughout history, women have also had less control over the means and results of such activity than men, again, *in connection with* those very rules which organize marriage and sexuality in kinship-organized societies.

The conclusion of this recognition, however, is that gender, certainly in kinship-organized societies, and perhaps to varying extents in societies following, should be viewed as a significant class division even following a traditional understanding of class. In other words, even if we subscribe to the traditional Marxist translation of production to refer to activities concerned with the making of food and objects, then gender relations, since historically involving different access to and control over these activities, constitute class relations. This point takes us beyond the traditional feminist castigation of Marxism for its sole focus on production. Part of the limitation of that castigation was that it shared with Marxists the belief in the separability of productive and reproductive activities. But if we recognize this separability as historically tied to a form of social organization where the principle of exchange has replaced the principle of kinship as a means of organizing the production and distribution of goods, then our comprehension of the limitations of Marxism on gender is deepened.

Another means of explicating this point is by noting that when Marx and Marxists use the category of "class," they have most paradigmatically in mind the examples of such societies as capitalism or feudalism. In feudal society kinship relations to a significant extent still organize production relations, but gender here may be less fundamental in some instances in indicating relation to the "means of production" than connection with a specific parental lineage. In capitalist societies, connection with a specific parental lineage remains a component in constituting class, but only also in conjunction with the actions of the market. Neither society, however, illuminates the case of more "egalitarian" societies where differences in parental lineages among men may be less important an indicator of differences in control over production than gender. In other words, whether gender is or is not an important class indicator must be empirically determined in every instance and we cannot assume, as do many Marxists, that gender and class are inherently distinct. Rather the evidence seems to be that in many early societies gender is a fundamental class indicator, a fact resonating throughout subsequent history, though also in conjunction with, and at times in subordination to, other factors.

This last point brings us finally to the issue of Marxism's ability to analyze gender in capitalist society. Much of my criticism of Marx has rested on the claim that he falsely generalizes features of capitalist society onto societies where such features do not hold and that this failure accounts for the theory's weaknesses in analyzing gender. The implication of this argument would be that the theory is adequate as an account of capitalism and as an account of gender relations within capitalist society. One problem with this conclusion is that it ignores the fact that capitalist society contains aspects of precapitalist societies within it which are highly relevant to gender. For example, it is true that in capitalist society the economy does become more autonomous of other realms than has been true of any earlier society. But insofar as Marxist theory treats the "economic" as autonomous, it loses sight of the ways in which even capitalist economies grew out of and continue to be affected by "noneconomic" aspects of human existence. Indeed, Marxism, by attributing autonomy to the "economic," comes close to that liberal position which would deny the influence over the market of such factors as gender, religion, ideology, etc. Of course, in specific contexts and in specific disagreements with liberals and conservatives, Marxists often argue for the determinacy of such noneconomic factors. Again, however, Marxism as historical analysis appears incompatible with Marxism as cross-cultural theory.

The way out of this dilemma for Marxists would be to eliminate the cross-cultural theory and more consistently follow the historical analysis. This would mean describing the progressive domination of the state and later the market over kinship as a historical process.[51] This type of approach could enable Marxism to correct two failures which are linked within the theory: its failure in explaining gender and the history of gender relations, and its failure to be adequately cognizant of the historical limitedness of certain of its claims. By recognizing that the progressive domination of the market has been a historical process, it might avoid the latter failure. By recognizing both the centrality of kinship in structuring early societies and its centuries-long interaction with such other institutions as the state and the market, it could provide itself with a means for analyzing gender. In an earlier chapter I noted that Marxists have occasionally described radical feminism as ahistorical. Whereas radical feminism pointed to the universality of the family, Marxists argued that this institution is always the changing effect of developments in the economy. Ironically, however, it may be a function of Marxism's failure to pay sufficient enough attention to the fundamentality of kinship and its changing relation to other social institutions and practices that has caused the theory to become falsely ahistorical itself.

MARXISM AND FEMINISM

From the above analysis we can resolve certain disputes among contemporary Marxist feminists. In particular, we can better assess the merits of each side in the dispute over "dual systems theory" discussed briefly in an early chapter. Marxist feminists have recognized that Marx's category of "production" leaves out of account many traditional female activities. In response, some have argued that we need to augment the category with the category of "reproduction." This, for example, is the position of Mary O'Brien: "What does have to be done is a modification of Marx's sociohistorical model, which must now account for two opposing substructures, that of production and that of reproduction. This in fact improves the model."[52]

Other Marxist feminists offer similar or somewhat revised models. Ann Ferguson and Nancy Folbre, for example, prefer to label the augmented category "sex-affective production" rather than "re-production." They note that the term "reproduction" is used by Marx to describe the "economic process over time." To employ it to refer to activities such as childbearing and childrearing might result in some confusion. Moreover, they argue, by including those traditionally female-identified tasks under the category of "pro-duction," we are reminded of the social usefulness of such tasks.[53]

As discussed earlier, such proposals have been described by Iris Young as constituting variants of what she labels "dual systems theory." Young also recognizes the narrowness of Marx's category of production:

> Such traditional women's tasks as bearing and rearing chil-dren, caring for the sick, cleaning, cooking, etc. fall under the category of labor as much as the making of objects in a factory. Using the category of production or labor to des-ignate only the making of concrete material objects in a modern factory has been one of the unnecessary tragedies of Marxian theory.[54]

Young, however, does not approve of focusing on those activities which have fallen outside this category to make Marxism more explanatory of gender. One weakness in such a solution is that it fails to account for gender relations which occur within "pro-duction."[55] In other words, Young is making the point stated earlier in this chapter: that gender has been a significant variable even among those activities concerned with the making of food and objects. Thus any analysis of gender must do more than enlarge the traditional category.

The basic problem of dual systems theory, according to Young, is that it does not seriously enough challenge the very framework of Marxism.[56] That this framework is gender blind must indicate a serious deficiency, whose remedy cannot merely be supplemen-tation. Moreover, dual systems theory, by making the issue of women's oppression separate and distinct from that which is covered by Marxism, reinforces the idea that women's oppression is merely a supplemental topic to the major concerns of Marxism.

The analysis in this chapter enables us both to understand the attractiveness of dual systems theory and to meet Young's challenge. Dual systems theorists are correct in recognizing that an important source of Marxism's inability to analyze gender is the narrowness of its category of production. Where they go wrong, however, is in not seeing this problem as in turn a function of Marxism's engulfment within the categories of its time. Marx's exclusion of certain activities from "production" is not sufficiently appreciated as a symptom of the particular period the theory is reflecting. Within industrial society many of those activities the category leaves out do become identified with women and become viewed as outside production. This very exclusion is reflected in Marx's categories.

This assessment of the failure of Marx's category provides us with a different remedy from that proposed by dual systems theorists. While we might agree with such theorists that the addition of the category of "reproduction" to the category of "production" might be necessary for understanding gender relations within industrial society, neither category is necessarily useful for analyzing earlier societies. Indeed, since there is no reason to believe that the kinds of social divisions expressed by these categories played a significant role in structuring gender relations within such societies, there would be no reason for employing them. This is not to say, of course, that gender did not play a significant role in earlier societies. It is rather that the categories through which we need to grasp it have to be understood as historically changing, reflecting the changing emergence, dominance, and decline of different institutions. Thus in early societies it appears that the key institution in structuring gender, as well as those activities we would label political or economic, is kinship. Social theory must focus on the differential power relations expressed within this institution to explain relations between men and women as well as among men as a group and women as a group. For later periods, we need to focus on the transformation of kinship into family, the emergence of the economy and the state, and the interaction among these. In short, we need to do the type of historical work described in chapter 4. As noted there, many feminist historians have come to recognize the historicity of many modern institutions and the need to be aware of such historicity if we are to explain gender. It is time for feminist theorists, including Marxist feminist theorists, to join in this recognition.

CHAPTER SEVEN

CONCLUSION

FROM THE ABOVE ANALYSIS of seventeenth-century liberalism and nineteenth-century Marxism, we can generate the outlines of a historical pattern of the modern period: the continual decline of kinship as a means of organizing society. In the very early modern period this was manifest first in the growth of the state and in the increasing restriction of kinship to the sphere of domesticity. Kinship and domesticity became joined in the "family," an institution which thus arose in conjunction with the state. Another means of labeling this change would be as the emerging separation of the "private" and the "public," with the former designating that which concerned the family and the latter as that which concerned the state. This historical change was in turn reflected in liberalism's theoretical separation of the two realms. This seventeenth-century separation of the private and public, while ancestral to the one existing today, is not the same as the one of today. The sphere of the "private" in the seventeenth century, insofar as it focused on the "individual," focused ambiguously on either the individual household or the individual man as head of household. This ambiguity in turn generated a contradiction in seventeenth-century liberalism, between its claims about the rights of "individuals" and its denial of such rights to women. In the course of the eighteenth and nineteenth centuries, this contradiction intensified insofar as the rule of kinship, even within the family, began to decline. The decline was in part a function of the growth of industrialization, which undermined the individual family/household unit as a productive unit. This meant the beginning of the possibility of men and women relating to the outside world as individuals rather than as heads of households or as dependents of such heads.

One consequence of industrialization was the emergence of Marxism, which recognized the increasing "nonprivate" nature of production and the interconnection between the state and the economy. Thus Marxism reflected in its theory the fact that the old lines which had separated the "private" from the "public" had changed in consequence of the movement of production outside the home. However, as liberalism was not aware of the historical nature of the separation of the family and the state—tending to reify that separation in its theory—so also Marxism was not sufficiently aware of the historical nature of the separation of the economic from the domestic, also tending to reify this separation in its cross-cultural theory.

The above historical pattern is in accord with the analysis I made in chapter 2 about the context of nineteenth-century American feminism. There I also noted the continuing decline of the importance of kinship in that century, one manifestation of which was that women were increasingly functioning as individuals in the nondomestic realm. This increase in women active outside the home was itself both a result of changes already occurring in the relation between the two spheres of "private" and "public" and a contributor to such changes. Industrialization brought new jobs for women: either directly, for example, as mill hands, or indirectly, as teachers or social workers of those who were being called to work in the new factories. Such jobs in turn affected women's sense of self and their position within the family. A wage-earning job raised the possibility that a woman could exist outside a family or within a family as an individual contributor. Moreover, it was not only as economic agents that women were beginning to relate to the social order as individuals rather than as members of families. While white, middle-class women may have begun their involvement in abolition or temperance work as a function of their ascribed private roles as moral guardians, the increased politicization of these movements, and the public activities women had to engage in to be involved, also contributed to changes in women's relation to society.

If women began to act outside familial roles in the nineteenth century, this movement has intensified during the twentieth century. During this century, women, and increasingly even married women and women with children, have entered the labor force in such new occupations as secretary, saleswoman, waitress, receptionist, flight attendant, nurse, dental technician, etc. As this list of occupations itself reveals, the world of work has become a more encompassing and complex one than that of previous centuries. Many types of activity formerly carried out in the home, such as health care, education, entertainment, and food production, are now being carried out in nonfamilial institutions. Moreover, not only women but also men have been leaving the home as changing careers and ideology have been defining men less as heads of households and more as individuals.

These contemporary changes in the relation of the familial to the nonfamilial have brought us to the point where the lines separating the two spheres are, in some instances, on the verge of disappearing altogether. The emergence of psychoanalysis, which makes into a licensed occupation the analysis of private feelings, is one manifestation of such a realignment. The growth of the welfare state and laws regulating interfamilial relations is another such example.

Contemporary feminist theoretical work stands at a particular crossroads in regard to such changes. Because feminist theory represents the voice of those whose lives most embody many of these new changes, its task has been in part to attack the theoretical reflections of previous forms of this separation. Thus coming out of women's studies is scholarship which helps us see the limitations of past theoretical work which assumed a certain form of the separation of private and public. On the other hand, feminist theory, like liberalism in the seventeenth century and Marxism in the nineteenth, also contains a tendency to reify the new changes in social organization it is helping to defend.

In other words, on the one hand, the very upheavals in the relation of private and public which have brought forth the contemporary women's movement have made it possible for feminists to play a leading role in seeing through buried assumptions of our culture. On the other hand, insofar as feminist theory is not sufficiently cognizant of the historical context which gives it such power, then like liberalism and Marxism before it, it runs the danger of distorting the insights it provides. The key element here is the extent to which contemporary feminist theory can extend the historical consciousness it inherited from the Marxist tradition to lay bare those historical patterns Marxism itself could not see. Marxism, in large part as a consequence of Hegel and of the historical consciousness which emerged during the nineteenth century, made an enormous contribution to a correct understanding of social theory. It helped us recognize that "human nature" is not a biological given but results from the interaction of inherited forms of human consciousness with changing circumstances. It also revealed many aspects of the social organization of its time, of a capitalist economy and a democratic state, as nonuniversal outcomes of a certain history. However, as I have argued, there were certain key features of this history which Marxism itself could not see, weakening the theory's ability to account for gender. To the extent that contemporary feminist theory can lay bare those features while extending the historical consciousness which Marxism began to provide, to that extent does it provide a powerful source for societal self-understanding. Insofar as it loses sight of this historical consciousness, then the insights it provides becomes muddied and the political directions it points to become partially oppressive.

For example, part of the historical context which has given modern feminism much of its meaning has been the exclusion of women from public activities. Thus to a significant extent, modern Western feminism speaks for those attempting to become public beings. One result, however—and this has been particularly true for nineteenth-century feminism and twentieth-century liberal feminism—is that it has sometimes slipped into the role of uncritical accomplice to the increasing publicization of private life which has both made possible and been extended by feminism's success. Thus we witness such phenomena as "dress for success feminism" or feminism using uncritically the same language of "rights" of liberalism, many of whose weaknesses have long been pointed out by Marxists.

In recognition of the dangers of such a direction, many contemporary radical and socialist feminists have accompanied their rejection of the traditional privatization of women with strong criticisms of the existing public sphere. They have pointed to the bureaucratic, hierarchical, competitive, and alienating nature of this sphere and its alliance with modern conceptions of the masculine. They have extended the existing critique of the left by looking to women's experiences as a countervoice to the claims of universality and authority of this sphere. This type of direction is evidenced in some of the most prominent contributors to contemporary feminist theory, such as Nancy Chodorow and Carol Gilligan. Thus Chodorow links aspects of our contemporary public world to personality characteristics of males and finds interrelated problems with both. Similarly, Carol Gilligan looks to women's traditionally assigned personality traits and behavior patterns as a partial corrective to the modes that are prevalent in masculine personality structures and public life.[1]

One problem, however, has been that even here there has been a tendency to lose sight of the historical context which both gives substance and provides limitations to the analysis. In Gilligan's case this tendency manifests itself both in her attempt to create a stage theory of moral development, modeled after Lawrence Kohlberg's, and in her tendency to speak of "a woman's voice" and "woman's development." The use of such expressions without supplementation by a historical account which would make clear which women under what circumstances her descriptions might be generally true of leads to a certain false generalization. What tends to get ignored are such facts as class, race, and sheer changes in history as variables in the analysis.

Many feminists of color have pointed to the dangers resulting from white and middle-class feminists universalizing from their own experiences. The contemporary women's movement has given much attention to this problem. It is my contention, however, that it will continually resurface without adequate attention to the methodological inclinations feminist theory has inherited from the larger culture. In particular, contemporary feminism must reverse that culture's tendency to ignore the phenomenon of history in accounting both for its own and others' practices and values. Feminism must thus, more consistently than other political movements and theories before it, come to see itself as well as its predecessors and antagonists within history.

Feminism must also come to understand women's oppression historically. Feminist practice and theory have made a most powerful challenge to the prevailing cultural assumption that gender is not a problem and thus facts such as women's lesser access to money, power, status, leisure, sense of self-worth, etc. are not an issue. Feminist practice and theory, in its continuing struggle to make the dominant culture accept the point that gender indeed is a problem, must now come to see that defining the problem as heterogeneous does not diminish any sense of its seriousness.

This call for feminists to recognize diversity in the content and causes of women's oppression has different implications for different sections of the contemporary women's movement. For Marxist feminists it means relinquishing the belief that some particular aspect of "production," such as women's specific contribution to the laboring process, can provide any ultimate clue in explaining or solving the problem. Nor can appeals to "mothering," or sexuality, factors more currently favored by radical feminists, provide the ultimate answer. Thus I am arguing that there is no one shortcut to aid us in figuring out what has brought us to our present state nor in figuring out what kind of future we wish to create.

This is not to claim that, at least in regard to analyzing our past, there have not been certain factors which have played highly significant roles. For example, it is most likely that sexuality has been a crucial factor in the construction of gender relations for much of our history. A point to note, however, is that the specific meaning sexuality has assumed in the structuring of gender has varied historically. Similarly, while I have been asserting that the separation of private and public has played a major role in the structuring of gender in the modern West, I have also been contending that the specific meaning of this separation, and thus its specific import in structuring gender, has been continuously in flux in this period. Moreover, the fact of connection between this separation and women's oppression in our past does not entail any necessary connection between this separation and women's oppression in our future. As traditional patriarchy existed prior to the creation and separation of family and state, so also could there exist a future type of society where a separation of private and public plays no, or a very minimal, role in generating male dominance. Indeed, there are signs that elements of such a possibility are present today, in the emergence of what some theorists have identified as "public patriarchy."

In short, I am arguing against a conception of feminist theory as totalizing. Sometimes the rejection of a totalizing theory is equated with a rejection of theory altogether. This latter equation is a mistake, for without any reflection on our practice and on the history which preceded it, we are led to unthinkingly replicate it. Thus rejecting a totalizing theory does not mean rejecting theory; it is rather to understand that theory as historical in both its creation and its content.

For feminist theory to come to see its own work in such a way would provide it both with that needed humbleness asked of it by many nonwhite feminists and with a greater awareness of its own importance. Both points are illustrated in the argument of this book concerning the role of private and public in structuring gender. The dynamic between private and public which forms the context for the emergence of modern feminism is a dynamic occurring primarily in Western Europe and North America. It has been the urban, bourgeois, and later professional class which generated many of the changes constituting it. Family types that were later to be adopted by persons outside this class were often first and most fully embodied by persons within this class. Thus it would follow that many of those who have been active in the contemporary women's movement have come from the white middle class of North America and Western Europe and that many of the messages of feminism have most resonance for persons of this group.

For feminism to see itself within history is thus to recognize that the historical pattern which was important in its emergence is only one pattern in a larger world history and culture. On the other hand, a historical perspective should also contribute to feminism having a justifiable sense of its own importance. The dynamic of change between private and public, while only one dynamic of change, is highly significant. It has greatly affected the lives of many, including those whose lives have not been Western, white, or of the middle class. Associated with the economic and cultural dominance that Western Europe and North America have exerted over other parts of the world in the modern period, and that certain groups within it have exerted over others, has also been a type of "social-organizational" dominance. Thus Western forms of the separation between private and public have frequently been imposed on non-Western countries and family forms first inaugurated by certain groups within Western countries have become the norm to which others have been taught to aspire. Insofar as contemporary feminism has called for the critical examination of these forms of social organization, it has also undermined the belief in their inherent "naturalness" or "superiority."

Moreover, even if we grant that the particular dynamic of private and public which brought forth contemporary feminism is specific to a certain society and time period, this does not mean that the issues generated by this dynamic are only relevant to that society and time. Modern forms of gender inequality, while not identical with, do connect with other forms of gender inequality, such as associated with kinship and older forms of a domestic/public separation. Attending to our present forms can partially illuminate these older forms, as has been revealed by contemporary feminist scholarship. Indeed, what this scholarship has shown is that contemporary feminist concerns provide a starting point for investigating patterns fundamental to much of world history, though crucially ignored for most of that history.

Notes

ONE The Contemporary Women's Movement

1. This is not to deny that there were many women who saw themselves as feminists and worked for feminism in a variety of ways during this period. As Dale Spender's book *There's Always Been A Women's Movement This Century* (London: Pandora Press, 1983) shows, feminists have existed throughout the twentieth century, and increased research will undoubtedly further support her thesis. The point here is only that the feminism engaged in by these women did not receive the kind of public attention given to the campaigns of the nineteenth century and to those since the early 1960s.

2. Barbara Sinclair Deckard, *The Women's Movement*, 2d ed. (New York: Harper and Row, 1979), pp. 342–43.

3. Judith Hole and Ellen Levine, *Rebirth of Feminism* (New York: New York Times Book, 1971), pp. 23–24.

4. Deckard, *The Women's Movement*, p. 347.

5. Hole and Levine, *Rebirth of Feminism*, p. 88.

6. *Ibid.* For a fuller elaboration of the demands see pp. 439–40.

7. Deckard, *The Women's Movement*, pp. 38 and 187.

8. Jo Freeman also notes this tendency in the movement of NOW to a more personally radical direction. As evidence she points to its change from being antilesbian in 1969 and 1970 to an increasing support for lesbianism in later years. Freeman claims that such factors as an overlap of membership in the "younger" and "older" branches of the movement can account for this tendency toward unity. See Jo Freeman, *The Politics of Women's Liberation* (New York: David MacKay, 1975), pp. 97–99. Zillah Eisenstein in *The Radical Future of Liberal Feminism* (New York: Longman, 1981), pp. 195–96 also notes how NOW became more radical during the course of the 1970s, though as she points out, it is not clear how one relates the more radical positions with the more standard ones. She notes a contrast between the national programs and the understanding of some state and local chapters.

9. This was a concept introduced first by Hannah Arendt in *The Human Condition* (Chicago: University of Chicago Press, 1958). Jacques Donzelot elaborates on this new hybrid of the private and the public in *The Policing of Families*, trans. Robert Hurley (New York: Random House, 1979). Nancy Fraser relates the new domain of state activity to feminist concerns in "Feminism and the Social State," *Salmagundi*, forthcoming.

10. However, as Alison Jaggar has pointed out to me in communication, liberal feminists also defend the right to privacy in a variety of areas, including sexual preference, abortion, and pornography. See her discussion of liberal feminism's complicated stance on the relation of private and public in *Feminist Politics and Human Nature* (Totowa, NJ: Rowman and Allenheld, 1983), pp. 173–206.

11. For an excellent theoretical discussion of the identification of abstraction and masculinity see Nancy Hartsock, *Money, Sex, and Power* (New York: Longman, 1983), pp. 230–47.

12. Both reflecting and reinforcing this position are the writings of Michel Foucault.

13. Carol Brown's work has been important in first articulating this point. See "Mothers, Fathers and Children: From Private to Public Patriarchy," in Lydia Sargent, ed., *Women and Revolution*, pp. 239–67 (Boston: South End Press, 1981). For an excellent critique of bureaucracy and the ways in which it is antiwomen see, Kathy Ferguson, *The Feminist Case Against Bureaucracy* (Philadelphia: Temple University Press, 1984).

14. As follows from this analysis, I would disagree with aspects of the account of liberal feminism found in Zillah Eisenstein's influential book, *The Radical Future of Liberal Feminism* (see note 8 above). In this work Eisenstein argues that liberal feminism's challenge to the separation of private and public undermines the liberal state as that state was created and maintains itself through the establishment of this separation. Here I would note—what will be a continuing theme throughout this book—the historically changing nature of the relation of private and public in the modern period and also the historically changing nature of liberalism. As we shall see in subsequent chapters, while from the seventeenth century to the present, the state has exerted considerable energy in creating and maintaining the family, and often in particular the ideology of the family, it has frequently done so while simultaneously undermining it. Especially in the nineteenth and twentieth centuries, the state has frequently justified its own intervention in family affairs with the need to "save the family." Eli Zaretsky, for example, points to this contradictory stance of the state in "The Place of the Family in the Origins of the Welfare State," in Barrie Thorne with Marilyn Yalom, eds., *Rethinking the Family*, pp. 188–224 (New York: Longman, 1982).

The point here is that while liberalism historically *has been* premised on the separation of the private and the public, liberalism is not inevitably tied to such a separation or at least not to that version of it found in previous centuries. In this respect, it is important that we understand liberalism, like any other political theory and movement, as having a history, such that later versions may be crucially different from earlier forms.

This recognition of the historically changing nature of liberalism is recognized more by Eisenstein in her more recent book, *Feminism and Sexual Equality: Crisis in Liberal America* (New York: Monthly Review Press, 1984). For example, on pp. 16–17 she notes that the earlier division of state and family has been challenged by the welfare state. She claims that in response to the subversion of old divisions between home and market made by wage-earning women, the state has stepped in to protect the distinctiveness of woman from man in new forms.

15. Hole and Levine, *Rebirth of Feminism*, p. 90.

16. N.Y. Radical Feminists, "Politics of the Ego: A Manifesto for N. Y. Radical Feminists," in Anne Koedt, Ellen Levine, and Anita Rapone, eds., *Radical Feminism*, pp. 379 and 381 (New York: New York Times Book, 1973). For other sources on early radical feminism see Kate Millet, *Sexual Politics* (New York: Doubleday, 1970); Shulamith Firestone, *The Dialectic of Sex* (New York: Bantam, 1970); and Robin Morgan, ed., *Sisterhood Is Powerful* (New York: Vintage, 1970). For an excellent survey and discussion of radical feminism as well as other sections of the contemporary women's movement, see Jaggar, *Feminist Politics and Human Nature* and Alison M. Jaggar and Paula Rothenberg Struhl, eds., *Feminist Frameworks: Alternative Theoretical Accounts of the Relations Between Women and Men* (New York: McGraw Hill, 1978). An insightful criticism of radical feminism is in Joan Cocks, "The Oppositional Imagination: Critical Reflections on Radical Feminism," manuscript.

17. Deckard, *The Women's Movement*, p. 352. Note that New York Radical Women and New York Radical Feminists were not the same. Radical Women in New York was formed in 1967 by Shulamith Firestone and Pam Allen. New York Radical Feminists developed later out of the Stanton-Anthony Brigade. See *ibid.*, pp. 351–56.

18. This is not to deny that some feminist theorists have forcefully argued psychoanalytic theory's usefulness for feminist theory. Gayle Rubin, for example, has drawn interestingly on Freud as elaborated by Lacan. See Gayle Rubin, "The Traffic in Women," in Rayna R. Reiter, ed., *Toward an Anthropology of Women*, pp. 157–210 (New York: Monthly Review Press, 1975). Other examples of the use of Freud or psychoanalytic theory for feminist theory can be found in the writings of Nancy Chodorow, such as *The Reproduction of Mothering: Psychoanalysis and the Sociology of Gender* (Berkeley: University of California Press, 1978); Jane Flax, "Political Philosophy and the Patriarchal Unconscious: A Psychoanalytic Perspective on Epistemology and Metaphysics," in Sandra Harding and Merrill B. Hintikka, eds., *Discovering Reality: Feminist Perspectives on Epistemology, Metaphysics, Methodology, and Philosophy of Science*, pp. 245–81 (Dordrecht, Holland: D. Reidel, 1983); and Jessica Benjamin, "Master and Slave: The Fantasy of Erotic Domination," in Ann Snitow, Christine Stansell, and

Sharon Thompson, eds., *The Powers of Desire,* pp. 280–99 (New York: Monthly Review Press, 1983).

19. Firestone, *The Dialectic of Sex,* p. 12.

20. *Ibid.,* p. 11.

21. Heidi Hartmann, "The Unhappy Marriage of Marxism and Feminism: Towards A More Progressive Union," in Sargent, *Women and Revolution,* p. 14. Early versions of this essay, coauthored with Amy B. Bridges, appeared in draft form in 1975 and 1977. A version very similar to the one published in the *Women and Revolution* collection was published in *Capital and Class* (Summer 1979), 8:1–33.

22. On the complicated relation of radical feminist theory to biological explanations, see Jaggar, *Feminist Politics and Human Nature,* pp. 83–113.

23. This point has been made most explicitly by French radical feminists. Specifically, Monique Wittig in 1979 at The Second Sex Conference in New York City read a paper, "One Is Not Born a Woman." See *ibid.,* p. 98. Even earlier, Simone de Beauvoir made the point that one is not born but becomes a woman in *The Second Sex* (New York: Knopf, 1970), p. 270.

24. Attention to issues of race and class is evidenced in the concern of such organizations as the National Women's Studies Association (NWSA) with these topics. This association includes as members many who would identify themselves as radical feminists. It is difficult to point to the political statement of organizations specifically identified with radical feminism as evidence of this change, since there are today few such organizations. The coming together of the various components of feminism in "the" women's movement has meant that much contemporary feminist organizing has taken place in program-oriented organizations such as the NWSA, various women's centers, or organizations devoted to specific political issues such as abortion rights, antinuclear activity, and women's safety. The reason I feel justified in making this claim of radical feminism is that there appears widespread agreement throughout these organizations on giving attention to matters of race and class. However, as Asoka Bandarage has pointed out to me in communication, this attention on the part of radical feminism to race and class has not been incorporated within radical feminist theory.

25. Jaggar, *Feminist Politics and Human Nature,* pp. 86–87.

26. I will discuss the emphasis within radical feminism on mothering at greater length in chapter 3. However, for now, one important book which can be noted as evidencing this concern is Adrienne Rich's *Of Woman Born* (New York: Norton, 1976).

27. Radicalesbians, "The Woman Identified Woman," in Koedt, Levine, and Rapone, *Radical Feminism,* pp. 240–45.

28. Adrienne Rich, "Compulsory Heterosexuality and Lesbian Existence," *Signs* (Summer 1980), 5(4):648–49.

29. Catharine A. MacKinnon, "Feminism, Marxism, Method, and the State: An Agenda for Theory," *Signs* (Spring 1982), 7(3):533–44.

30. *Ibid.*, p. 516.

31. Frederick Engels, *The Origin of the Family, Private Property, and the State*, ed. Eleanor Burke Leacock (New York: International Publishers, 1972).

32. Engels, *Origin*, pp. 119–21.

33. For helpful elaborations of the meaning of socialist feminism see Jaggar, *Feminist Politics and Human Nature* and Jaggar and Struhl, *Feminist Frameworks*. See also Zillah Eisenstein, ed., *Capitalist Patriarchy and the Case for Socialist Feminism* (New York: Monthly Review Press, 1979) and Sargent, *Women and Revolution*.

34. Hartmann, "The Unhappy Marriage of Marxism and Feminism," pp. 2 and 10–11.

35. *Ibid.*, pp. 19–29.

36. *Ibid.*, p. 33.

37. In conjunction with reprinting Hartmann's article, Sargent's entire collection *Women and Revolution* is devoted to a discussion of it.

38. Iris Young, "Beyond the Unhappy Marriage: A Critique of the Dual Systems Theory," in Sargent, *Women and Revolution*, pp. 47–48.

39. *Ibid.*, p. 48.

40. *Ibid.*, p. 49.

41. To stress the point, it is not *just* a "mode of production," since it organizes sexuality, culture, religion, etc. as well as work. Moreover, in distinction from a traditional Marxist position, I do not believe that modes of production universally organize all else in society. This point will be further elaborated in the last chapter on Marx.

That capitalism and patriarchy are sometimes at odds with each other is a point that Ann Ferguson and Nancy Folbre also make in "The Unhappy Marriage of Patriarchy and Capitalism," in Sargent, *Women and Revolution*, pp. 313–38.

TWO From Suffrage to Sexuality

1. Barbara J. Berg, *The Remembered Gate: Origins of American Feminism* (New York: Oxford University Press, 1978); Nancy F. Cott, *The Bonds of Womanhood: "Woman's Sphere" in New England, 1780–1835* (New Haven: Yale University Press, 1977); Nancy F. Cott and Elizabeth H. Pleck, eds., *A Heritage of Her Own: Toward a New Social History of American Women* (New York: Simon and Schuster, 1979); Carl Degler, *At Odds: Women and the Family in America from the Revolution to the Present* (Oxford: Oxford University Press, 1980); Ann Douglas, *The Feminization of American Culture*

(New York: Avon, 1977); Ellen Dubois, "The Radicalism of the Woman Suffrage Movement: Notes Toward the Reconstruction of Nineteenth-Century Feminism," *Feminist Studies* (Fall 1975), 3:(1–2):63–71; Ellen Dubois, "The Nineteenth-Century Woman Suffrage Movement and the Analysis of Women's Oppression," in Zillah Eisenstein, ed., *Capitalist Patriarchy and the Case for Socialist Feminism*, pp. 137–50 (New York: Longman, 1981); Ellen Carol Dubois, *Feminism and Suffrage: the Emergence of An Independent Women's Movement in America, 1848–1969* (Ithaca: Cornell University Press, 1978); Barbara Easton, "Feminism and the Contemporary Family," in Cott and Pleck, *A Heritage of Her Own*, pp. 555–77 and in *Socialist Review* (May–June 1978), 8(3):11–36; Jean Bethke Elshtain, "Moral Woman and Immoral Man: A Consideration of the Public Private Split and Its Political Ramifications," *Politics and Society* (1974), 4(4):453–73; Eleanor Flexner, *Century of Struggle: the Woman's Rights Movement in the United States*, rev. ed. (Cambridge, MA: Harvard University Press, 1975); Linda Gordon, "Why Nineteenth Century Feminists Did Not Support 'Birth Control' and Twentieth Century Feminists Do: Feminism, Reproduction, and the Family," in Barrie Thorne and Marilyn Yalom, eds., *Rethinking The Family*, pp. 40–53 (New York: Longman, 1983); Dolores Hayden, *The Grand Domestic Revolution: A History of Feminist Designs for American Homes, Neighborhoods, and Cities* (Cambridge, MA: MIT Press, 1981); Aileen Kraditor, *Up from the Pedestal* (Chicago: Quadrangle, 1968); William Leach, *True Love and Perfect Union: The Feminist Reform of Sex and Society* (New York: Basic, 1980); William L. O'Neill, *Everyone Was Brave: The Rise and Fall of Feminism in America* (Chicago: Quadrangle, 1969); William L. O'Neill, "Feminism as a Radical Ideology," in Alfred F. Young, ed., *Dissent: Explorations in the History of American Radicalism*, pp. 273–300 (DeKalb: Northern Illinois University Press, 1968); Carroll Smith-Rosenberg, "The Female World of Love and Ritual: Relations Between Women in Nineteenth-Century America," in Cott and Pleck, *A Heritage of Her Own*, pp. 311–42 and in *Signs* (Autumn 1975), 1(1):1–29; Mary P. Ryan, "Femininity and Capitalism in Antebellum America," in Eisenstein, *Capitalist Patriarchy and the Case for Socialist Feminism*, pp. 151–68; Mary Ryan, *Womanhood in America, from Colonial Times to the Present* (New York: New Viewpoints, 1975); Kathryn Kish Sklar, *Catherine Beecher: A Study in American Domesticity* (New Haven: Yale University Press, 1973).

2. Douglas, *The Feminization of American Culture*, p. 56.

3. *Ibid.*, p. 63.

4. *Ibid.*, p. 64.

5. Cott, *The Bonds of Womanhood*, p. 97.

6. Flexner, *Century of Struggle*, pp. 45–46.

7. *Ibid.*, p. 42.

8. *Ibid.*, pp. 71–74.

9. *Ibid.*, pp. 7–8.

10. Alice Rossi, ed., *The Feminist Papers: From Adams to Beauvoir* (New York: Columbia University Press, 1973), pp. 416–17.

11. Dubois, "The Radicalism of the Woman Suffrage Movement," p. 64.

12. *Ibid.*, p. 65.

13. The theme of the removal of many formerly family activities to industry and bureaucracy is important in the work of Ivan Illich. See, for example his *Tools for Conviviality* (New York: Harper and Row, 1973). On the destruction of the family by the ever increasing encroachments of the outside world, see also Christopher Lasch, *Haven in a Heartless World: The Family Besieged* (New York: Basic, 1977). As noted in chapter 1, a major work discussing the changing alignments of the nineteenth- and twentieth-century family to the state and economy is that by Jacques Donzelot, *The Policing of Families*, trans. Robert Hurley (New York: Random House, 1979). Also, it should again be emphasized that the decrease of the scope and autonomy of the family in the nineteenth and twentieth centuries that these writers and I point to is not incompatible with the kind of increase in the ideological importance of the family that Eli Zaretsky discusses in "The Place of the Family in the Origins of the Welfare State," in Thorne and Yalom, *Rethinking the Family*, pp. 188–224. Zaretsky notes that the state often justified intervention into the "abnormal" family by invoking an ideal of a "normal" family as a private and autonomous institution.

14. Lawrence Stone, *The Family, Sex, and Marriage in England, 1500–1800* (New York: Harper and Row, 1979), pp. 221–69; Degler, *At Odds*, pp. 8–25.

15. Carl Degler, *At Odds*, pp. 347–49 and 357–59. A similar argument on the greater appeal of the WCTU had been made by Ellen Dubois in "The Radicalism of the Woman Suffrage Movement," pp. 68–69.

16. Elshtain, "Moral Woman and Immoral Man," pp. 453–73.

17. As examples of this type of criticism see Kraditor, *Up from the Pedestal*, and O'Neill, "Feminism as Radical Ideology." Zillah Eisenstein makes a similar type of criticism in "Developing a Theory of Capitalist Patriarchy," in Eisenstein, ed., *Capitalist Patriarchy and the Case for Socialist Feminism*, p. 16, as well as in *The Radical Future of Liberal Feminism* (New York: Longman, 1981), pp. 145–73.

18. Hayden, *The Grand Domestic Revolution.*

19. Degler, *At Odds*, p. 344.

20. Barbara Deckard, *The Women's Movement*, 2d ed. (New York: Harper and Row, 1979), p. 327.

21. Judith Hole and Ellen Levine, *Rebirth of Feminism* (New York: New York Times Book, 1971), p. 24.

22. Sara Evans, "The Origins of the Women's Liberation Movement," *Radical America* (1975), 9(2):3–4.

23. Christopher Lasch, *The Culture of Narcissism: American Life in an Age of Diminishing Expectations* (New York: Norton, 1978).

24. Barbra Ehrenreich, *The Hearts of Men: American Dreams and the Flight from Commitment* (New York: Doubleday, 1983).

25. Carol B. Stack, *All Our Kin: Strategies for Survival in a Black Community* (New York: Harper and Row, 1974).

26. For illustrations of this point see Barbara Smith, ed., *Home Girls: A Black Feminist Anthology* (New York: Kitchen Table: Women of Color Press, 1983).

27. See, in addition to the above article by Sara Evans (see note 22), her book *Personal Politics: The Roots of Women's Liberation in the Civil Rights Movement and the New Left* (New York: Random House, 1979) and Barrie Thorne, "Women in the Draft Resistance Movement: A Case Study of Sex Roles and Social Movements," *Sex Roles* (1975), 1(2):179–95.

THREE Toward a Method for Understanding Gender

1. Gayle Rubin, "The Traffic in Women," in Rayna R. Reiter, ed., *Toward an Anthropology of Women*, p. 159 (New York: Monthly Review Press, 1975).

2. Michelle Zimbalist Rosaldo, "Woman, Culture, and Society: A Theoretical Overview," in Michelle Zimbalist Rosaldo and Louise Lamphere, eds., *Woman, Culture, and Society*, p. 18 (Stanford: Stanford University Press, 1974).

3. *Ibid.*, pp. 19–20.

4. Rubin, "The Traffic in Women," p. 160.

5. Rosaldo, "Woman, Culture, and Society," p. 21.

6. *Ibid.*, pp. 23–24.

7. *Ibid.*, p. 24.

8. *Ibid.*, p. 41.

9. Sherry Ortner, "Is Female to Male as Nature Is to Culture?" in *Woman, Culture, and Society*, pp. 67–87.

10. *Ibid.*, p. 79.

11. *Ibid.*, p. 80.

12. See Nancy Chodorow, "Being and Doing: A Cross-Cultural Examination of the Socialization of Males and Females," in Vivian Gornick and Barbara K. Moran, eds., *Woman in Sexist Society: Studies in Power and Powerlessness*, pp. 173–97 (New York: Basic, 1971); "Family Structure and Feminine Personality," in Rosaldo and Lamphere, *Woman, Culture, and Society*, pp. 43–66; "Oedipal Asymmetries and Heterosexual Knots," in

Social Problems (1976), 23(4):454–68, and *The Reproduction of Mothering: Psychoanalysis and the Sociology of Gender* (Berkeley: University of California Press, 1978).

13. Chodorow, "Family Structure and Feminine Personality," p. 51.

14. Rosaldo, "Woman, Culture, and Society," p. 25.

15. *Ibid.*, p. 26.

16. Ortner, "Is Female to Male as Nature Is to Culture?" pp. 78–79.

17. Michelle Zimbalist Rosaldo, "The Use and Abuse of Anthropology: Reflections on Feminism and Cross-Cultural Understanding," *Signs* (1980), 5(3):389–417.

18. Rosaldo, "The Use and Abuse of Anthropology," pp. 399–400.

19. *Ibid.*

20. *Ibid.*, p. 405.

21. *Ibid.*, p. 407.

22. Carol MacCormack, "Nature, Culture, and Gender: A Critique," in Carol MacCormack and Marilyn Strathern, eds., *Nature, Culture, and Gender*, p. 14 (Cambridge: Cambridge University Press, 1980). MacCormack here references Esther Boserup, *Women's Role in Economic Development* (London: Allen and Unwin, 1970), pp. 79–80 and Carol P. MacCormack, "The Compound Head: Structures and Strategies," *Africana Research* Bulletin 6 (July 1976), 4(4):44–64.

23. Susan Carol Rogers, "Woman's Place: A Critical Review of Anthropological Theory," *Comparative Studies in Society and History* (January 1978), 20(1):146.

24. Sylvia Junko Yanagisako, "Family and Household: The Analysis of Domestic Groups," in Bernard J. Siegel, Alan R. Bates, and Stephen A. Tyler, eds., *Annual Review of Anthropology* (1979), 8:191.

25. Rogers, "Woman's Place," p. 145.

26. *Ibid.*, p. 148.

27. *Ibid.*, pp. 143–44.

28. Louise Lamphere in her review essay on anthropology in *Signs* (Spring 1977), 2(3):617, identifies as upholders of this position: Leacock, Rohrlich-Leavitt, Nash, Sutton, Klein, and Sacks.

29. Rosaldo, "The Use and Abuse of Anthropology," p. 401.

30. Martin King Whyte, *The Status of Women in Preindustrial Societies* (Princeton: Princeton University Press, 1978), p. 167.

31. For a collection of essays entirely devoted to this topic see MacCormack and Strathern, *Nature, Culture, and Gender*. On the point on Rousseau see Carol P. MacCormack's article in this collection, "Nature, Culture, and Gender: A Critique," p. 20. On the identification of men with the natural and wild from this same article, see p. 8.

32. Rayna Rapp, review essay on anthropology in *Signs* (Spring 1979), 4(3):510.

33. *Ibid.*

34. Rayna Rapp, "Family and Class in Contemporary America: Notes Toward an Understanding of Ideology," in *Science and Society* (Fall 1978), 42(3):280.

35. This idea of the modernity of the family will be discussed at greater length in the next chapter.

36. Amy Swerdlow, Renate Bridenthal, Joan Kelly, and Phyllis Vine, *Household and Kin: Families in Flux* (Old Westbury, NY: Feminist Press, and New York: McGraw Hill, 1981), p. xvii.

37. This point is also suggested by Joan Kelly in "Family Life: An Historical Perspective," in *ibid.*, p. 13.

38. There also emerged during the course of the modern period the other meaning of family as extended kinship network. A more extensive discussion of the history of this term can be found in chapter 4.

39. Kelly, "Family Life: An Historical Perspective," p. 1; Carl Degler in *At Odds: Women and the Family in America from the Revolution to the Present* (Oxford: Oxford University Press, 1980), p. 4. Degler, while arguing for the universality of the family, similarly notes this exception. He also points to the work of anthropologist George P. Murdock who, in analyzing 500 different cultures, noted that in about one-fourth of them the father, for a certain period of time, lives apart from the mother and children. Degler claims, in qualification, that in most of these cases the distance between father and mother is slight (pp. 3–4).

40. Kelly, "Family Life: An Historical Perspective," pp. 1 and 5–6. See also Lawrence Stone, *The Family, Sex, and Marriage in England, 1500–1800* (New York: Harper and Row, 1977), pp. 105–14.

41. Sylvia Junko Yanagisako, "Family and Household," pp. 196–99.

42. *Ibid.*, p. 199.

43. Chodorow, *The Reproduction of Mothering*, p. 169.

44. *Ibid.*, pp. 7, 10, and 215–16.

45. *Ibid.*, p. 214.

46. Judith Lorber, Rose Laub Coser, Alice S. Rossi, and Nancy Chodorow, "On *The Reproduction of Mothering*: A Methodological Debate," *Signs* (Spring 1981), 6(3):508–9.

47. Chodorow, *The Reproduction of Mothering*, pp. 9–10.

48. Iris Marion Young, "Is Male Gender Identity the Cause of Male Domination?" in Joyce Trebilcot, ed., *Mothering: Essays in Feminist Theory*, pp. 129–46 (Totowa, NJ: Rowman and Allanheld, 1984). Roger Gottlieb has made a similar point, noting that exclusively female parenting reproduces patriarchy only in a society already characterized by patriarchy, that is, in a society where women are politically, culturally, and economically devalued. Roger Gottlieb, "Mothering and the Reproduction of Power: Chodorow, Dinnerstein, and Social Theory," *Socialist Review* (1984),

77:99–100. See also the reply to his article by Chodorow and Dinnerstein and his further reply to both in Nancy Chodorow, Dorothy Dinnerstein, and Roger Gottlieb, "Mothering and the Reproduction of Power: An Exchange," *Socialist Review* (1984), 78:121–30.

49. Chodorow also notes this cultural difference in the intensity of the mothering relationship and is aware of its mitigating effect on the universality of her account. The issue, however, is the extent to which she consistently abides by this awareness.

50. Chodorow notes this point of the family being a social structure in "On The Reproduction of Mothering: A Methodological Debate," p. 502.

51. Aspects of Wilhelm Reich's account in *The Mass Psychology of Fascism,* trans. Vincent R. Carfagno (New York: Farrar, Strauss, and Giroux, 1970) might be so construed, as also the analysis by T. W. Adorno and others, *The Authoritarian Personality* (New York: Harper, 1950).

52. Rosaldo, "The Use and Abuse of Anthropology," pp. 390–91.

53. Karen Sacks makes this point in "Engels Revisited: Women, The Organization of Production, and Private Property," in Reiter, *Toward an Anthropology of Women,* pp. 211–34, as also does Peter Aaby in "Women and Anthropology," in *Critique of Anthropology* (1977), 3:27.

54. This is a point originally brought to my attention by Roger Gottlieb in conversation.

55. Isaac Balbus, *Marxism and Domination: A Neo-Hegelian, Feminist, Psychoanalytic Theory of Sexual, Political, and Technological Liberation* (Princeton: Princeton University Press, 1982), p. 81. Balbus points to another inconsistency in Engel's account. He notes that for Engels, men even have certain privileges, such as polygamy and occasional infidelity, in early communistic societies prior to the introduction of private property. This, he claims, is inconsistent with Engels' argument that it is monogamy and the introduction of private property which are responsible for gender antagonism.

56. June Nash, "The Aztecs and the Ideology of Male Dominance," *Signs* (1978), 4(2):349–62.

57. Viana Muller, "The Formation of the State and the Oppression of Women: Some Theoretical Considerations and a Case Study in England and Wales," *Review of Radical Political Economics* (1977), 9(3):13.

58. Whyte, *The Status of Women in Preindustrial Societies,* p. 164.

59. Jane F. Collier and Michelle Z. Rosaldo, "Politics and Gender in Simple Societies," in Sherry B. Ortner and Harriet Whitehead, eds., *Sexual Meanings: The Cultural Construction of Gender and Sexuality,* p. 281 (Cambridge: Cambridge University Press, 1981).

60. *Ibid.,* pp. 284 and 285.

61. *Ibid.,* p. 285.

62. *Ibid.*, p. 284.
63. Rubin, "The Traffic in Women," p. 174.
64. *Ibid.*, p. 175.
65. This argument accords with a type of analysis put forth by Rayna Reiter in "Men and Women in the South of France: Public and Private Domains," in Reiter, *Toward an Anthropology of Women*, pp. 252–82. There she suggests that preexisting divisions of labor and geographical space become transformed into divisions with different status as the state asserts its own legitimacy and attempts to devalue the authority of kinship groups (p. 279). Lawrence Stone makes a similar point when he notes the process by which the state in early modern England devalued forms of social organization external to itself as a means of legitimating itelf. See Stone, *The Family, Sex, and Marriage in England*, p. 153.
66. Peggy Reeves Sanday, *Female Power and Male Dominance: On the Origins of Sexual Inequality* (Cambridge: Cambridge University Press, 1981).
67. Rosalind Petchesky, "Dissolving the Hyphen: A Report on Marxist-Feminist Groups 1–5" in Eisenstein, *Capitalist Patriarchy and the Case for Socialist Feminism*, pp. 376–77.

FOUR **Gender and Modernity: Reinterpreting the Family, the State, and the Economy**

1. Joan Kelly-Gadol, "The Social Relations of the Sexes: Methodological Implications of Women's History," *Signs* (Summer 1976), 1(1):811. See also her article, "Did Women Have a Renaissance?" in R. Bridenthal and C. Koonz, eds., *Becoming Visible*, pp. 137–64 (Boston: Houghton Mifflin, 1976). This point is also made by Carolyn C. Lougee, "Review Essay on Modern European History" in *Signs* (Spring 1977), 2(3):632. There is now a large literature on the general methodological implications of inserting women in history. Examples are to be found in Berenice A. Carroll, ed., *Liberating Women's History* (Urbana: University of Illinois Press, 1976); Gerda Lerner, *The Majority Finds Its Past* (Oxford: Oxford University Press, 1979); and as referenced by Kelly-Gadol, *Conceptual Frameworks in Women's History* (Bronxville, NY: Sarah Lawrence Publications, 1976). Natalie Zemon Davis summarizes some of the important issues in " 'Women's History' in Transition: The European Case," in *Feminist Studies* (Spring–Summer 1976), 3(3–4):83–103.

2. The issue as to how cross-culturally applicable is the concept of the "economy" will be discussed at length in chapter 6. For now, however, the point can be made that it is only some societies which evidence an "economy" as a separable sphere of social life.

3. This, for example, is how Lawrence Stone defines the family in *The Family, Sex, and Marriage in England, 1500–1800* (New York: Harper and Row, 1979), p. 21.

4. See for example, Rayna Rapp, Ellen Ross, and Renate Bridenthal, "Examining Family History," *Feminist Studies* (Spring 1979), 5(1):174–200, as well as Barrie Thorne, "Feminist Rethinking of the Family: An Overview," in Barrie Thorne with Marilyn Yalom, eds., *Rethinking the Family*, pp. 21–24 (New York: Longman, 1982). A major exponent of the importance of a historical conception of modern social divisions for a feminist perspective has been Eli Zaretsky in *Capitalism, the Family, and Personal Life* (New York: Harper and Row, 1976). In this work Zaretsky argued that many of the divisions which the women's movement first confronted, i.e., between the personal and the political, the family and the economy, need to be understood historically within the context of the changing dynamics of a capitalist society (p. 31). Zaretsky focused particularly on the manner in which industrialization created our modern sphere of home and personal life in opposition to the increasingly socialized sphere of production. Zaretsky's work has been important for my own thinking and particularly to my own understanding of the manner in which industrialization contributed to the shaping of contemporary social divisions. However, one important difference between Zaretsky's theoretical framework and mine is that Zaretsky explains these contemporary social divisions by situating them within the context of capitalism as a mode of production. I, as will become evident in my later discussion of Marx, wish to argue that such a framework, i.e., one which separates "modes of production" from other aspects of social life, such as the family, itself reflects and therefore cannot explain the divisions being described. Zaretsky's specific claim, moreover, seems undermined by that historical work which shows the nuclearization of the family as a phenomenon predating, not postdating, industrialization. These issues will be discussed at greater length later in this chapter and in chapter 6.

5. There are many writers who have pointed out how recent this field is. See, for example, Carl Degler, *At Odds: Women and the Family in America From the Revolution to the Present* (Oxford: Oxford University Press, 1980), p. v. Peter Laslett also notes it in his introduction to Peter Laslett, ed., *Household and Family in Past Time* (Cambridge: Cambridge University Press, 1972), p. 1. Stone similarly speaks of the rapid acceleration of work on family history in the period from the early 1940s to the 1970s and then an even more rapid growth in the 1970s in his review article on family history in the 1980s, "Past Achievements and Future Trends," *Journal of Interdisciplinary History* (Summer 1981), 22(1):51.

6. An important contributor to this idea was Frederic Le Play. See Catherine Bodard Silver, ed. and trans., *Frederic Le Play on Family, Work, and Social Change* (Chicago: University of Chicago Press, 1982).

7. Laslett, *Household and Family in Past Time*, pp. 130–33 and p. 61.

8. Peter Laslett, *The World We Have Lost* (New York: Scribner's, 1965).

9. Jean Louis Flandrin, *Families in Former Times*, trans. Richard Southern (Cambridge: Cambridge University Press, 1979), p. 57.

10. Laslett, *Household and Family in Past Time*, p. 1.

11. Philippe Ariès, *Centuries of Childhood: A Social History of Family Life*, trans. Robert Baldick (New York: Knopf, 1962), p. 353.

12. *Ibid.,* p. 364.

13. *Ibid.,* p. 356.

14. Flandrin, *Families in Former Times*, p. 9.

15. *Ibid.,* p. 5.

16. *Ibid.,* pp. 6–7.

17. *Ibid.,* p. 18.

18. Stone, *The Family, Sex, and Marriage*, p. 89.

19. Karl Marx, *Critique of Hegel's Philosophy of the State* (1943), in Loyd D. Easton and Kurt H. Guddat, eds. and trans., *Writings of the Young Marx on Philosophy and Society*, p. 176 (Garden City, NY: Doubleday, 1967). The quotation was brought back to my attention by Zaretsky's "The Place of the Family in the Origins of the Welfare State," in Thorne and Yalom, *Rethinking the Family*, p. 188.

20. Isaac Balbus makes this point in *Marxism and Domination: A Neo-Hegelian, Feminist, Psychoanalytic Theory of Sexual, Political, and Technological Liberation* (Princeton, NJ: Princeton University Press, 1982), p. 329. The sources Balbus in turn referenced are: Morton Fried, *The Evolution of Political Society* (New York: Random House, 1967); Elman R. Service, *Origins of the State and Civilization* (New York: Norton, 1975); S. Lee Seaton and Henri M. Claessen, *Political Anthropology: The State of the Art* (The Hague: Mouton, 1979). Other writers who Balbus notes agree on the antinomy of the hegemony of state and kinship are: Aidab Southall, "Typology of States and Political Systems," in *Political Systems and the Distribution of Power*, ASA Monographs 2 (London: Tavistock, and New York: Praeger, 1965); Stanley Diamond, *In Search of the Primitive* (New Brunswick, NJ: Transition, 1974) and Jürgen Habermas, *Communication and the Evolution of Society* (Boston: Beacon, 1979).

21. Balbus, *Marxism and Domination*, p. 328. Balbus here references M. Fortes and E. E. Evans-Pritchard, *African Political Systems* (London: Oxford University Press, 1940), pp. 6–7, John Middleton and David Tait, eds., *Tribes Without Rulers* (London: Routledge and Kegan Paul, 1958) and Fried, *The Evolution of Political Society*.

22. Marilyn Arthur, " 'Liberated' Woman: The Classical Era," in Bridenthal and Koonz, *Becoming Visible*, p. 67.

23. *Ibid.,* p. 67.

24. *Ibid.,* pp. 67–70.

25. *Ibid.,* p. 62.

26. Hannah Arendt, *The Human Condition* (Chicago: University of Chicago Press, 1958), p. 24.

27. Stone, *The Family, Sex, and Marriage*, p. 133.

28. *Ibid.*, pp. 132–33.

29. *Ibid.*, pp. 133–34.

30. *Ibid.*, p. 154.

31. Arthur, " 'Liberated' Woman," p. 69.

32. This controversy, with its respective adherents, is noted by Sarah Pomeroy in *Goddesses, Whores, Wives, and Slaves: Women in Classical Antiquity* (New York: Schocken Books, 1975), pp. 58–60.

33. Arthur, " 'Liberated' Woman," p. 75.

34. See above note 32.

35. Arthur, " 'Liberated' Woman," p. 75.

36. *Ibid.*, p. 78.

37. Stone, *The Family, Sex, and Marriage*, p. 141.

38. Roberta Hamilton, *The Liberation of Women: A Study of Patriarchy and Capitalism* (London: Allen and Unwin, 1978), pp. 56–57.

39. Alice Clark, *Working Life of Women in the Seventeenth Century* (New York: Augustus M. Kelley, 1968), pp. 6–7; Louise A. Tilly and Joan W. Scott, *Women, Work, and Family* (New York: Holt, Rinehart, and Winston, 1978), pp. 227–28.

40. Clark, *Working Life of Women*, p. 10.

41. Tilly and Scott, *Women, Work, and Family*, pp. 123–24.

42. Other examples can also be found. Mary Ryan points to the note made by colonial historians of the centrality of certain ties of kinship and marriage alliances in making possible the phenomenon of the merchant capitalist. See her article, "The Explosion of Family History," in *Reviews in American History* (December 1982), 10(4):183. Even more dramatically, Barbara Harris argues that factors such as the stem family, late marriage, and high rates of celibacy, by keeping the population of the West low and raising standards of living, made possible the market conditions necessary for industrialization. Barbara J. Harris, "Recent Work on the History of the Family: A Review Article," in *Feminist Studies* (Spring–Summer 1976), 3(3–4):165.

Also of interest here, for underlining the possible causal efficacy of changes in marriage rules, is Jack Goody's *The Development of the Family and Marriage in Europe* (Cambridge: Cambridge University Press, 1983). Goody points to changes in marriage rules in the centuries after Christ, promulgated by the church, whose effect was both to contribute to an emphasis on conjugality and to vastly increase the property of the church.

43. Joan W. Scott and Louise A. Tilly, "Women's Work and the Family in Nineteenth Century Europe," *Comparative Studies in Society and History* (January 1975), 17(1):53.

44. *Ibid.,* p. 54.

45. This story is recounted by Tilly and Scott in *Women, Work, and Family,* p. 117.

46. Michele Barrett and Mary McIntosh also point to the historical continuities in home and paid labor in *The Anti-Social Family* (London: Verso, 1982), pp. 88–89.

47. Natalie Zemon Davis, "Ghosts, Kin, and Progeny: Some Features of Family Life in Early Modern France," *Daedalus* (Spring 1977), 106:87–91.

FIVE John Locke: The Theoretical Separation of the Family and the State

1. For Laslett's argument here see his introduction to John Locke, *Two Treatises of Government,* ed. Peter Laslett, rev. ed. (New York: New American Library, 1965). All future references to Locke's *Two Treatises* will be to this edition. All references to Filmer will be to *Patriarcha and Other Political Works of Sir Robert Filmer,* ed., Peter Laslett (Oxford: Basil Blackwell, 1949). That the 1949 edition of Filmer represented the first republication of his works since 1696 was pointed out by Gordon Schochet in *Patriarchalism in Political Thought* (New York: Basic, 1975), p. 4. Schochet's work itself stands as an important example of this new tradition of reading Locke. Another example is R.W.K. Hinton, "Husbands, Fathers, and Conquerors: I," *Political Studies* (1967), 15(3):291–300 and "Husbands, Fathers, and Conquerors: II," *Political Studies* (February 1968), 16(1):55–67. It is interesting to note that while Hinton disagrees with Laslett on the point that it is Filmer and not Hobbes who serves as Locke's major opponent in the *Second Treatise,* he agrees with him that patriarchalism serves as the important context of Locke's writing. Indeed, he argues that Hobbes' patriarchalism was a more important obstacle to Locke than Filmer's because it was based on consent. "Husbands, Fathers, and Conquerors: II," p. 62.

2. As examples see Teresa Brennan and Carole Pateman, " 'Mere Auxiliaries to the Commonwealth': Women and the Origins of Liberalism," *Political Studies* (June 1979), 27(2):183–200; Melissa Butler, "Early Liberal Roots of Feminism: John Locke and the Attack on Patriarchy," *American Political Science Review,* (March 1978), 72(1):135–50; Zillah Eisenstein, *The Radical Future of Liberal Feminism* (New York: Longman, 1981); Jean Bethke Elshtain, *Public Man, Private Woman* (Princeton: Princeton University Press, 1981); Lorenne M. G. Clark, "Women and Locke: Who Owns the Apples in the Garden of Eden?" in Lorenne M. G. Clark and Lynda Lange, eds., *The Sexism of Social and Political Theory,* pp. 16–40 (Toronto: University of Toronto Press, 1979).

3. This is not an original claim. It has been made by Laslett in his introduction to *Two Treatises,* p. 91; by Schochet, *Patriarchalism,* pp.

259–60; by John Dunn, "Consent in the Political Theory of John Locke," *Historical Journal* (1967), 10(2):177; and by J.G.A. Pocock, *The Ancient Constitution and the Feudal Law* (Cambridge: Cambridge University Press, 1957), pp. 235–37.

4. Jürgen Habermas, for example, uses Hobbes as a major representative of this methodological position in his essay "The Classical Doctrine of Politics in Relation to Social Philosophy," in Jürgen Habermas, *Theory and Practice*, trans. John Viertel, pp. 41–81 (London: Heinemann, 1974).

5. Laslett, in his introduction to *Patriarcha*, p. 15.

6. Gayle Rubin makes this point on the distinction between "patriarchy" and "male dominance" in "The Traffic in Women: Notes on the 'Political Economy' of Sex," in Rayna R. Reiter, ed., *Toward an Anthropology of Women*, pp. 167–68 (New York: Monthly Review Press, 1975).

7. Hinton, "Husbands, Fathers, and Conquerors: I," p. 292. The reference is to Laslett's introduction to *Patriarcha*, p. 26.

8. Hinton, "Husbands, Fathers, and Conquerors: I," pp. 292–93.

9. Mary Lyndon Shanley, "Marriage Contract and Social Contract in Seventeenth Century English Political Thought," *Western Political Quarterly* (March 1979), 32(1):80–81.

10. *Ibid.*, pp. 83–85.

11. Lawrence Stone notes how the new Renaissance state deliberately encouraged the supremacy of the father in the family on the grounds of an analogy between the family to its head and subjects to their sovereign. However, as noted, my point is that Filmer's position here is different insofar as it goes beyond the claim of an analogy. See Lawrence Stone, *The Family, Sex, and Marriage in England, 1500–1800* (New York: Harper and Row, 1979), p. 110.

12. Don McIntosh aided me in elaborating this point.

13. Locke, *Two Treatises*, 1, p. 294 (par. 153).

14. *Ibid.*, p. 277 (par. 135).

15. *Ibid.*, p. 296 (par. 157).

16. *Ibid.*, p. 216 (par. 55).

17. Locke, *Two Treatises*, 2, p. 364 (par. 81).

18. Locke, *Two Treatises*, 1, p. 248 (par. 93).

19. Stone, *The Family, Sex, and Marriage*, p. 73.

20. Locke, *Two Treatises*, 1, p. 256 (par. 105). On this argument of Locke's that either every father is a king or there is only one true king, see also pp. 284–85 (par. 142). Hinton discusses this problem in "Husbands, Fathers, and Conquerors: I," p. 299.

21. Locke, *Two Treatises*, 1, p. 256 (par. 105).

22. J.G.A. Pocock, *The Ancient Constitution*, pp. 47–48. Christopher Hill makes the same point in *The Century of Revolution, 1603–1714* (New York: Norton, 1966), p. 65.

23. Locke, *Two Treatises,* 2, p. 380 (par. 103).

24. Dunn, "Consent in the Political Theory of John Locke," pp. 157–58. Richard Ashcraft makes the same point in "Locke's State of Nature: Historical Fact or Moral Fiction?" *American Political Science Review* (September 1968), 62(3):912.

25. Dunn, "Consent in the Political Theory of John Locke," p. 180.

26. Locke, *Two Treatises,* 2, p. 381 (par. 105).

27. *Ibid.,* p. 283 (par. 107).

28. *Ibid.,* pp. 386–87 (par. 110).

29. *Ibid.,* p. 387 (par. 111).

30. *Ibid.,* p. 308 (par. 2).

31. C. B. Macpherson, *The Political Theory of Possessive Individualism* (Oxford: Oxford University Press, 1970), pp. 221–47.

32. Locke, *Two Treatises of Government,* 2, p. 308 (par. 2).

33. *Ibid.,* p. 356 (par. 71).

34. It is to be understood that Locke interprets the term "property" broadly, to include life and liberty as well as possessions. Macpherson claims, as will be noted later in this discussion, that there is an important ambiguity in Locke's use of this term.

35. Locke, *Two Treatises,* 2, pp. 362–63 (par. 79).

36. *Ibid.,* p. 362 (par. 78).

37. *Ibid.,* p. 396 (par. 125).

38. *Ibid.,* p. 364 (par. 82).

39. Clark, "Women and Locke," p. 19.

40. Locke, *Two Treatises,* 2, p. 239 (par. 27).

41. *Ibid.,* p. 438 (par. 183).

42. Clark, in "Women and Locke," also notes this contradiction between Locke's theory of property and his denial of property rights to women (pp. 31 ff.).

43. Macpherson, *Possessive Individualism,* pp. 247–48.

44. Clark, "Women and Locke," pp. 36–38.

45. Schochet, *Patriarchalism,* pp. 21–24.

46. Eisenstein, *The Radical Future of Liberal Feminism,* p. 33.

47. Clark, "Women and Locke," pp. 22 ff.

48. Butler, "Early Liberal Roots of Feminism," pp. 142–50; Shanley, "Marriage Contract and Social Contract," pp. 87–91.

49. Clark, "Women and Locke," p. 34, for example, finds it inconsistent to call Locke a promulgator of the new modern-style "companionate" marriage because of his patriarchal views on property. But if one views Locke's theory as a reflection of a particular historical attitude and recognizes that such attitudes are not necessarily consistent in reference to modern positions, then the above labeling of Locke appears valid.

50. Locke's theory of tacit consent, as a response to such an objection, suffers from a number of problems. One obvious one stems from its stretching of the notion of choice to include that situation where an individual does not abandon her or his society of origin to begin anew.

51. Elshtain, *Public Man, Private Woman*, pp. 118–19.

52. *Ibid.*, p. 120.

53. Lawrence A. Blum, "Kant and Hegel's Moral Paternalism: A Feminist Perspective," *Canadian Journal of Philosophy* (June 1982), 12:287–88.

SIX Karl Marx: The Theoretical Separation of the Domestic and the Economic

1. Habermas has also distinguished Marx's concrete historical work from his philosophical self-understanding concerning the role symbolic interaction plays within the theory. See Jürgen Habermas, *Knowledge and Human Interests*, trans. Jeremy Shapiro (Boston: Beacon Press, 1972), p. 42.

2. For two early and important formulations of this position see Frederick Engels, *Herr Eugen Duhring's Revolution in Science* (Anti-Duhring), trans. Emile Burns and ed. C. P. Dutt (New York: International Publishers, 1966), and Georgy Plekhanov, *Fundamental Problems of Marxism* (New York: International Publishers, 1969).

3. As revealed in the title of his collection of essays, *Zur Rekonstruktion des Historischen Materialismus* (Frankfurt: Suhrkamp, 1976).

4. See, as just a few examples: Nancy Hartsock, "The Feminist Standpoint: Developing the Ground for a Specifically Feminist Historical Materialism," in Sandra Harding and Merrill Hintikka, eds., *Discovering Reality: Feminist Perspectives on Epistemology, Metaphysics, Methodology, and the Philosophy of Science*, pp. 283–310 (Dordrecht: Reidel, 1983); Sandra Harding, "What Is the Real Material Base of Patriarchy and Capital?" in Lydia Sargent, ed., *Women and Revolution*, pp. 135–63 (Boston: South End Press, 1981); and Ann Ferguson, "Women as a New Revolutionary Class in the United States," in Pat Walker, ed., *Between Labour and Capital*, p. 280 (Hassocks, Sussex: Harvester Press, 1979).

5. Karl Marx, *A Contribution to the Critique of Political Economy*, ed. Maurice Dobb (New York: International Publishers, 1970), pp. 20–21.

6. Karl Marx and Frederick Engels, *The German Ideology* (Moscow: Progress Publishers, 1968), p. 39.

7. Loyd D. Easton and Kurt H. Guddat, eds. and trans., *Writings of the Young Marx on Philosophy and Society* (Garden City, NY: Anchor, 1967), pp. 294–95.

8. Shlomo Avineri, *The Social and Political Thought of Karl Marx* (Cambridge: Cambridge University Press, 1968), p. 76.

9. Many of the writers in this tradition of reading Marx have pointed out the similarities between this reading and American instrumentalism or pragmatism. Examples are: Sidney Hook, *From Hegel to Marx: Studies in the Intellectual Development of Karl Marx* (Ann Arbor: University of Michigan Press, 1962), pp. 6–7; Richard J. Bernstein, *Praxis and Action: Contemporary Philosophies of Human Activity* (Philadelphia: University of Pennsylvania Press, 1971), pp. 227–28; Norman E. Livergood, *Activity in Marx's Philosophy* (The Hague: Martinus Nijhoff, 1967), p. 22; Habermas, *Knowledge and Human Interests*, p. 43 as well as Avineri himself, *The Social and Political Thought of Karl Marx*, p. 74.

10. Karl Marx, *Capital: A Critique of Political Economy*, trans. from 3d German ed. by Samuel Moore and Edward Aveling, ed. Frederick Engels, and amplified according to the 4th German ed. by Ernest Untermann (New York: Charles H. Kerr, 1906), p. 198.

11. Karl Marx, "Theses on Feuerbach," 1, in Marx and Engels, *The German Ideology*, p. 659.

12. Frederick Engels, *The Origin of the Family, Private Property, and the State*, ed. Eleanor Burke Leacock (New York: International Publishers, 1972), pp. 72–73.

13. Avineri, *The Social and Political Thought of Karl Marx*, p. 77.

14. Marx and Engels, *The German Ideology*, p. 41.

15. Jürgen Habermas has made a similar objection to Marx's work. Habermas notes that while Marx does claim to incorporate the aspect of symbolic interaction, understood under the concept of "relations of production," within his theory, this aspect is ultimately eliminated within Marx's basic frame of reference. This point replicates the criticism of feminists in that in both cases Marx is cited for an ambiguity in his concept of production. In the problems pointed to by Habermas there is an ambiguity in Marx's inclusion under "production" of either both "the forces and the relations of production" or more narrowly of only "the forces of production." In the problems pointed to be feminists, there is an ambiguity concerning even what "forces of production" might include. In all cases, such ambiguity is made possible by Marx's moving from broader to narrower meanings of "production." For Habermas' critique see, *Knowledge and Human Interests*, pp. 25–63.

16. Nancy Holmstrom raised this objection in commenting on a paper of mine, "The 'Economic' and the Feminist Response to Marx," at the Eastern Division meeting of the American Philosophical Association in Boston, Mass., 1983.

17. Karl Marx, *Grundrisse*, trans. Martin Nicolaus (London: Penguin, 1973), p. 86.

18. *Ibid.*, pp. 88–89.

19. Letter of Marx to P. V. Annenkov, 1846, appendix to Karl Marx, *The Poverty of Philosophy* (New York: International Publishers, 1963), p. 180.

20. Within the group around *Socialisme ou barbarie*, one writer, Cornelius Castoriadis, is to be particularly noted for making this point. Georg Lukács also notes it in *History and Class Consciousness*, trans. Rodney Livingstone (Cambridge, MA: MIT Press, 1971), pp. 55 and 57. These references were first pointed out to me by Alasdair MacIntyre in communication. They are also noted by Isaac Balbus in *Marxism and Domination* (Princeton: Princeton University Press, 1982), p. 34. Balbus also references Baudrillard and Sahlins and discusses Lukács' ambiguous commitment to this point.

21. Again it is to Balbus, *Marxism and Domination*, p. 35, that I owe this reference. His citation is to Maurice Godelier, "Infrastructures, Societies, and History," *New Left Review* (November–December 1978), no. 112, p. 87.

22. Balbus, *Marxism and Domination*, pp. 35–36.

23. Marshall Sahlins, *Culture and Practical Reason* (Chicago: University of Chicago Press, 1976), p. 212.

24. The most famous work on this change in attitude is Max Weber's *The Protestant Ethic and the Spirit of Capitalism*, trans. Talcott Parsons and with a foreword by R. H. Tawney (New York: Scribner, 1930). Hannah Arendt also discusses this change in *The Human Condition* (Chicago: University of Chicago Press, 1958).

25. R. H. Tawney, *Religion and the Rise of Capitalism* (New York: New American Library, 1954), pp. 34–35. It was Heilbroner's excellent discussion of this issue which reminded me of these lines from Tawney. See Robert Heilbroner, *The Making of Economic Society* (Englewood Cliffs, NJ: Prentice-Hall, 1962), pp. 38–44.

26. Again for an excellent discussion of the creation of "labor," "land," and "capital" see Heilbroner, *The Making of Economic Society*, chapter 3.

27. Marx and Engels, *The German Ideology*, pp. 31 and 32.

28. Jean Baudrillard, *The Mirror of Production*, trans. Mark Poster (St. Louis: Telos Press, 1975), pp. 22, 35, and 17.

29. This criticism was raised in chapter 3, where I noted that it was Roger Gottlieb who first brought the point to my attention.

30. Marx and Engels, *The German Ideology*, p. 40.

31. Karl Polanyi, *The Great Transformation* (Boston: Beacon Press, 1957), p. 60.

32. *Ibid.*, p. 63.

33. As Polanyi argues, the absence of some regulation does not mean the absence of all regulation. On the contrary, he claims that markets and regulation grew up together.

34. Polanyi, *The Great Transformation*, p. 70.

35. *Ibid.*, p. 71.

36. *Ibid.*

37. *Ibid.*, p. 57.

38. G. A. Cohen, *Karl Marx's Theory of History* (Princeton: Princeton University Press, 1978), pp. 134–50.

39. *Ibid.*, pp. 143–44.

40. Polanyi, *The Great Transformation*, pp. 74–75.

41. Heilbroner, *The Making of Economic Society*, p. 74.

42. Karl Marx, *The Poverty of Philosophy* (New York: International Publishers, 1963), pp. 186–87.

43. Anthony Giddens, *Capitalism and Modern Social Theory: An Analysis of the Writings of Marx, Durkheim, and Max Weber* (Cambridge: Cambridge University Press, 1971), p. 10.

44. Marx, *Capital*, 1, p. 188. See also p. 87.

45. Marx, *The Poverty of Philosophy*, pp. 210–11.

46. *Ibid.*, p. 211.

47. Mary O'Brien, "Reproducing Marxist Man," in Lorenne M. G. Clark and Lynda Lange, eds., *The Sexism of Social and Political Theory*, p. 107 (Toronto: University of Toronto Press, 1979).

48. *Ibid.*, p. 102 and p. 111.

49. *Ibid.*, p. 105.

50. Marx, *The Poverty of Philosophy*, p. 180.

51. This point of the progression of kinship to state to market has been made often in the Marxist literature. See, for example, the quotation from Engels' *The Origin of the Family, Private Property, and the State* cited above in note 12. Jürgen Habermas takes the point further, noting similarly to Godelier, that in the progression of kinship to state to market we see also changes in those institutions through which access to the means of production is regulated. Jürgen Habermas, *Communication and the Evolution of Society*, trans. Thomas McCarthy (Boston: Beacon Press, 1979), p. 114.

52. O'Brien, "Reproducing Marxist Man," p. 114.

53. Ann Ferguson and Nancy Folbre, "The Unhappy Marriage of Patriarchy and Capitalism," in *Women and Revolution*, p. 318.

54. Iris Young, "Beyond the Unhappy Marriage: A Critique of Dual Systems Theory," in Sargent, *Women and Revolution*, p. 52.

55. *Ibid.*, p. 49.

56. *Ibid.*

SEVEN Conclusion

1. Carol Gilligan, *In a Different Voice* (Cambridge, MA: Harvard University Press, 1982).

Index

State *(Continued)*
  separated from family by Locke,
  133–66
State of nature, 147–52
Stone, Lawrence, 52, 113, 116–18,
  120–21, 128, 143
Street theater, 29
Subjective vs. objective, 5
Subjectivity, 5
Suffrage, 4, 20; and nineteenth-
  century women's movement, 49, 65
Suffrage movement, 53–54, 56

Tawney, R. H., 182
Teaching, 62, 202
Technological determinism, 188–90
Temperance movement, 53, 202
Theses on Feuerbach (Marx), 172
Tilly, Louise, 123–26
Trade, 122, 129, 185–92
Two Treatises of Government (Locke),
  133, 143, 148, 152

Unger, Roberto, 162
Unions, 22
United Auto Workers, 22
Universalists, 70–76

Vassalage, 139
Voting rights, *see* Suffrage

Warfare, specialization of men in, 95
WEAL (Women's Equity Action
  League), 22, 28
Welfare agencies, 24
Welfare state, 54, 203
Welfare state liberalism, 5, 25
Whyte, Martin King, 80, 95, 100
Wittgenstein, Ludwig, 134

Women's Bill of Rights (NOW), 21–22
Women's Christian Temperance
  Union, 53
Women's liberation, 5, 19
Women's movement: contemporary, 4,
  17–42, 56–65, 203; diversity within,
  19–41; and growth of nondomestic
  sphere, 56–62; nineteenth-century,
  43–56
Women's Rights Convention (Seneca
  Falls, New York), 48
"Women's rights" movement vs.
  "women's lib," 19
Women's status: anthropological view
  of, 70–91; in brideservice societies,
  96–100; and domestic/public
  separation, 73–91, 95, 101–2, 104,
  208; and historical separation of
  family and state, 118; indicators of,
  80; liberal feminist view of, 20–26;
  Marxist view of, 36, 192–97; need
  for historical view of, 6, 10–12, 105,
  206–8; and production, 93–95;
  psychological implications of, 64–65;
  radical feminist view of, 26–35;
  search for cross-cultural causes of,
  7–10, 70–76, 88–89; and social
  forms, 113–21
Women's studies, 203
Women, Work, and Family (Tilly and
  Scott), 123
Woodhull, Victoria, 55
*Working Life of Women in the
  Seventeenth Century* (Clark), 123
World Anti-Slavery Convention, 47
World We Have Lost, The (Laslett), 109

Yanagisako, Sylvia Junko, 83
Young, Iris, 40–41, 198–99